IMAGES
of America
DELTA COUNTY

On the Cover: Taken shortly after 1890, the picture shows the third courthouse built in the center of the square of the Delta County seat, Cooper, Texas. (Courtesy of the Quentin Miller family.)

IMAGES
of America

DELTA COUNTY

Judy Falls, Sylvia Wood, and
Friends of Delta County Public Library

ARCADIA
PUBLISHING

ISBN 978-0-7385-7932-0

Published by Arcadia Publishing
Charleston, South Carolina

Printed in the United States of America

Library of Congress Control Number:

For all general information, please contact Arcadia Publishing:
Telephone 843-853-2070
Fax 843-853-0044
E-mail sales@arcadiapublishing.com
For customer service and orders:
Toll-Free 1-888-313-2665

Visit us on the Internet at www.arcadiapublishing.com

Contents

ACKNOWLEDGMENTS

This book owes everything to the unfailing support of so many people who hold Delta County dear. The authors especially thank the members of the Delta County Public Library Board of Directors, the Patterson Memorial Museum Board of Directors, and Delta County Historical Commission. In addition, we wish to thank the people of Delta County who have unselfishly given both their family pictures and pictures of the community.

Also, thanks to Richard Duncan of the Clara Slough Museum. Duncan has been relentless in his quest to accurately locate the old communities in the area surrounding Enloe. His work was invaluable in creating the map of communities. Additionally, the authors wish to thank Hunter Sissons for his artwork for the map.

Thanks also to Dr. James Conrad, the former archivist of Texas A&M University–Commerce, who provided advice and assistance as to the content of this book; Jim Ainsworth, local author and Cooper High School graduate, who provided valuable editing advice; Larry Stowers, English teacher at Cooper High School, for comments and proofing the written materials; and another Bulldog, Merry Williams Ressler, who provided help with writing the history and proofing the pages. Finally, we are indebted to the Nabors sisters, Katie and Shirley, who have contributed their time, knowledge, and energy to getting this book to publication, and all others who volunteered to help with identification of the myriad of faces and places depicted in the photographs.

The authors wish to acknowledge that many of the pictures used in this book were identified by the families or the staff at the library and museums. We endeavored to ensure the accuracy of all information, using materials obtained from the backs of pictures, personal interviews, or handwritten notes that accompanied pictures. However, memories, like eyesight, fade over time, and we apologize for any errors. For questions about the book, contact Sylvia Wood at P.O. Box 463, Klondike, Texas, 75448 or sylwood2@yahoo.com; Judy Falls at the Delta County Public Library, 300 West Dallas Avenue, Cooper, Texas, 75432 or deltalib@neto.com; Nancy and Richard Duncan at the Clara Slough Museum, P.O. Box 63, Enloe, Texas, 75441; or the Patterson Museum at 700 West Dallas Avenue, Cooper, Texas 75432.

INTRODUCTION

Early settlers crisscrossed the land now known as Delta County as early as the 1820s. They found prairies and thickets, and also buffaloes, turkeys, prairie chickens, raccoons, possums, wolves, bears, polecats, deer, squirrels, and cottontail rabbits. The area began to see large numbers of settlers by the 1840s, when extended families from the South established homes in the area.

The Civil War brought disagreements between different groups and families. When Sam Houston called for a statewide vote on secession, Hopkins County voted to leave the Union, while Lamar County voted to stay. As tensions grew during the Civil War, 15 men in Hunt, Lamar, and Hopkins Counties were hanged. The Sons of Washington, a pro-South vigilante group, hanged Henry, Thomas, and James Howard and Jonathan and James E. Hemby on the banks of the South Sulphur River near Charleston, Texas. Other people left Delta County to avoid persecution by the Sons of Washington.

During Reconstruction, many Texas counties petitioned for border realignment. As a result of this request, Delta County was created in 1870 from parts of Hopkins and Lamar Counties, bounded by the North and South Sulphur Rivers. The first commissioners, James Hamilton, John P. Boyd, Joel Blackwell, Thomas Lane, and J. W. Iglehart, were delegated the task of creating precincts. The area known as Yates Prairie was renamed for state senator L. W. Cooper and was designated the county seat with the final organization of the county on October 6, 1870. The first commissioner's court met under a live oak tree around a wagon in February 1871. One of the first orders of business was the construction of the initial jail, a small one-room wooden structure frequently set on fire by prisoners.

Settlers to the area primarily came from the Old South "Cotton Belt." They found the dark, fertile, and easily cultivated Houston-Wilson soils of the region to be perfectly suited for cotton production. Along the northwest corner of the county, there is a ledge of limestone that appears along the surface of the land, and gray land lies on the north side of the South Sulphur. But the majority of the county has black, waxy, thick, and rich soil—the gumbo soil that a public-spirited newspaperman described as so fertile that "when tickled with a hoe, it laughs back with a bounteous harvest."

Along with being productive, the land was reasonably priced. By the 1890s, advertised land prices were averaging $3 an acre. Cotton, grains, and livestock thrived for the yeoman farmers willing to work the land.

With an initially sparse population, early farmers united to take their crops to Jefferson, Texas. The Bonham-Jefferson Road passed near Pecan Gap, Lone Star, Antioch, Liberty Grove, and Granny's Neck before crossing the South Sulphur River into Hopkins County. Roads and weather, which could lengthen the time for the trip, continued to be a concern and a factor for growth in Northeast Texas, especially in Delta County. Because of the roads, often all but impassable when the rains turned the gumbo soil to glue, families rarely did business, socialized, or sought medical attention farther than 3 miles from their homes.

By 1880, the county had its own newspaper, the *Delta Courier*, and the population had grown to almost 5,600, of whom approximately 600 were African American. Twenty years later, several communities had not only their own newspapers but also thriving businesses. Today the *Cooper Review* and J. F. Henslee Hardware are the two oldest surviving businesses in Delta County.

Records of various communities indicate that local doctors took care of neighbors and families. Dr. O. Y. Janes opened the original Janes Hospital in nearby Prattville but later moved to Cooper because the doctor said people did not want to be sick in the middle of a cotton patch—they wanted to be sick in town. Eventually the Janes Hospital was operated by three brothers—Drs. Olen, Gaza, and Osler Janes, the sons of Dr. O. Y. Janes. The brothers served the people of Delta County until the last and youngest, Gaza, retired. The clinic was sold to the Paris Regional Medical Center, which closed in 2008.

Fraternal organizations, such as Woodmen of the World, the Praetorians, the Masons, the Knights of Pythias, and others, were active in the county at the beginning of the 20th century. Two Masonic lodges have been located at Cooper, but only one remains in operation. Lake Creek, Ben Franklin, Yowell, and Charleston also had active lodges. The Masonic sister organization, the Order of the Eastern Star, begun in 1908, involved many local women, and the Rebekah Assembly, affiliated with the Odd Fellows, organized in 1913. The Independent Order of Odd Fellows (IOOF) gained their charter in 1874, and the group was instrumental in developing the first county cemetery, Oaklawn.

The Santa Fe Railroad arrived in the county in 1890 with stops in Pecan Gap and Ben Franklin. Cooper, the county seat, got its first railroad in 1896. The Southern Pacific Railroad later bought the Texas Midland, and trains ran until 1973, when serious flooding destroyed the railroad trestle on the North Sulphur River. With railroads, farm life and production shifted from a subsistence level to cash crops. Families purchased flour delivered by trains instead of raising wheat or corn, freeing acreage for the more lucrative cotton.

Financing to run the farms and homes became easier when the first bank began operation in Cooper in 1889. The First National Bank, originally located inside a grocery store, was followed the next year by Delta National Bank. Several other banks opened across the county in the ensuing years, and both landowners and tenants came to depend on them. Several of the banks struggled and failed in the Depression years, taking the hard-earned savings of farmers and other clients with them. By the 21st century, the only remaining banks are First National Bank in Cooper and Enloe State Bank.

Even the early rural communities had some type of schools. Sylvia Wood compiled this list from various newspaper articles and library archives. Schools in existence in 1932 are listed in *Loose Leaves* by Ilkie Gray Patteson. The schools listed in parentheses are area schools that consolidated with other schools over a period of time: Amy (Hobbs Thicket), Antioch, Bagley School (Mohegan), Ben Franklin, Bethany School, Booker T. Washington, Brushy Mound School (Petifils School), Cedar Creek (Daisy Mission), Charleston, Charleston College (Street School), Clark School, Cleveland (Red Branch-Edgar School), Cooper, Craig-Tranquil (Bloody Hollow), Cross Roads (Clem-Hog Waller-Union), Darwin School (Andersonville), Doctor's Creek, Enloe, Eureka School (Needmore), Giles Academy, Gough (Bittick Prairie), Greenwood, Hickory Grove, Horton, Kensing School (Red Branch–Cherry Mound), Klondike (Old Pleasant Grove–Kate), Lake Creek, Liberty Grove, Lone Star, Long Ridge School (Sharptown), Long Taw (Good's Chapel), Mayo College, Milam (Buzzard's Roost), Mount Joy, Mount Zion, Mulberry School, New Hope (Independence), Old Liberty (Billyville), Pacio School (Lone Elm School), Pecan Gap, Pecan Grove (Granny's Neck), Perkins School, Post Oak School (Brush Creek), Prairie Dell, Prattville, Price, Race Track School, Rattan (Blue Prairie), Shiloh, Simmons (Jackson's Chapel), Simmons Academy, Underwood School, Union Grove (Tichner School), Unitia, Vasco, Walker's Chapel, and Yowell.

Although there were already established community schools scattered around Delta County, Ada Patterson established the first known Cooper school in her residence. The second school was in a church, and the third was a joint-stock company school on East First Street, which was eventually purchased by W. L. Mayo and was a normal school known as East Texas Normal School. The building burned in 1894, and Mayo moved his school to Commerce.

The next school was a frame building in East Cooper. A brick two-story building was added to house grades 1 through 11. In 1906, a brick high school building was constructed on Southwest

Fourth Street. The brick building was demolished in 1926, and a new redbrick high school was constructed on this site. A new elementary school was constructed on the school complex in 1952, and other buildings were added through the years to house various needs. In 1998, high school students moved from the redbrick high school to a new school. In 2010, a new elementary school was added; both schools were on Farm-to-Market (FM) Road 1528.

County schools before 1966 included several schools for African American children only. Located in Cross Roads, Klondike, Ben Franklin, Pecan Gap, Enloe, Charleston, and Cooper, the schools slowly consolidated to bring all African American children to the Booker T. Washington campus in Cooper.

Common among all rural schools were small buildings and a lack of running water or indoor plumbing. Playground equipment consisted only of swings or seesaws, and the team sport was baseball, played in streets and open fields. Nevertheless, the schools are remembered by many because they were led by loving, strict, no-nonsense educators who wanted and expected their students to learn.

Booker T. Washington School, originally located at the end of Northwest Fifth Street, was later moved to larger accommodations at the corner of 500 Commerce Avenue. Before 1965, a lunchroom, a separate gymnasium, and a room for the visiting nurse were added. The school closed in 1967, causing much sadness among its alumni. With the closing of Booker T. Washington, all of the existing rural common and independent schools plus the African American schools were combined into one school in Cooper.

The Cooper school mascot was the bulldog, and today the Bulldogs are fiercely supported by the local communities, who travel to ball games, track meets, one-act plays, band events, University Interscholastic League competitions, and other student activities. Maroon and Gray scholarships help students advance in academics, and volunteers lend their support in every endeavor.

Delta schools did more than educate; they also provided a lively social outlet through sports. Early schools too small to field a football team had stellar tennis players, and baseball proved a popular sport. Beginning in 1900, baseball teams from Yowell, Klondike, Gough, Pecan Gap, Cooper, and Ben Franklin competed against each other as well as teams from surrounding counties. Cheering crowds gathered to watch the teams play at gin lots and in open fields while 300 to 400 people sat on cars, trucks, and the ground. Basketball occupied many girls and boys with team names like the Kensing Dragons or the Booker T. Wildcats. A Negro League played baseball in Cooper, and World War II saw a baseball team with 12 men from Delta County win the 49th Division Softball Championship for the 147th Armored Infantry Battalion.

Like many Texans, Delta County residents followed their talented athletes. Marshall Robnett from Klondike played on the 1939 Texas A&M national championship team and is a member of the Texas A&M Hall of Fame. He was named an All-America guard in 1940, was ninth in the Heisman Trophy ballot in 1940, and played for the Chicago Cardinals and Card-Pitt professional football teams. Another acclaimed athlete, David Floyd Weaver, was a Ben Franklin native and Paris Junior College graduate. Weaver still holds a junior college record in strikeouts and was a major-league pitcher for the Cleveland Indians, Chicago White Sox, and Milwaukee Brewers.

After World War II, returning veterans formed an organization with both sports and agriculture themes—a rodeo club. Every year, area residents are treated to both a junior and a professional rodeo at the Cooper Fairgrounds. Another popular sport in the county is golf, enthusiastically pursued by young and old alike. The Delta County Golf Links, located 5 miles east of Cooper, got their start before 1935 with an interested group of 20 area businessmen. Today the golf links are known as the Delta County Country Club. Many residents also learned to swim in the county's lakes and creeks, and fishing is a popular pastime.

The Cooper Lake was authorized by Congress in 1955, but it was 1993 before the Army Corps of Engineers opened the lake. Instrumental in helping the lake become a reality were Congressmen Wright Patman and Jim Chapman, Speaker of the House Sam Rayburn, and area residents including Grover Pickering, Quentin Miller, Morris Partain, and Don Abernathy. It is now a haven for sportsmen and naturalists.

Church and religious training were important to the citizens, even when only circuit riders pastored the flocks. Spiritual singing brought friends together around a piano in the evenings after work in the fields, cementing bonds that lasted lifetimes. Methodist circuit riders in the early 19th century included William Stevenson, John B. Denton, John B. Craig, C. A. Tower, L. P. Smith, and Redmond Boyd. There were 27 Methodist churches of record for the county. One of the first churches in the county, built in 1858, served as both a Baptist church and Giles Academy. The founder was Thomas Hart Benton Hockaday, whose daughter later founded the Hockaday School in Dallas.

Many buildings, constructed with donated materials and labor on donated land, served as both schools and churches. Church services, including revivals, did not always meet indoors. Many lively services were conducted at brush arbor meetings, which sometimes lasted up to two weeks in the fall after harvest. Baptisms, commonly held in lakes and the North Sulphur River, were a cause of much celebration. The county was home to 36 churches at the beginning of the 21st century.

Today Delta County residents fondly remember other institutions, including the Parkhill Café, located on the west side of the square. Owned by Bill and Maude Parkhill, the restaurant served many meals and countless cups of coffee. The Sparks family owned two theaters on the north side of the square. Many residents recall seeing Bessie Sparks hurry down the sidewalk with husband Henry Sparks three steps behind. Hooten Drug, on the southwest corner of the square, and Miller's Pharmacy, on the southeast corner, competed for prescription service and soda fountain business. Miller's Pharmacy still features homemade ice cream, which is still served by Mabel Wheat. Miller's is one of the few remaining soda fountains in the state. The lunch counter at Silman's Grocery on the east side of the square served residents for over 40 years. It was initially owned by J. J. Silman, and Jack and Joyce Silman soon became the owners of the store, which began as a grocery store and meat market. A lunch counter was added, and the menu included hamburgers, cheeseburgers, chili, stew, barbeque, and other assorted goodies, served with coffee. These items were served by Maggie Bowers, Hester Hooten, Effie Kizer, Mozelle Bettes, and Billy Robinson.

Agriculture must be at the forefront of any description of Delta County. Beginning with rich, fertile land, the county fielded generations of hardy farmers—landowners, tenants, and sharecroppers alike—all avid to make another bale of cotton. It has been said that a man could make a better living by accident on the dense black soil than by trying hard on neighboring sandy land. Raising fine crops did not guarantee a prosperous living, however. Area farmers were hit hard in the Depression years by a double blow of low prices and record boll weevil infestation. From a state-high rural density of 61 persons per square mile in 1927, Delta County population dwindled over the years. Mechanization meant fewer men working more land, and better roads led people to abandon the small villages for better shopping in larger areas.

The trickle away from the farms became a flood after World War II, as returning veterans often left to seek higher wages in Dallas factories, Houston shipyards, or West Texas oil fields or cotton patches. Those remaining returned to cattle ranching and raised a diversity of crops. Cotton, which had brought so many families to the area, was no longer the only crop.

Still considered a rural area, the county seat's population is under 2,500, and the outlying areas are wide open once again. Regardless of the small population, the fiercely loyal residents love their county and fight to keep it from those who would flood parts of it to give metropolitan areas water. To those who grew up here, to those who moved here, or to those who merely remember living here, Delta County remains home, with all the sweet—and bittersweet—implications of the word.

One

Delta County

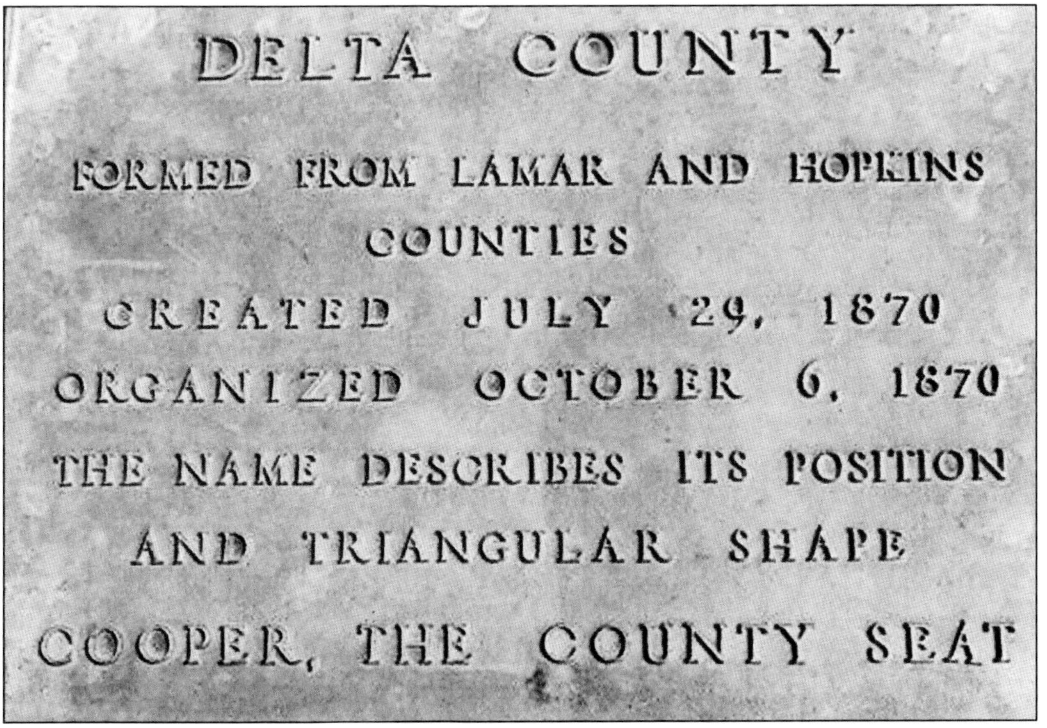

This 1936 Texas Highway Department centennial marker is located 2 miles east of Cooper at the junction of Highways 154 and 1529. It documents the fact that Delta County was officially designated on July 29, 1870. (Courtesy of Judy Falls.)

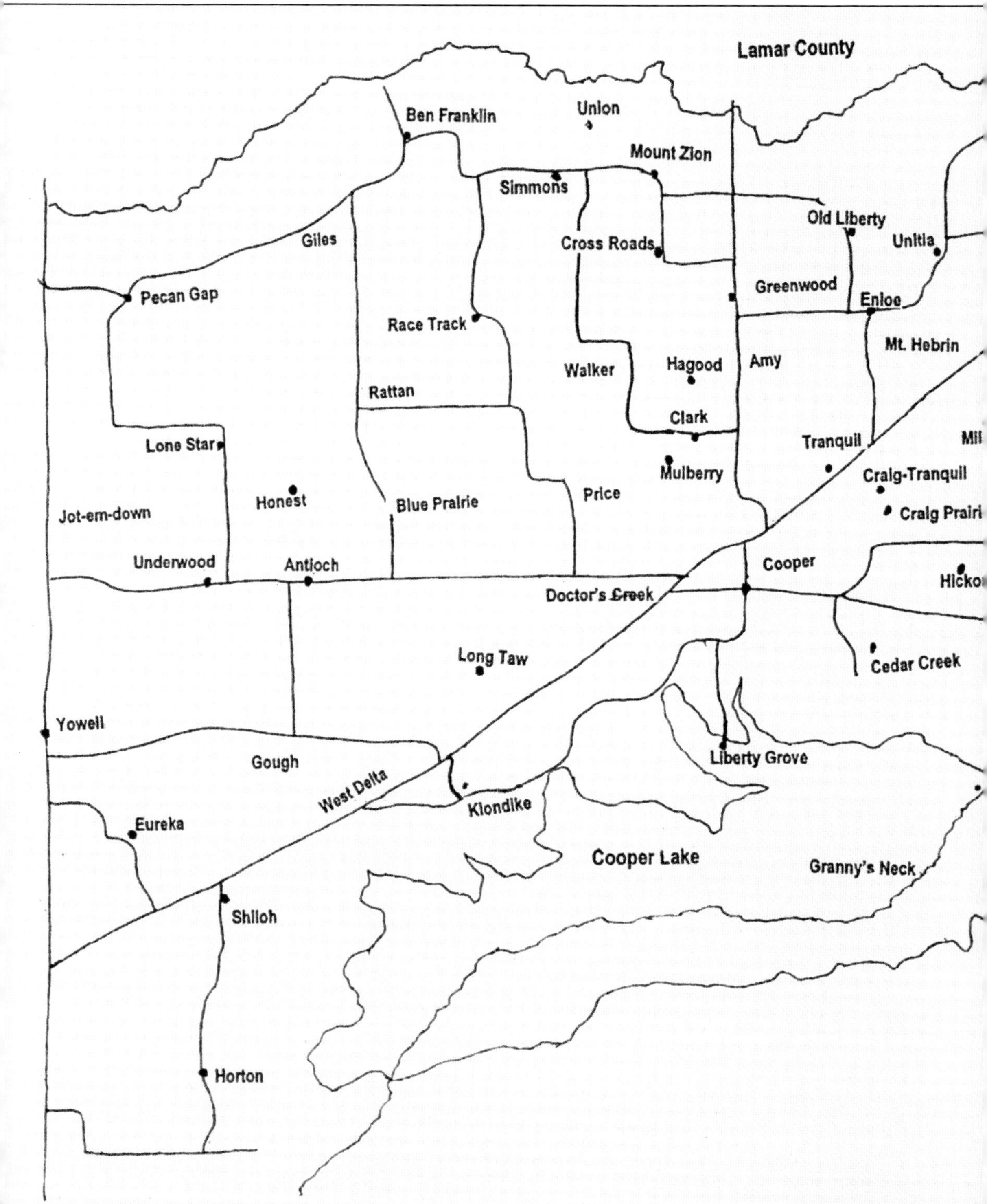

The map of Delta County, Texas, shows the rural communities and cities that existed at some time between the Sulphur Rivers since the mid-1800s. Most have left no visible

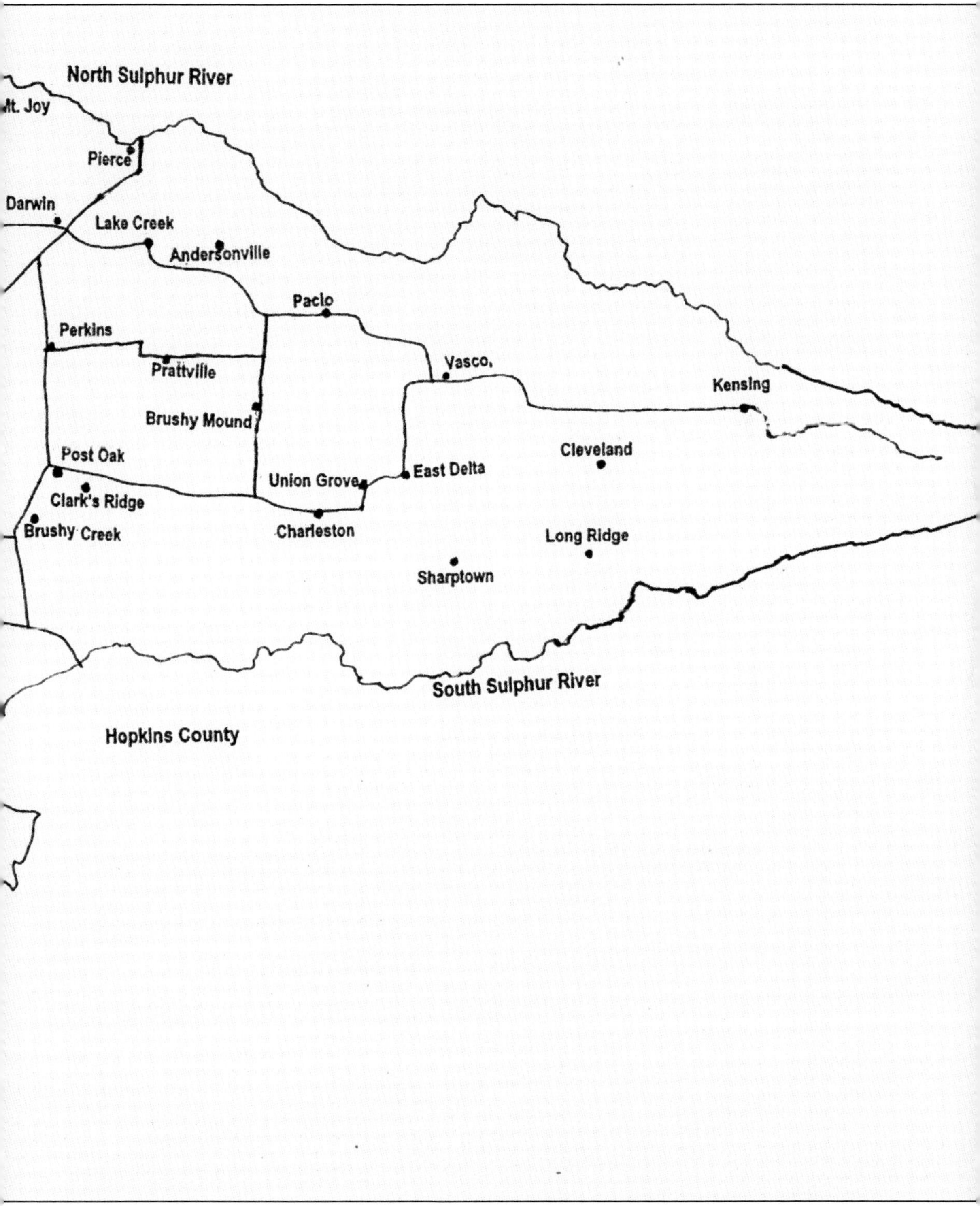

sign of existence. (Map by Hunter Sisson; research by Richard Hunter, Leo Millard, Shirley Smith, and Judy Falls.)

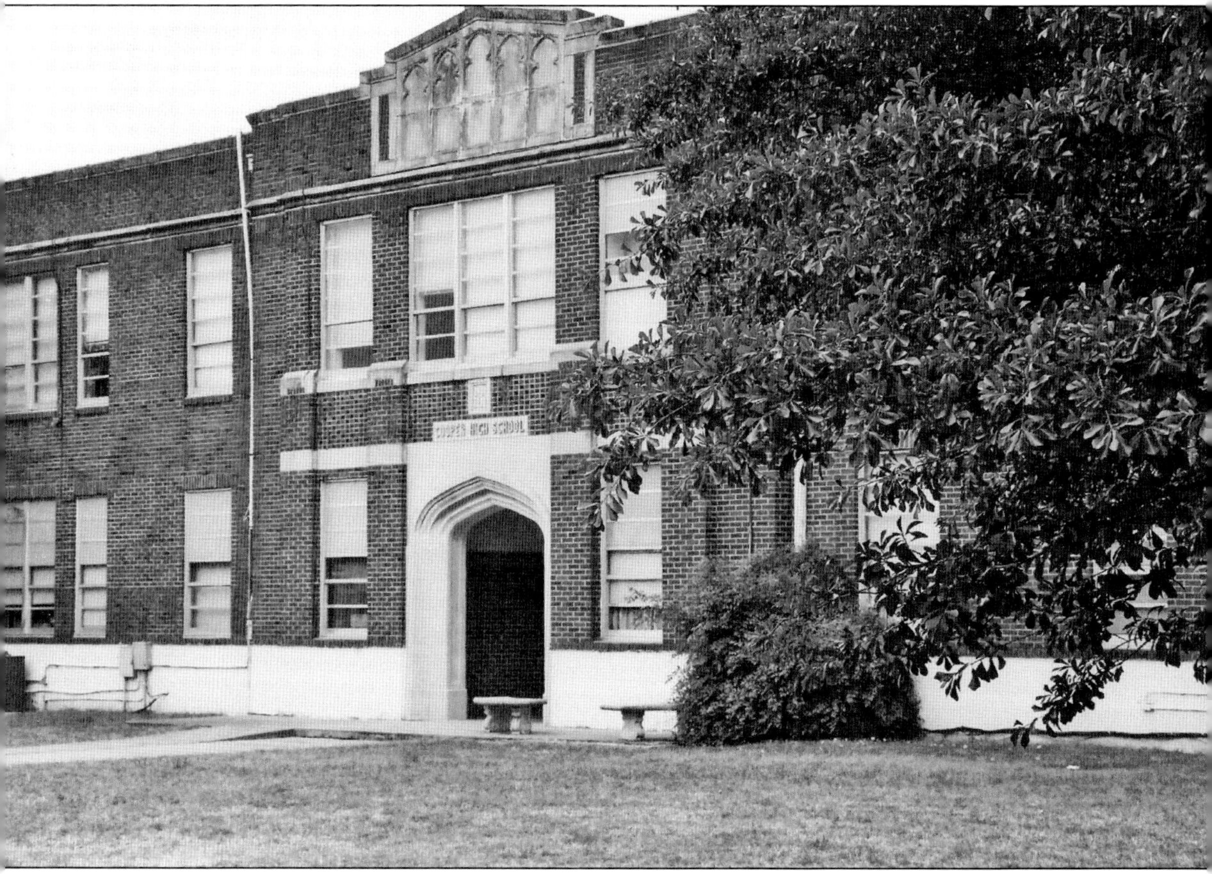

The redbrick Cooper High School was erected in 1925. The board of education in 1925 was comprised of Dr. C. C. Taylor (president), Joel H. Berry, J. W. Green, D. N. Mulligan, R. H. Foster, Dr. C. S. Ellington, and D. M. Fisher. J. H. Newton was the superintendent of school at that time. Elementary students used this building until the 2010 school year. (Courtesy of Judy Falls.)

Two

The North Side

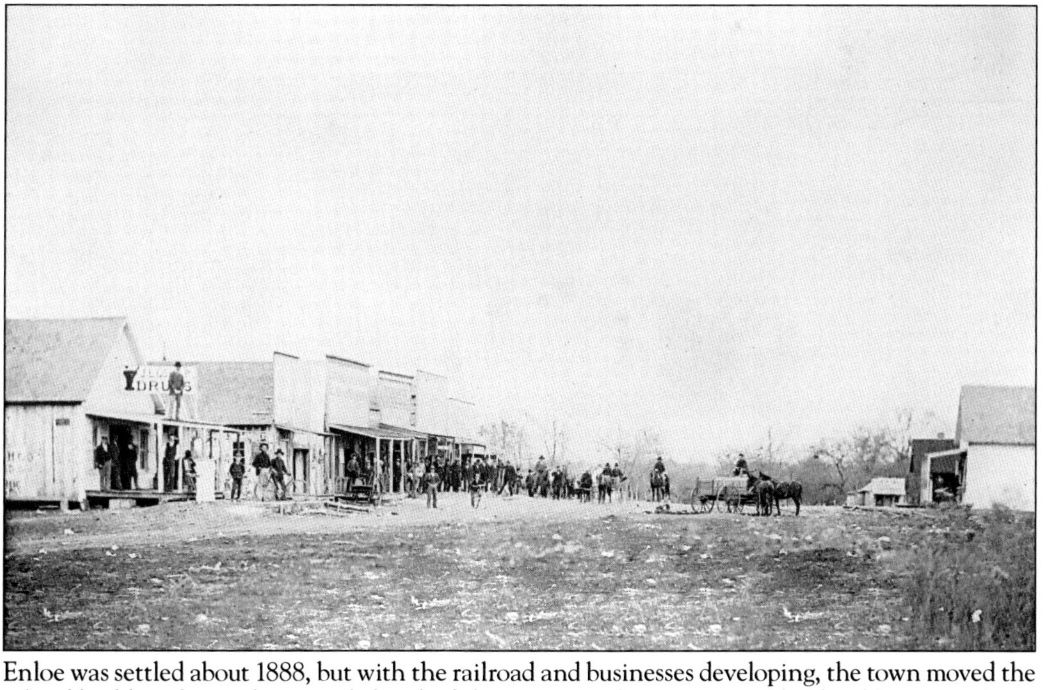

Enloe was settled about 1888, but with the railroad and businesses developing, the town moved the school building from Liberty and absorbed the Mount Hebron or Hagood School by 1897. This is a picture of the main street, along with banks, a telegraph office, a restaurant, general stores, an apothecary, a seed store, and a lumber company. (Courtesy of Clara Foster Slough Museum.)

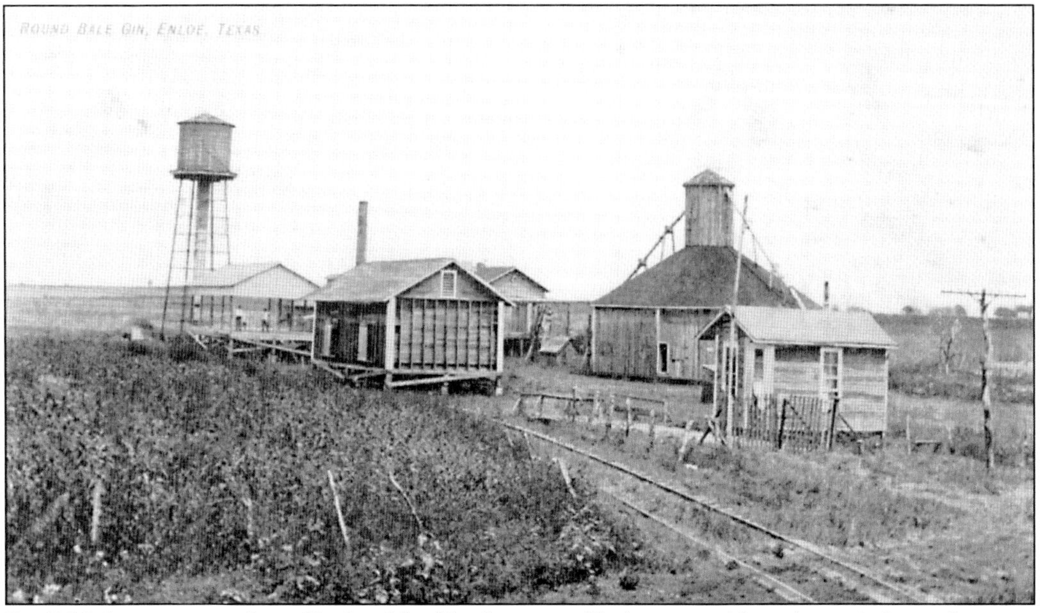

By 1908, businessmen from England had built a round bale gin and bought and shipped cotton directly back to England. This was the only known gin that put out round bales, at least in this area. A note on this postcard stated that more than 100 bales of cotton were sold in the streets of Enloe that day. (Courtesy of Clara Foster Slough Museum.)

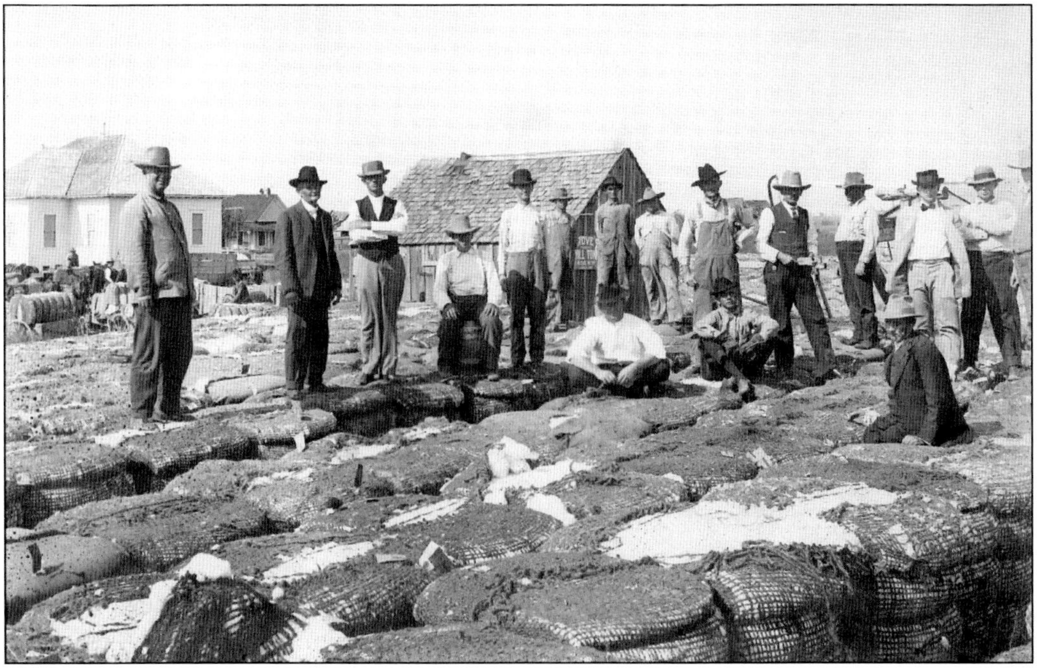

Cotton was the major industry and supported many cotton buyers with two gins. Pictured with this cotton around 1920 are, from left to right, (first row) Alfred Enloe, L. Stanley, and ? Anderson; (second row) J. A. Enloe, N. J. Huie, C. Kinard, R. E. Toon, Ras Stockton, two unidentified, F. A. Hooks, W. A. Watkins, unidentified, B. Anderson, unidentified, and Bob Mills. (Courtesy of Clara Foster Slough Museum.)

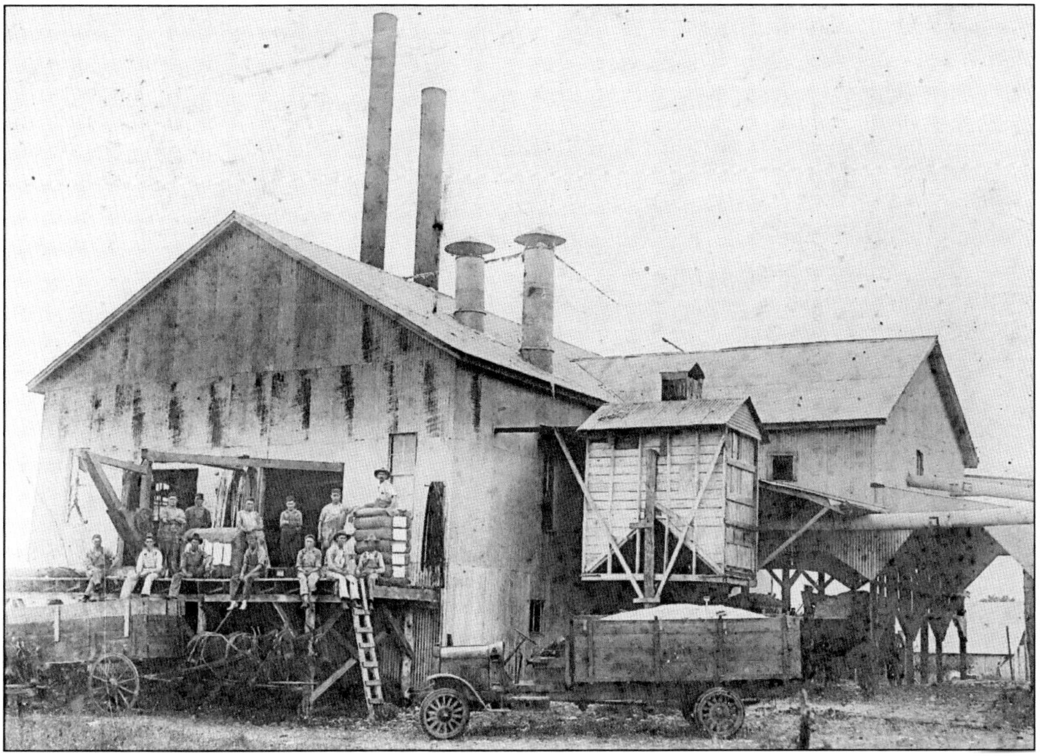

This gin was owned by Jackson-Mullens-Hull and later by Coleman. This gin at Enloe produced many bales of cotton. Note that some cotton was still brought in by horse-drawn wagon, but the truckload of cotton is impressive. (Courtesy of Clara Foster Slough Museum.)

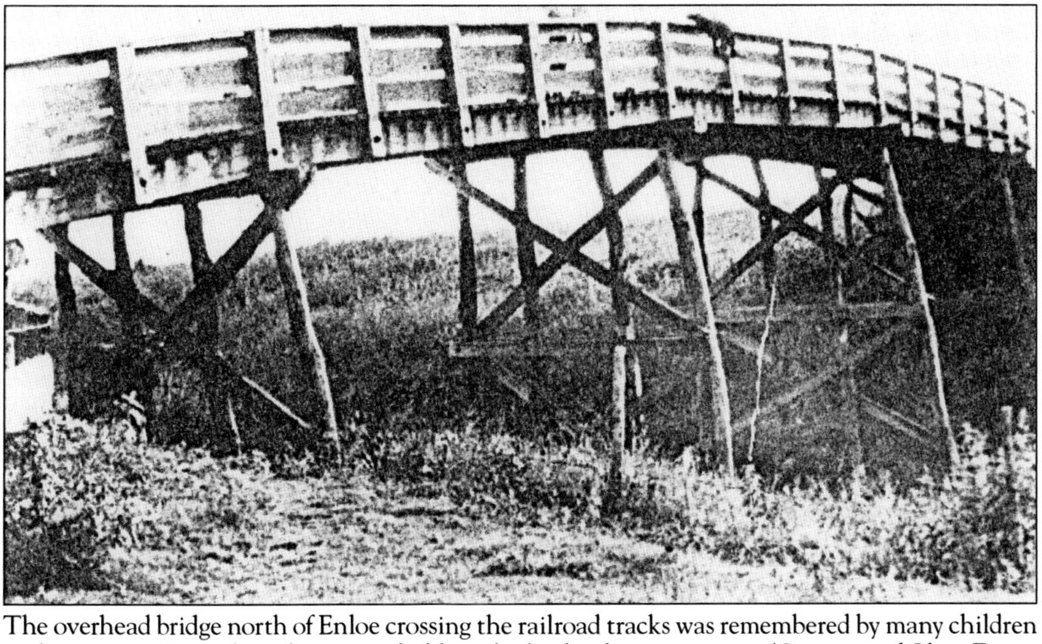

The overhead bridge north of Enloe crossing the railroad tracks was remembered by many children and teenagers. Large bois d'arc posts held up the bridge for many years. (Courtesy of Clara Foster Slough Museum.)

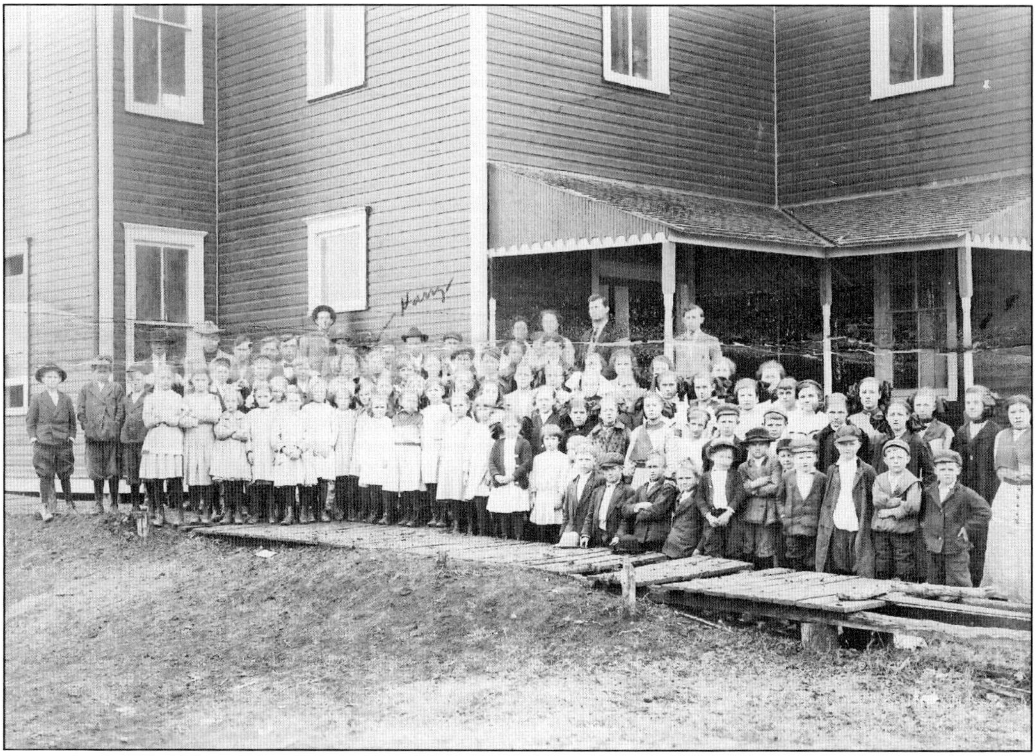

Shown above with many of its students, a new school was constructed by 1913 to replace the building moved from the Liberty community to use as an early Enloe school. This school lasted until 1924, when the brick building below was constructed. It was in use through 1960. (Both, courtesy of Patterson Museum.)

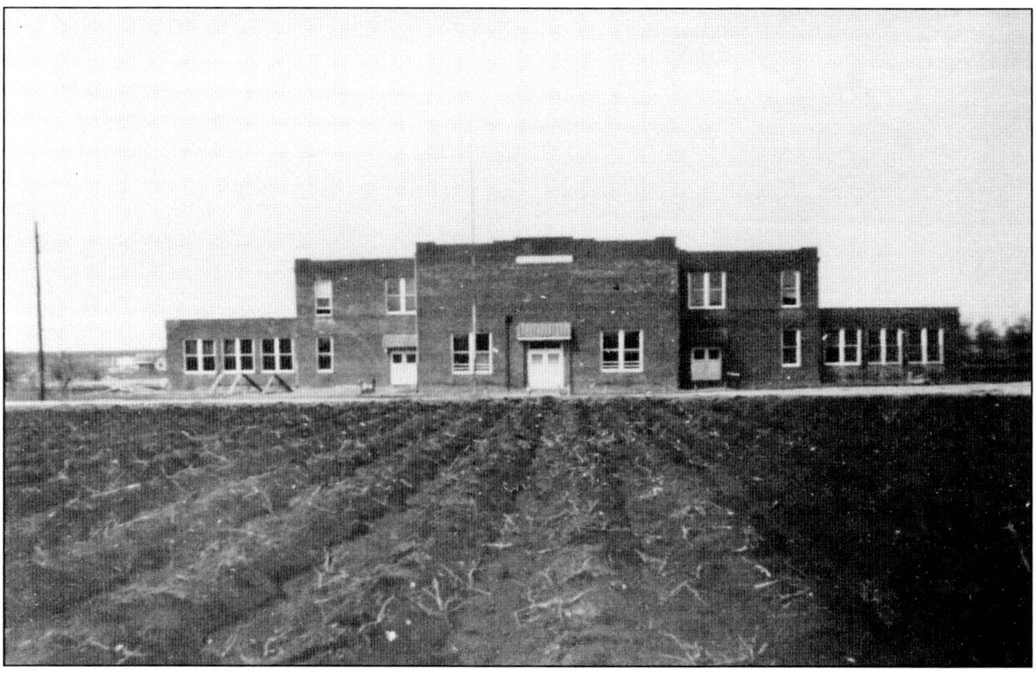

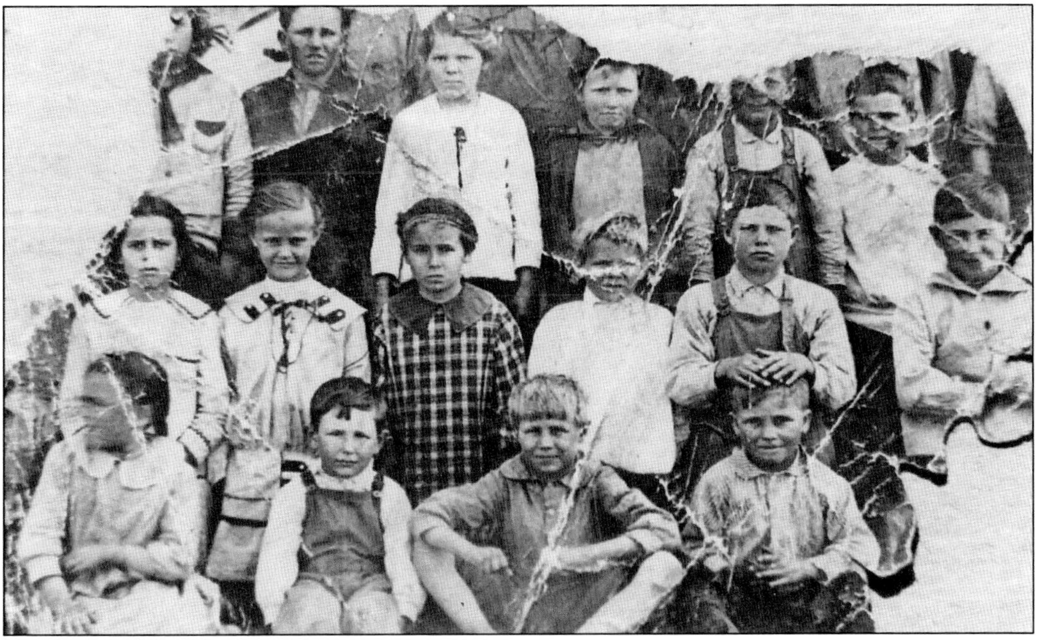

The Amy School was created about 1890, but the community started declining in 1905. Pictured about 1915, from left to right, are the following students: (first row) Sula Steed, J. W. Watson, Burton Moore, and Noble Dawson; (second row) Beatrice Sidle, Rea Davis, Irene Moore, Jack Brewer, Marvin Rose, and Foy Moore; (third row) unidentified, Dan Frazier, Ruby Brewer, Eunice Adams, unidentified, and Charlie Action. (Courtesy of Daphne Story.)

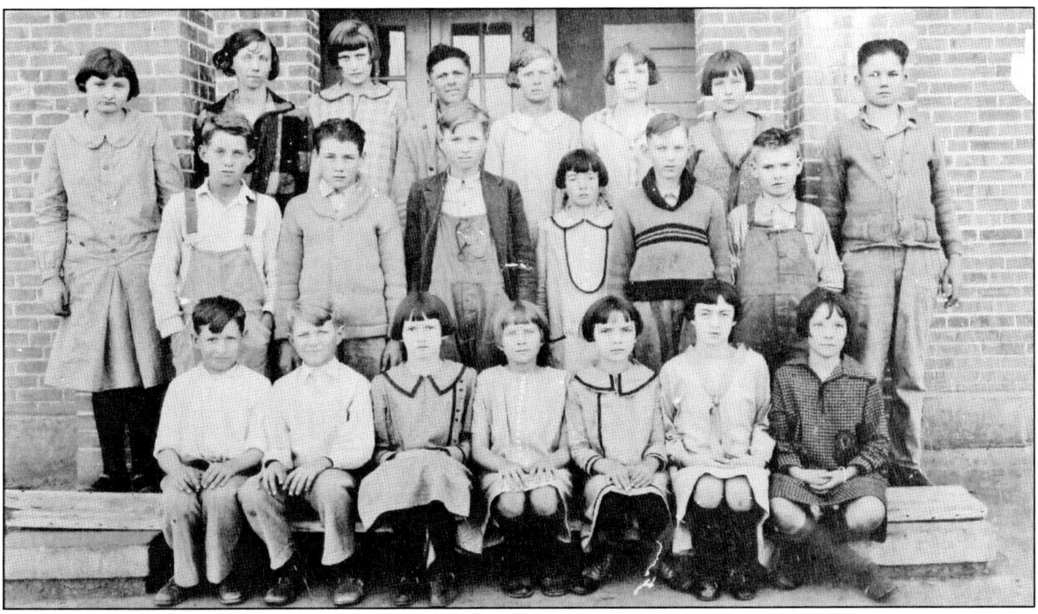

The Simmons family arrived in the area in 1835 and they were among the first settlers near Ben Franklin. The first school was probably established shortly after the Civil War. Records for 1918 indicate two schools, one for white children and one for black children. The community grew, declined, and then grew again several times over the next century. Students in the fifth and sixth grades in 1925 appear above. (Courtesy of Patterson Museum.)

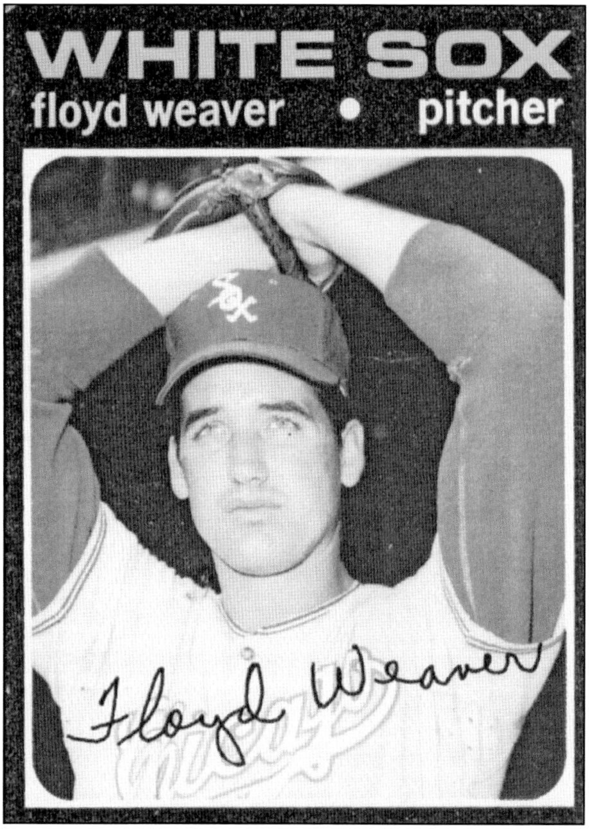

Floyd Weaver was born in Ben Franklin. While attending Paris Junior College, his baseball team went to the National Junior College Tournament, the world series for junior colleges. He set a strikeout record that still holds today—21 strikeouts in a nine-inning game. Shortly after setting this record, he turned professional, going with the Cleveland Indians in 1961. His career in baseball lasted from 1961 to 1973, and he played for teams including the Cleveland Indians, Chicago White Sox, New York Mets, Milwaukee Brewers, and Chicago Cubs. Some of his fondest memories were striking out Mickey Mantle and Carl Yastrzemski; playing with Willie Mays, Roger Maris, and Reggie Jackson; and rooming with Tommy John. After returning home, he completed his degree in education in 1976 at East Texas State University in Commerce. (Both, courtesy of Kay Weaver Heath.)

TOPPS 231

FLOYD WEAVER

CLEVE. INDIANS PITCHER

Ht: 6'04'' Wt: 195 Throws: Right
Bats: Right Born: May 21, 1941
Home: Ben Franklin, Texas

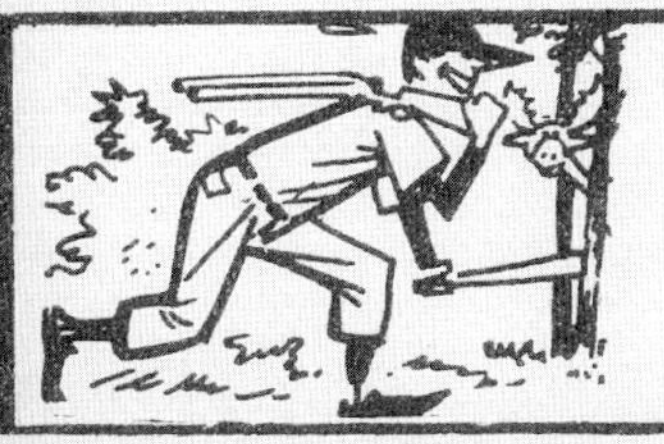

FLOYD LIKES TO HUNT AND FISH FOR RELAXATION

The young rookie righthander saw lots of action with the Indians in 1965. Floyd, a product of the Indians' farm system can throw hard. Mgr. Tebbetts expects Floyd to contribute heavily in the '66 flag bid.

COMPLETE MAJOR AND MINOR LEAGUE PITCHING RECORD

YEAR	TEAM	LEA.	G	IP	W	L	PCT	SO	BB	ERA
1961	Selma	Ala.-Fla.	3	16	1	2	.333	12	11	3.94
1961	Burlington	Carol.	15	83	6	4	.600	57	62	4.01
1962	Salt. L. City	P.C.L.	42	180	10	10	.500	88	82	5.50
1962	Cleveland	A. L.	1	5	1	0	1.000	8	0	1.80
1963	Jacksonville	Int.	14	46	1	7	.125	27	26	6.46
1963	Charleston	East.	13	91	7	3	.700	66	30	2.77
1964	Portland	P.C.L.	36	216	13	10	.565	178	91	2.75
1965	Cleveland	A. L.	32	61	2	2	.500	37	24	5.46
1965	Toledo	Int.	6	14	1	1	.500	8	8	1.93
Major League Totals		2 Yrs.	33	66	3	2	.600	45	24	5.18

©T.C.G. PRINTED IN U.S.A.

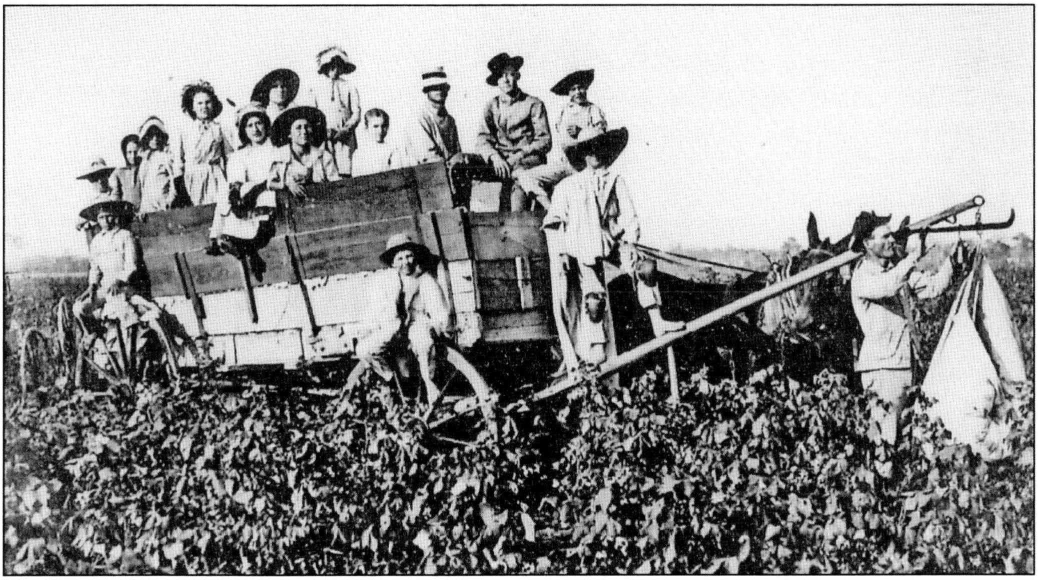

Cotton ginning and railroad shipment were major businesses in Ben Franklin, but others included a sawmill, a shingle manufacturer, a flour mill, and a feed mill. The town had general stores, hotels, livery stables, a saloon, a restaurant, an apothecary shop, doctors' offices, a barbershop, and a blacksmith shop. Pictured in August 1912, the cotton pickers above were from the Morehead, Edwards, Casey, Rorie, Mora, and Waters families. (Courtesy of Blanche Perkins.)

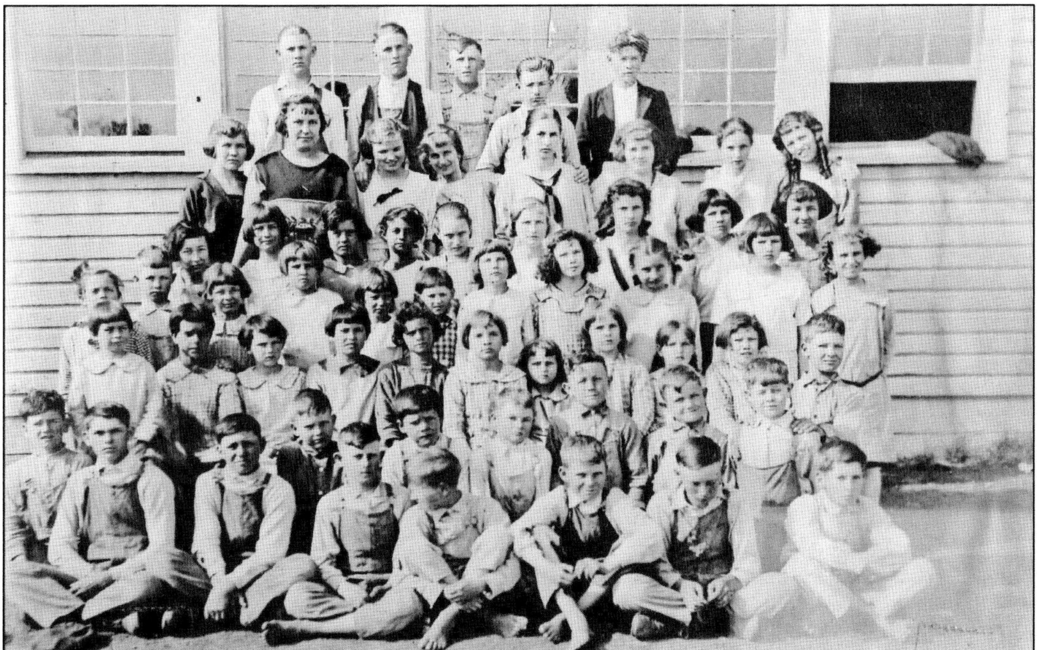

Giles Academy and Baptist Church was built in 1859 by settlers from Giles County, Tennessee. Thomas B. Hockaday was one of its first teachers. His daughter, Ela Hockaday, was the founder of Hockaday School for Girls in Dallas. Gen. Samuel Bell Maxey's 9th Texas Infantry performed drills in a nearby encampment. The date of the Giles School picture is unknown. (Courtesy of Patterson Museum.)

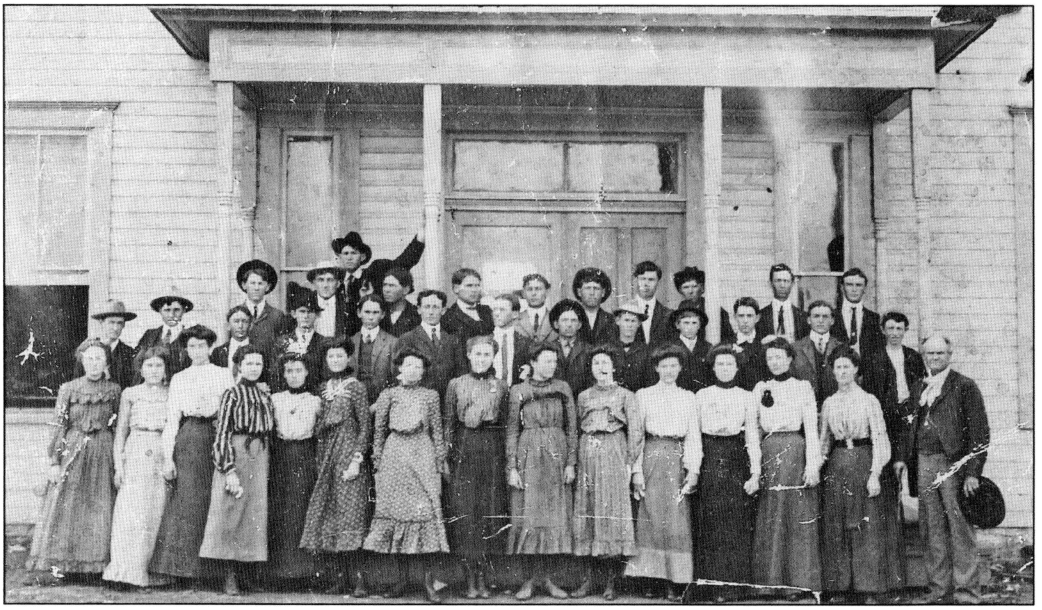

Among the early settlers from Giles County, Tennessee, were families with the names of Lane, Smith, Patteson, Moore, Nelson, and Kennedy. The Giles Academy continued to operate until it was annexed by Pecan Gap in 1949. The picture is believed to been taken after 1880. (Courtesy of Sharline Freeman.)

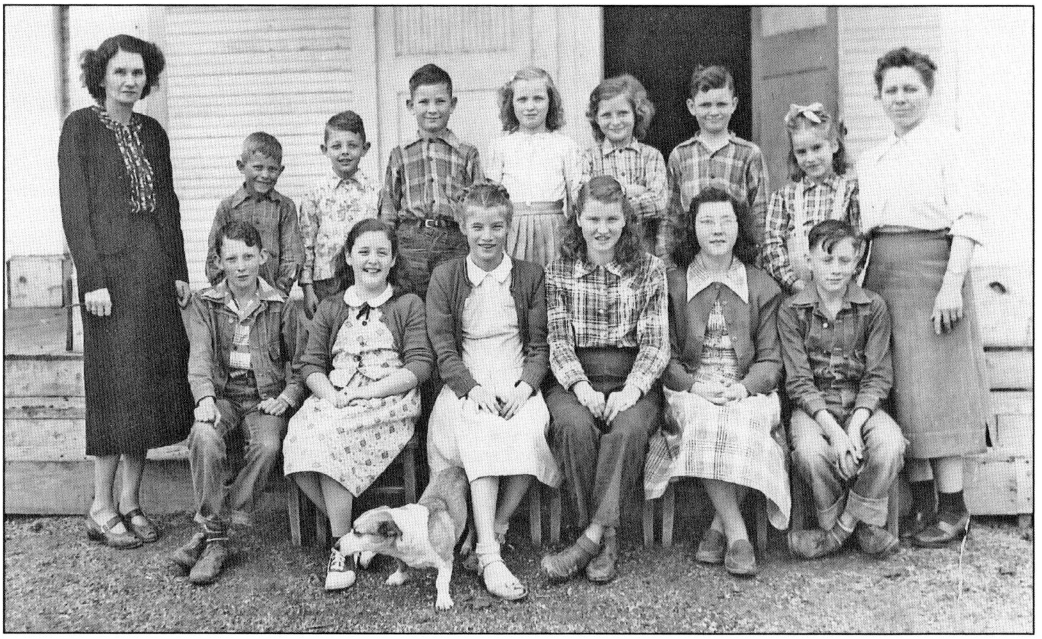

Cross Roads had several names, including Hog Wallow, Union, and Clem. The school was named Hog Wallow, but the Cross Roads name emerged because of its location. Pictured in 1948 are, from left to right, (first row) William Preston West, Peggy Garner, Ruby Jackson, Pat Grant, Glenna Stanley, Willie West; (second row) Jessie Mae Ellis, ? Roland, Roddy West, ? Roland, Betty Wood, Glynana Steward, ? Roland, Marva Hagood, Mrs. Hargraves (teacher) (Courtesy of Pat Grant and Glynana Steward.)

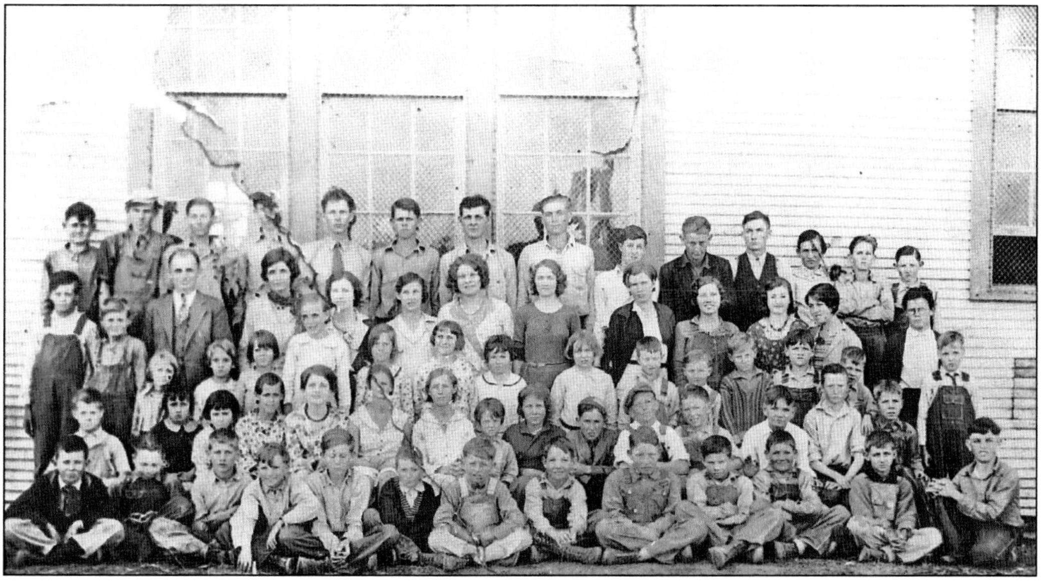

This picture shows the Craig Prairie School about 1908. Students pictured are from the Wester, Wickersham, Irby, Skinner, Young Kerbow, Rhodes, Skeen, Dodd, Robertson, Hurley, Calhoun, Stagner, Pickens, and Russell families. Alva Kerbow was the teacher. (Courtesy of Daphne Story.)

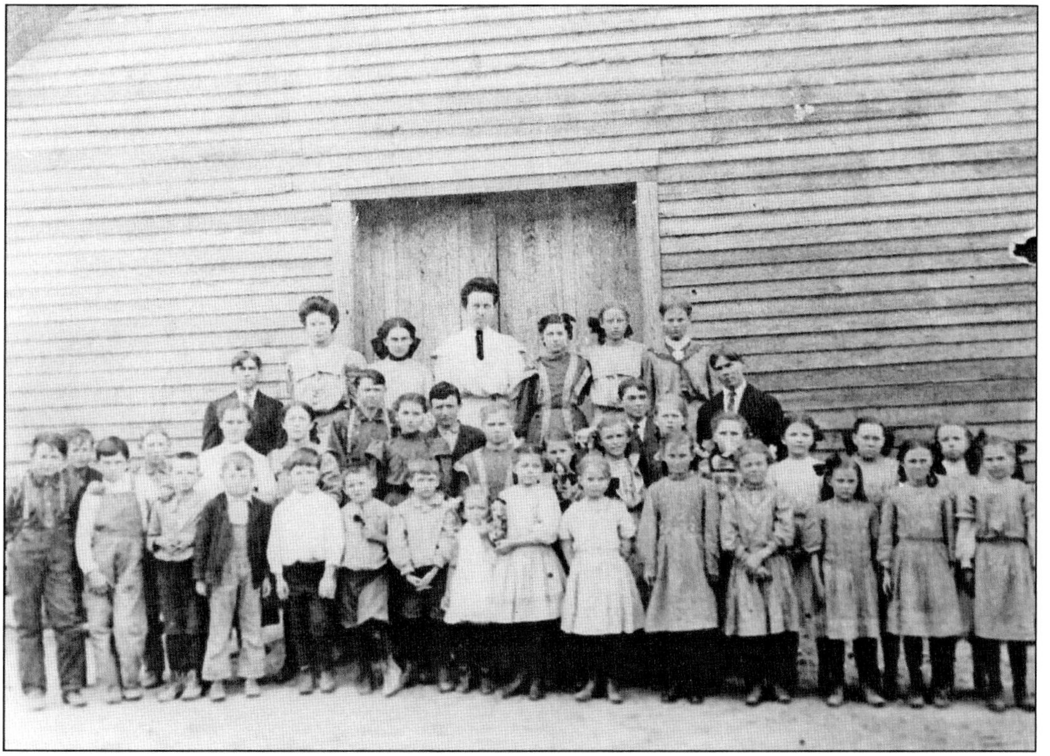

The area of Craig-Tranquil was settled in the mid-1850s. A Methodist Episcopal Church, South was established, and a school nicknamed Bloody Hollow was started about 1905. The students and teachers are shown above. The school was later merged with Craig Prairie. (Courtesy of Daphne Story.)

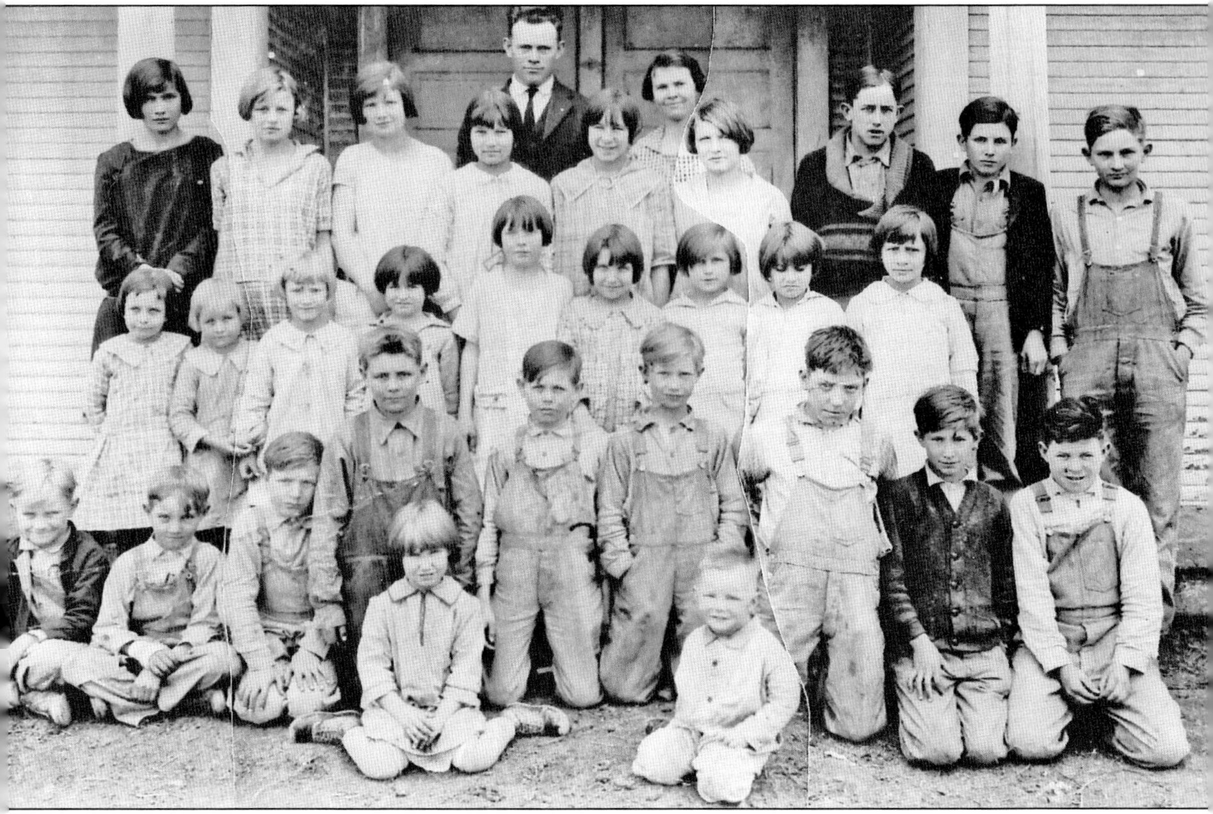

The 1926 Greenwood School picture includes the following students and visitors, from left to right: (first row) Clarice Pendergrass and W. O. Hendley Jr.; (second row) Cotton Echols, Jason Staley, Haskel Virgil, R. D. Walker, two unidentified, Ray Bush, unidentified, and Wilson Smith; (second row) Ethel Toppings, Lucille Toppings, ? Hurley, Lucille Walker, ? Bledsoe, Mildred Echols, Lorene Walker, Bill Echols, and Katherine Virgil; (third row) Opal Hurley, Inez Smith, Vessie Hurley, Ellene Stanley, Cora Toppings, Avis Brannon, J. C. Toppings, Houston Echols, and Wayne Stanley. The teachers, in back, are Mr. and Mrs. W. O. Hendley. (Courtesy of Daphne Story.)

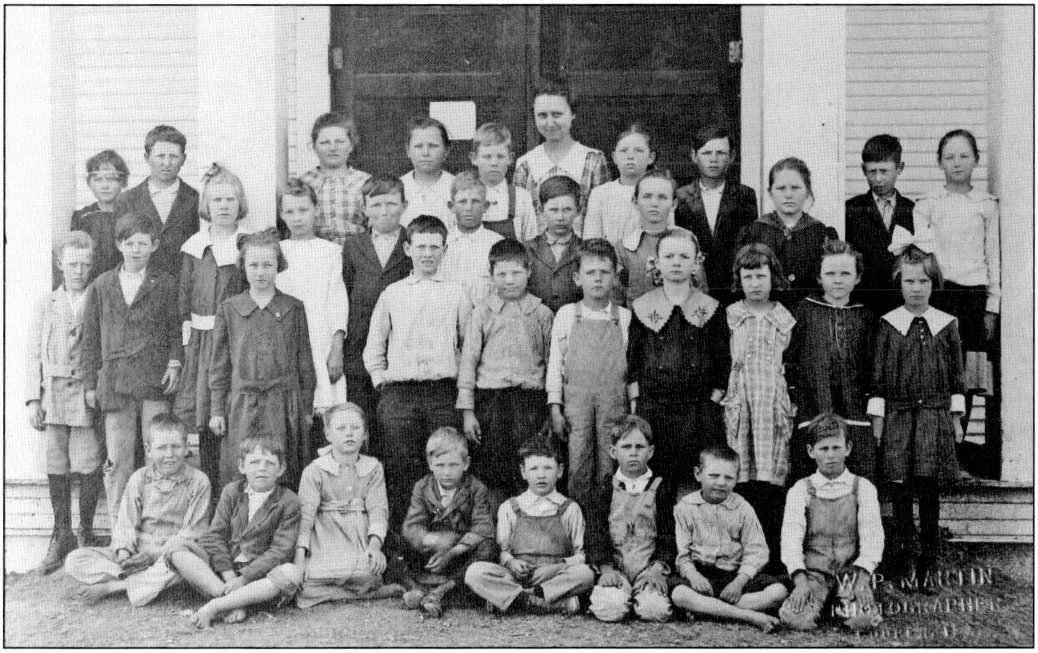

Mount Joy was a church community in northeast Delta County so named when a Virginia emigrant reached the area and expressed her relief at finally arriving safely at her new home. The school was established in 1897, and the students above attended in 1917–1918 with Ruth Stovall as teacher. (Courtesy of Patterson Museum.)

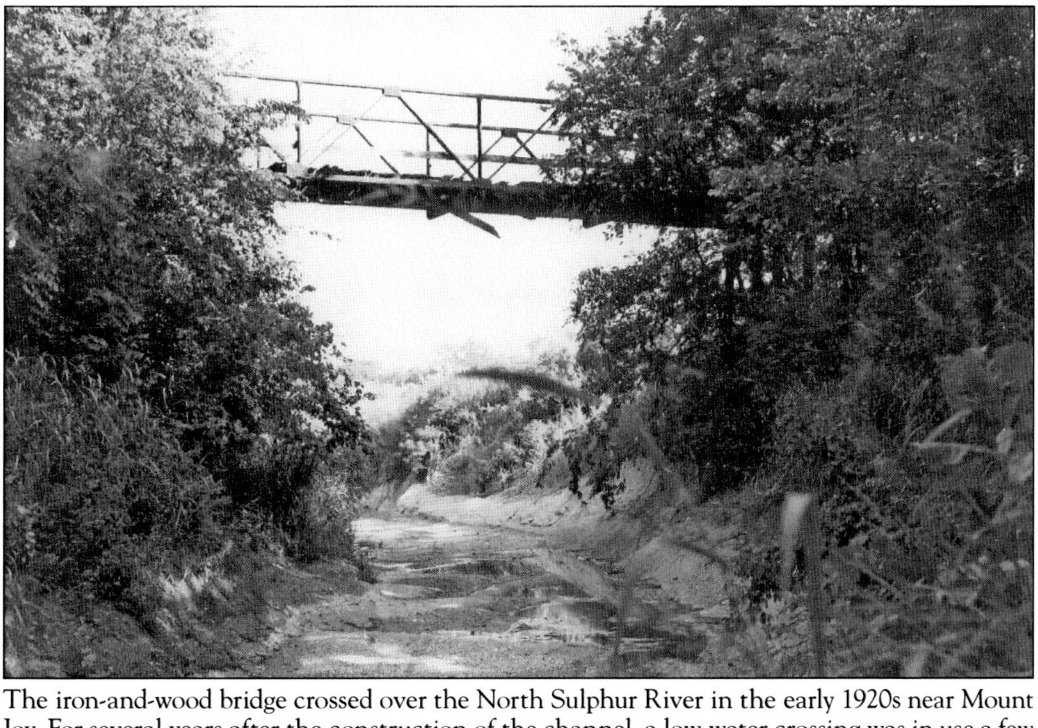

The iron-and-wood bridge crossed over the North Sulphur River in the early 1920s near Mount Joy. For several years after the construction of the channel, a low-water crossing was in use a few feet west of the old bridge. (Courtesy of Clara Foster Slough Museum.)

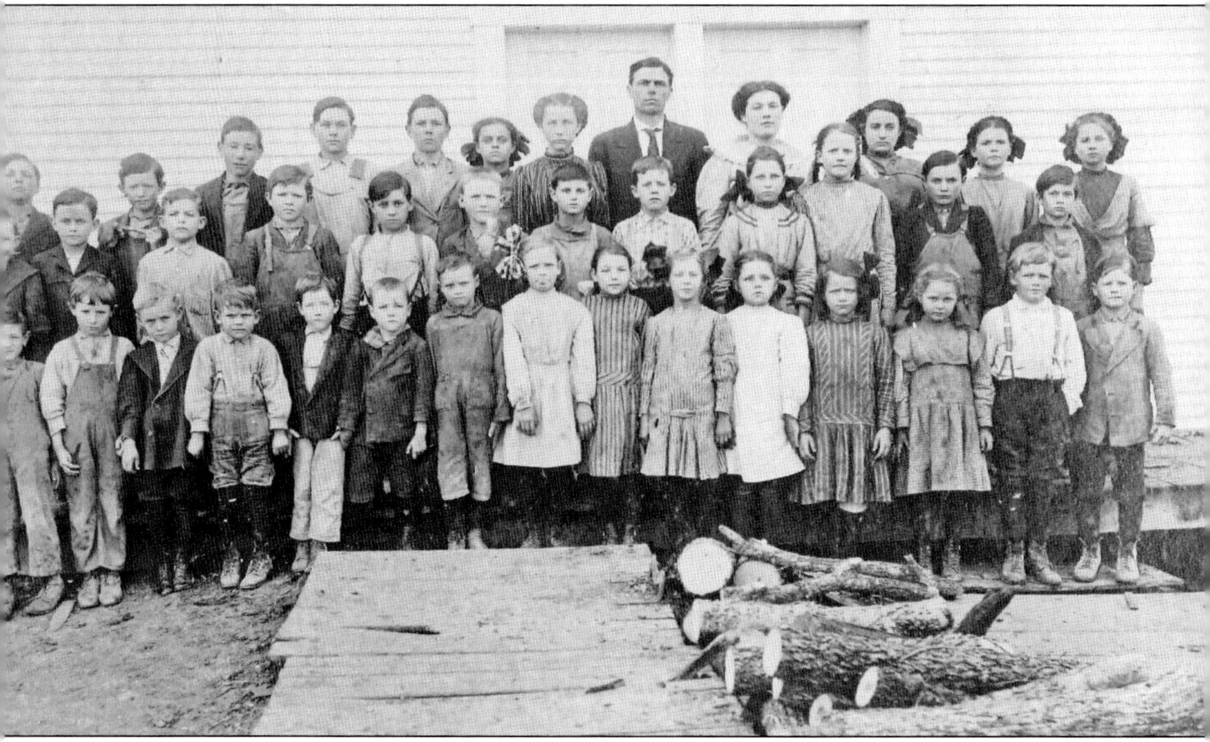

Race Track was a community located about 3 miles south of Ben Franklin and was so named because of the horse races held every Sunday on a prairie racetrack. About 1910, the teacher was Delmar Black, and students identified in the picture are J. W. Gideon, Frank Pitts, Earl Earnest, Walter Devers, Jennings Jordan, Pauline Morehead, Bessie Thompson, Hazel McMillian, ? Jordan, Herbert Ernest, Roy Fort, Herndon Gideon, Ollie Devers, ? Roberts, Ivor Mullican, Jessie Jordan, Thelma Morehead, Ocie Adams, Odessa Childers, Mary Clark, Bryan Brackeen, Bob Pitts, Alta Jordan, Veva Mullican, Beatrice Childers, Eula Childers, Lillie Belle Pitts, Ora Pitts, Maidea Black, Etta Mullican, Millie Golden, and Minerva Mullican. (Courtesy of Patterson Museum.)

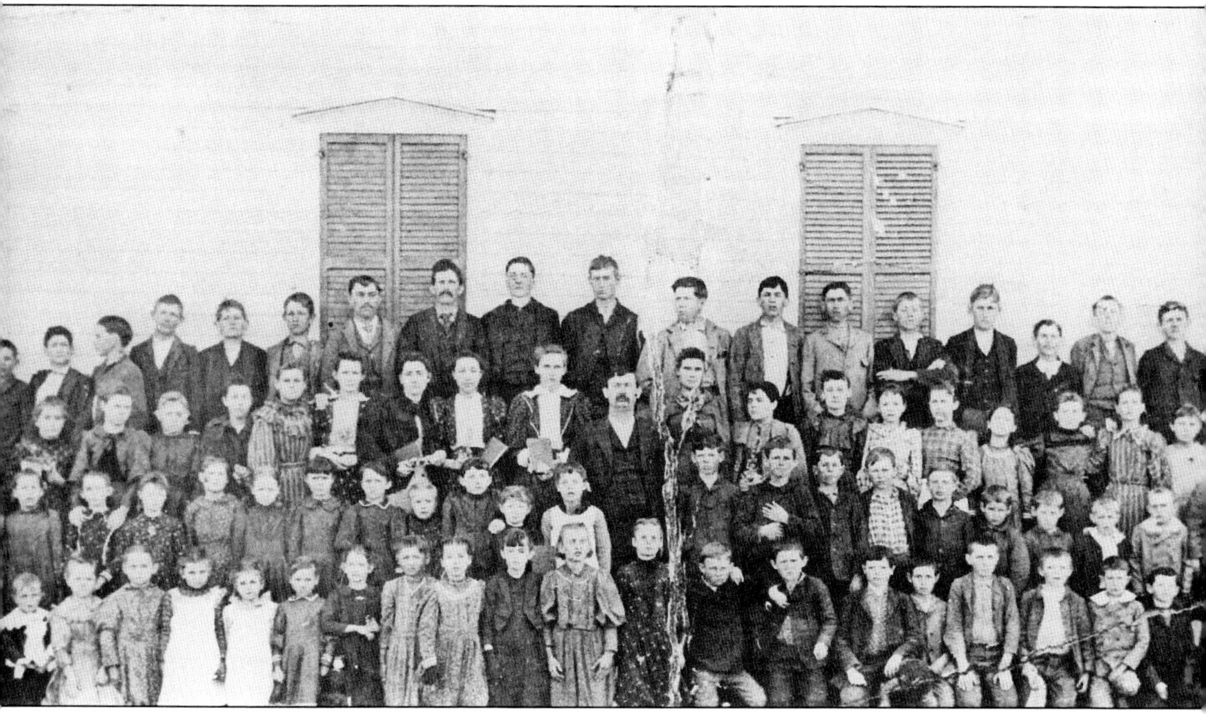

At Unitia in 1893–1894, Jim Wilkinson was the teacher. Students are, from left to right, (first row) Cora Shelton, Pierce Coston, Pearl Byrns, unidentified, Alice Moore, Carrie Moore, Addie Chappell, Mollie Patterson, Mary Vanderburg, Lucy Wilkinson, Alma Iglehart, Bessie Coston, Bessie Jackson, Elsie Kerbow, Ennis Parramore, Percy Garrett, Alfus Beckham, Will Iglehart, Bascum Patterson, Ernest Patterson, Avie Garrett, and Albert Aaron; (second row) Tommie Cooper, Minnie Shelton, Molly Patterson, Hettie Coston, Molly McWhorter, Lois Wallace, Nina Patterson, Mamie Chappell, Vera Jackson, Eunice Byrns, Maggie Shelton, Edward Moore, Tom Coston, Lee Jackson, Roger Kerbow, Hugh Moore, Elmer Coston, Elbert Coston, Charlie Coston, Fred Kerbow, and Dode Enloe; (third row) Audrey Patterson, Lillie McWhorter, Hattie Byrns, Laura Howell, Lula Jackson, Annie Patterson, Inez Patterson, Lou Howell, Lizzie Whitlock, Maggie Reynolds, Bessie Shelton, Gertrude Iglehart, Alva Patterson, Gertrude Shelton, Amelia Wilkinson, Minnie Guthrie, Jimmie Patterson, and Mattie Vanderburg; (fourth row) Bennett Kerbow, Joe Whitlock, George Patterson, Lee Wilkinson, Jud Coston, Edmund Coston, Will Maupin, Bill Whitlock, Floyd Cooper, Jim Coston, Eugene Slough, Marvin Patterson, R. E. DeWitt, Thurston Coston, Alex Coston, George Shelton, Lloyd Iglehart, and Elmer Patterson. (Courtesy of Daphne Story.)

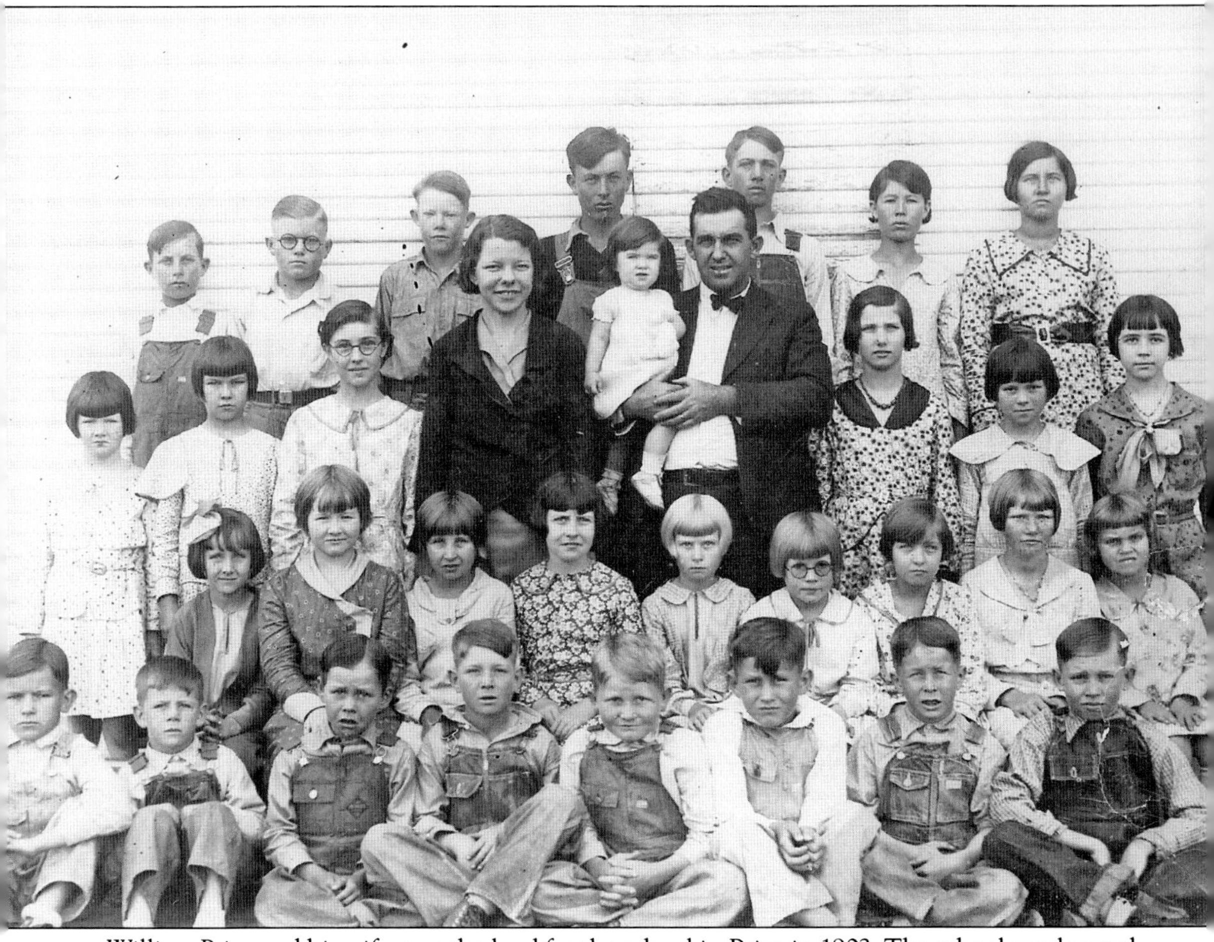

William Price and his wife gave the land for the school in Price in 1902. The school was located about 5 miles northwest of Cooper. Pictured about 1931–1932 are, from left to right, (first row) Coy Sansing, Ralph Smead, T. J. Shields, William McBrayer, Billy Mosley, Jack Taylor, Joe Kitchens, and unidentified; (second row) Dorothy Spees, Adeline Martin, Nell Cross, Billie Bruton, Nathalie Bogan, Bonnie Mosley, Jim Scott, and two unidentified; (third row) Elizabeth Smead, Helen Sansing, Mary Anita Scott, Christine Bledsoe (teacher), Cecil Toon (teacher, holding unidentified girl), unidentified, Lora Bell Shields, and Aileene Martin; (fourth row) James Moses, Louell Mosley, two unidentified, Charlie McBrayer, Jennie Moses, and Kay Kerbow. (Courtesy of Leo and Dorothy Millard.)

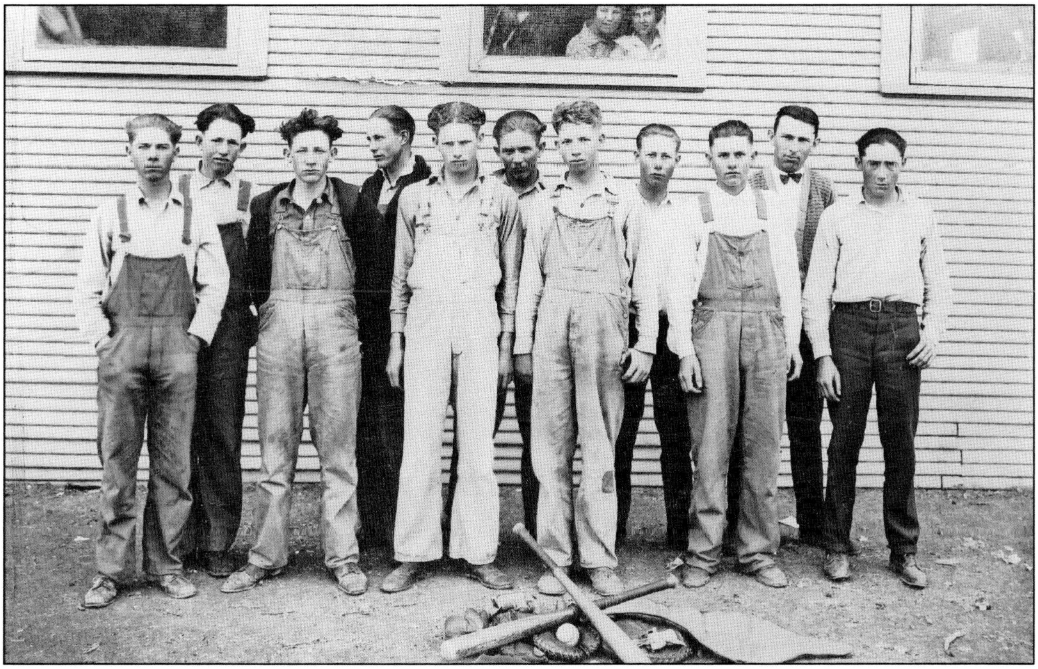

The community of Rattan developed in the late 1890s, and a school was established about 1900. The baseball team members in 1925–1926 were, from left to right, (first row) Ebb Neal, Trent McFerren, Foy Moss, Lee Roy Bailey, Bill Ellis, and Elmer Falkner; (second row) Ray Cauley, Edd Fowler, Coleman Cunning, Lee Roy Morris, and a Mr. Mason (teacher). (Courtesy of Patterson Museum.)

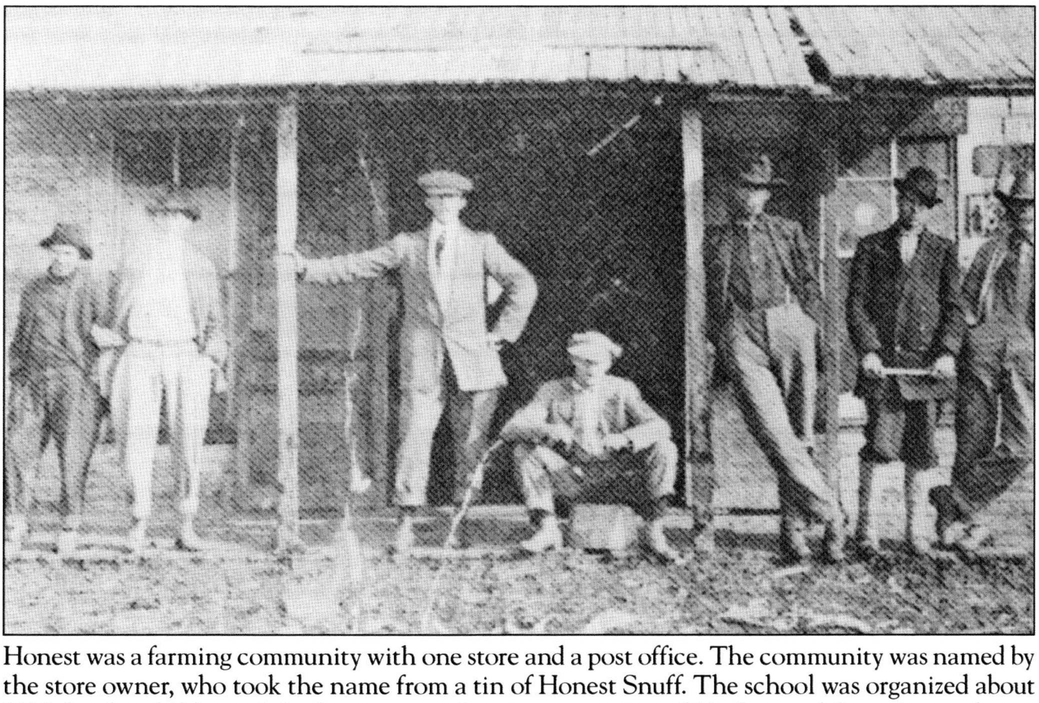

Honest was a farming community with one store and a post office. The community was named by the store owner, who took the name from a tin of Honest Snuff. The school was organized about 1915 for the children of the large tenant-farming operation of Underwood Farm in northwest Delta County. (Courtesy of Patricia Blundell.)

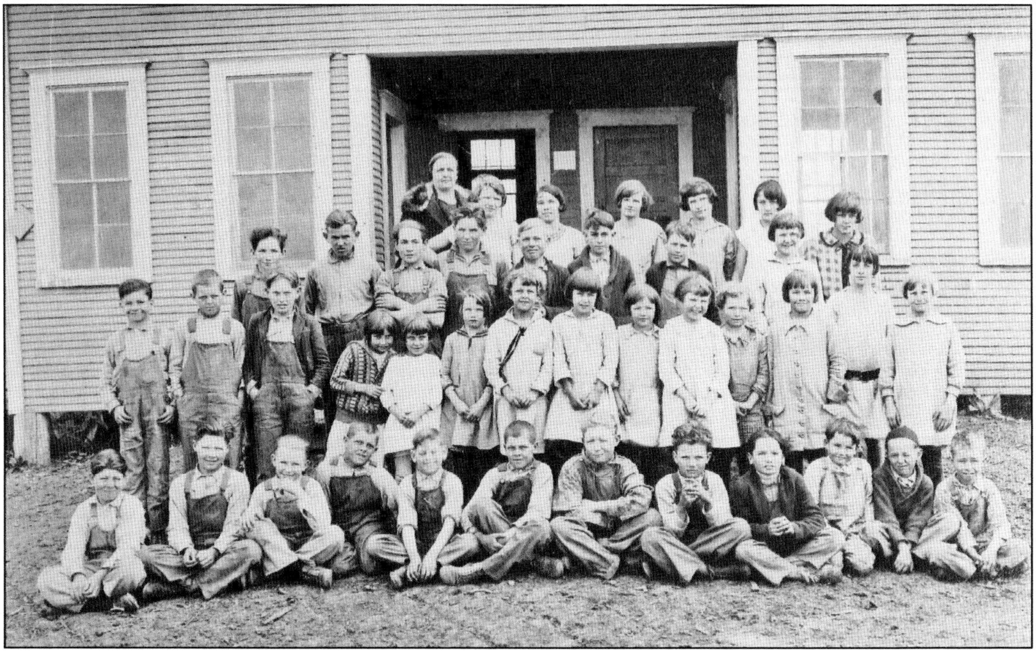

The Lone Star area was established around 1878 about a mile east of the county line and was on the Bonham–Jefferson Road. The above picture was of the students in 1924–1925 with Mrs. Keith Miller as the teacher. (Courtesy of Patterson Museum.)

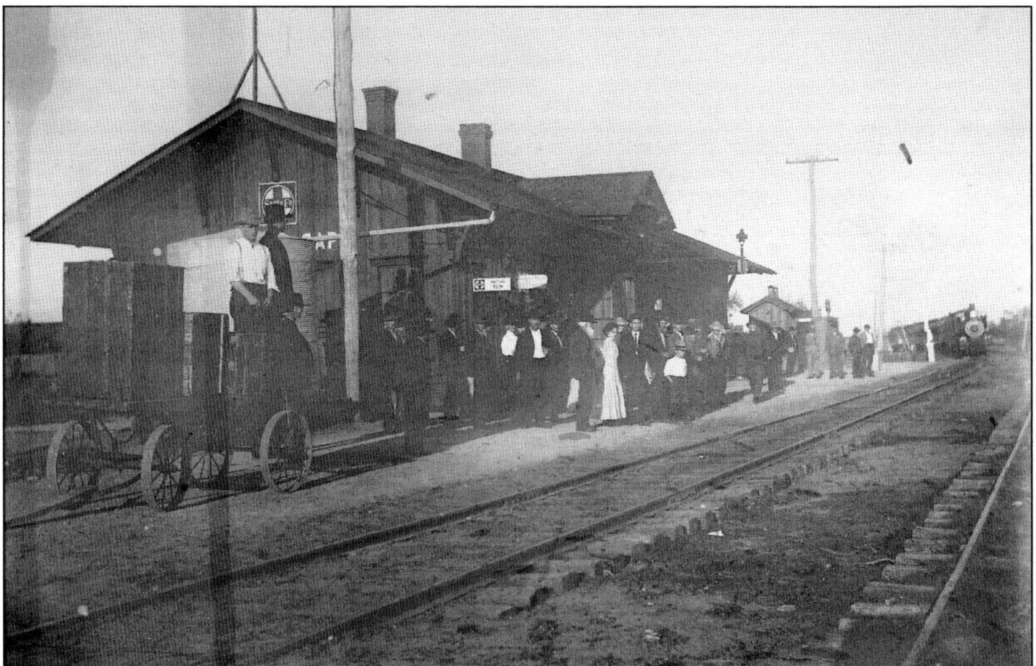

In 1888, the Santa Fe Railway came through Pecan Gap and built a depot. The town soon flourished, with general stores, a livery, a hotel, a telegraph office, gins, and lumberyards. The school was established by W. L. Mayo, who also established East Texas Normal College in Cooper then later in Commerce. (Courtesy of Nan Olson Beeler.)

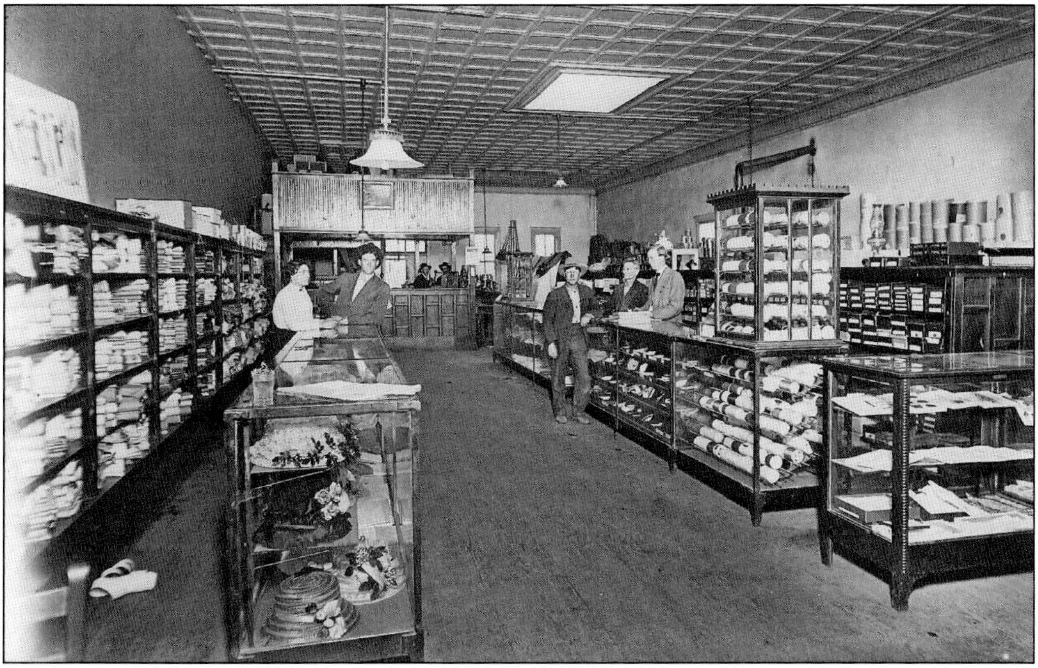

One of the many businesses in Pecan Gap was owned by John S. Reid and his family. The picture above is the dry goods store. Pictured from left to right are Modena Hensley, Bert Garson, W. S. Reid, Thomas Clower, and unidentified. Below is the Reid gas station in 1922. Businessmen are, from left to right, Adam Canup, ? Routt, Andrew Reid, unidentified, Noah Shaw, Tom McQuary, Houston Rhodes, two unidentified, Herschel Walker, George Braddock, and ? Armon. (Both, courtesy of Peggy Durham.)

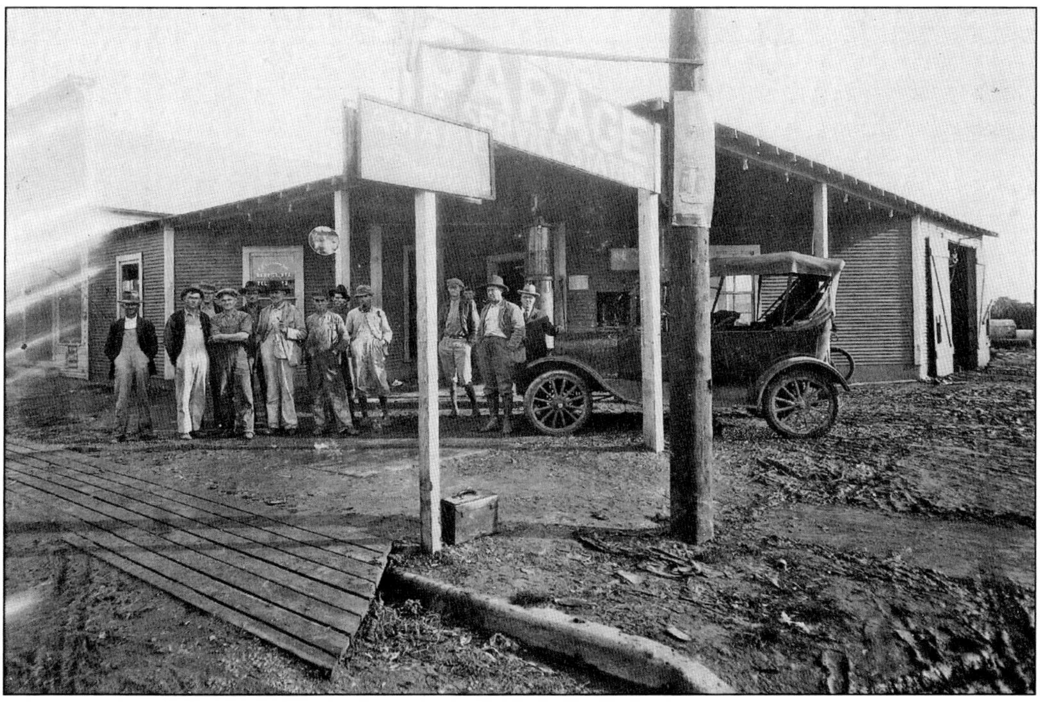

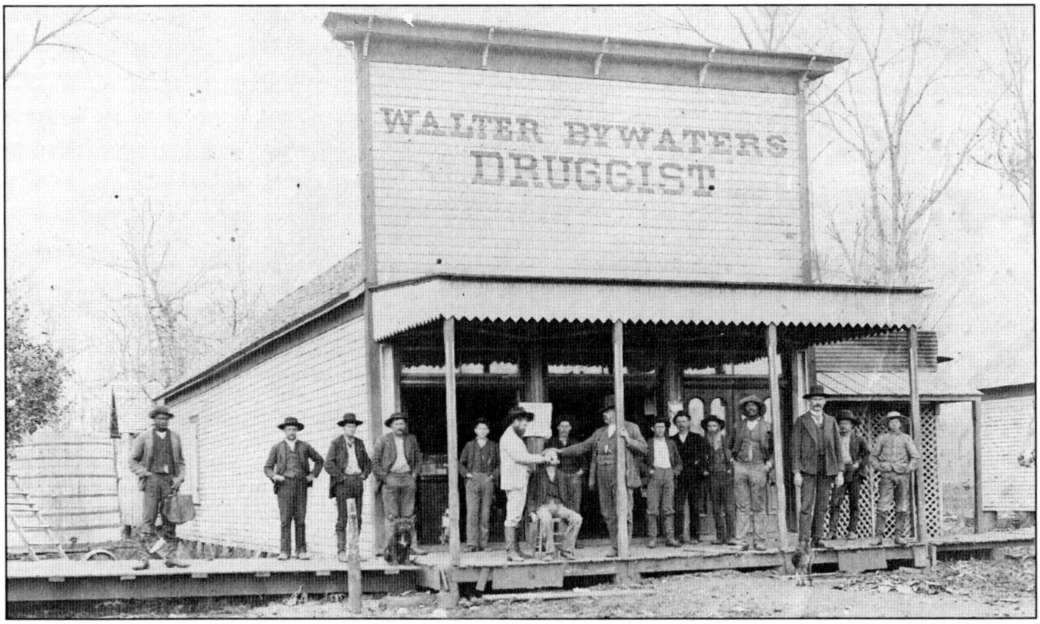

The community that had a drugstore was indeed fortunate, as these establishments not only had a druggist to compound drugs but also sold sundry items. Originally this drugstore was named the Walter Bywaters Drug Store, but the name was later changed to Hardy's Drug Store. (Courtesy of Sharline Freeman.)

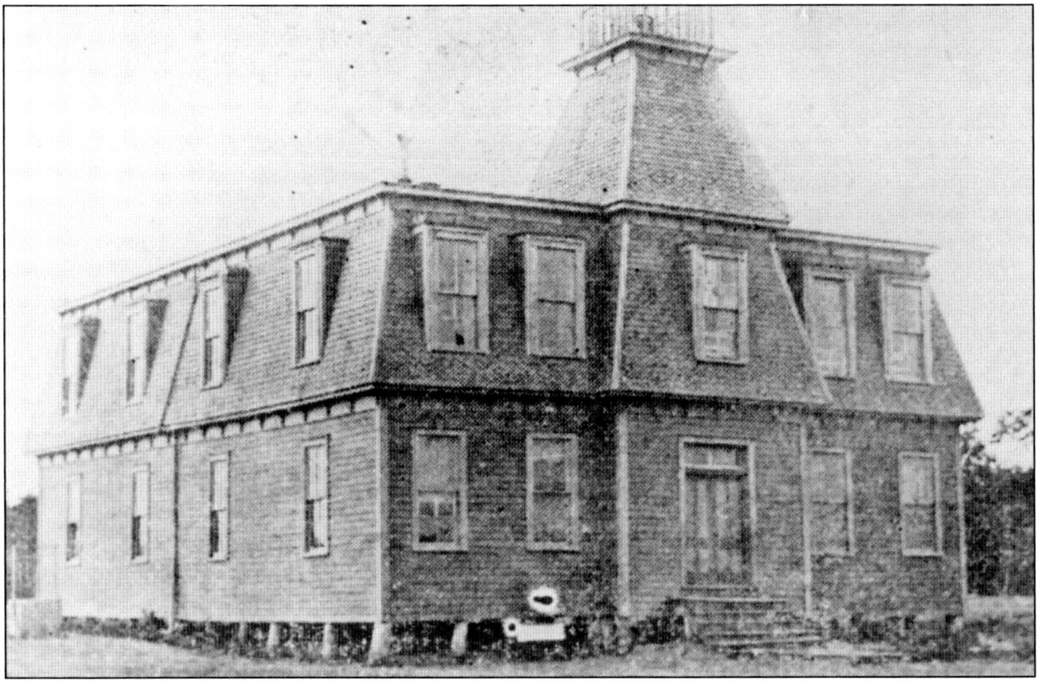

This picture shows the third Pecan Gap School building, the scene of debates on the second floor on Friday nights. Notes indicate that Sam Rayburn was a frequent visitor to the debates, walking from Dial to attend the festivities. This school operated until a new brick building was constructed with the merger of two districts after 1913. (Courtesy of Sharline Freeman.)

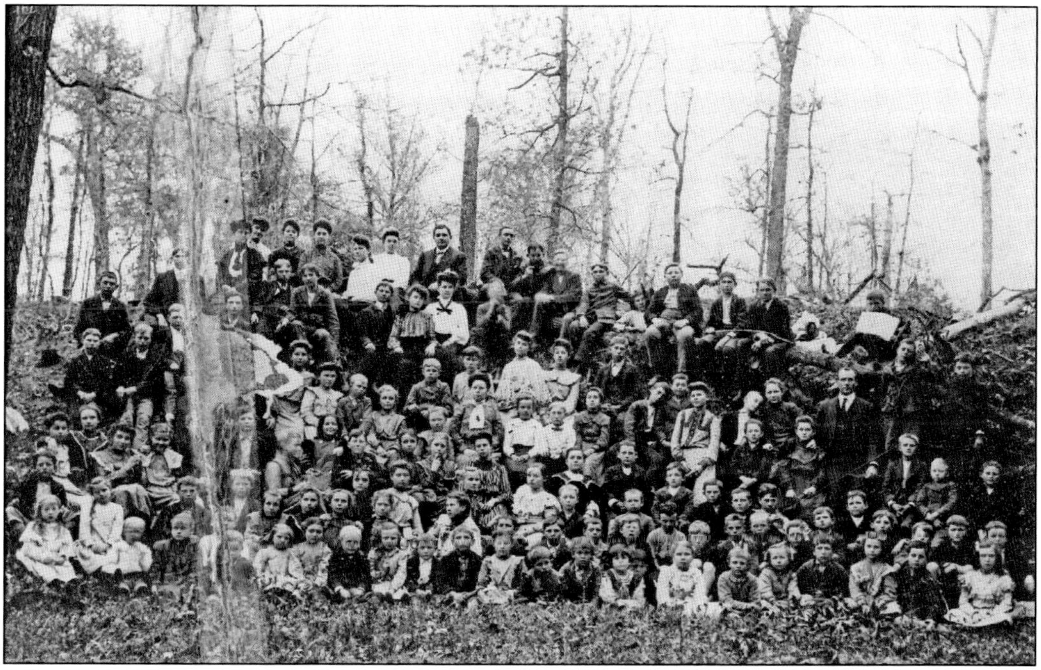

Schools in Delta County in the early 20th century taught large number of students, as evidenced by this photograph of the Pecan Gap school picnic in 1905. The end of the school year usually culminated with a picnic or social. (Courtesy of Sharline Freeman.)

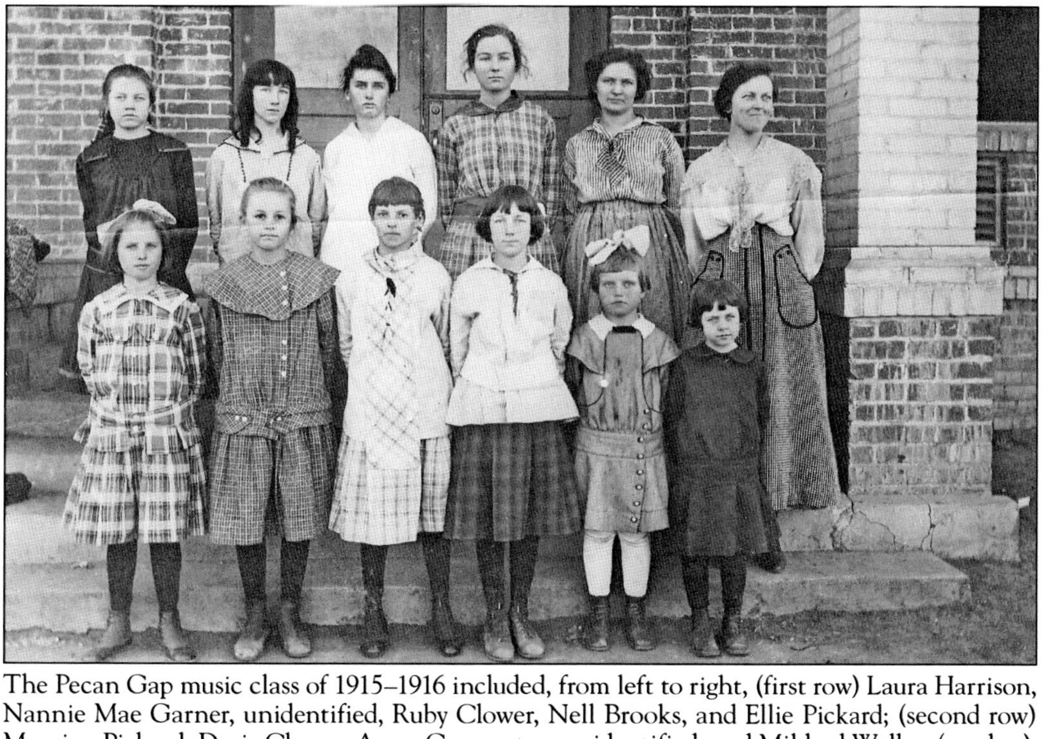

The Pecan Gap music class of 1915–1916 included, from left to right, (first row) Laura Harrison, Nannie Mae Garner, unidentified, Ruby Clower, Nell Brooks, and Ellie Pickard; (second row) Maurine Pickard, Doris Clower, Anna Garner, two unidentified, and Mildred Walker (teacher). (Courtesy of Delta County Library.)

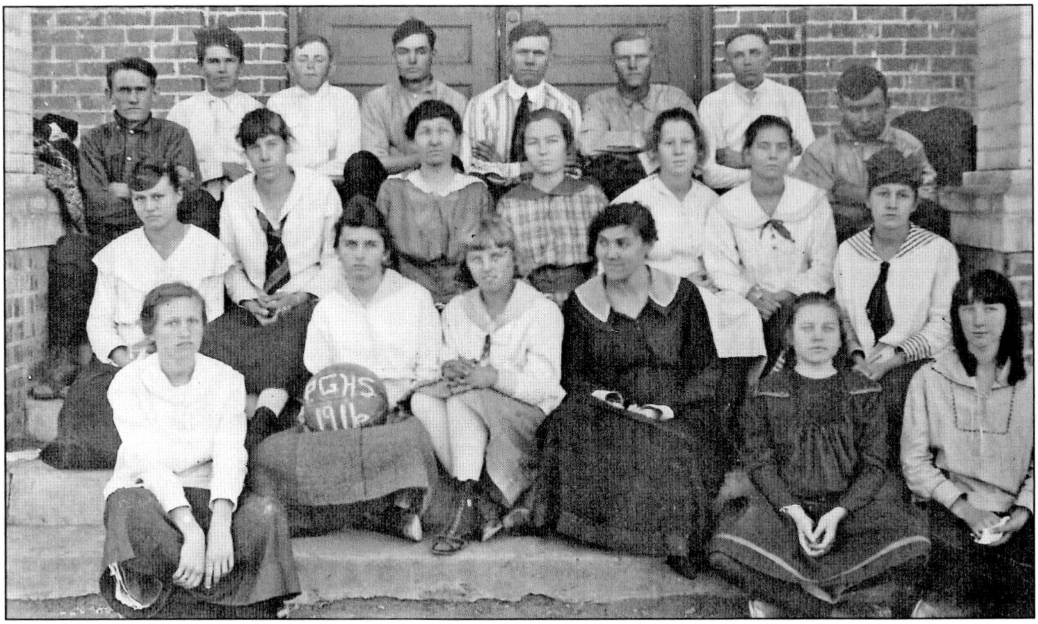

The Pecan Gap girls' and boys' basketball teams of 1915–1916 were, from left to right, (first row) Anice McCaslin, Anna Garner, Lucy Merrill, Leona Boyd (teacher and coach), Maurine Pickard, and Doris Clower; (second row) Ea McCollum, Alta Lee James, four unidentified, and Ruby Sockwell; (third row) two unidentified, Earl Bryant, Everett Reynolds, unidentified, Martin Newman, and two unidentified. (Courtesy of Delta County Library.)

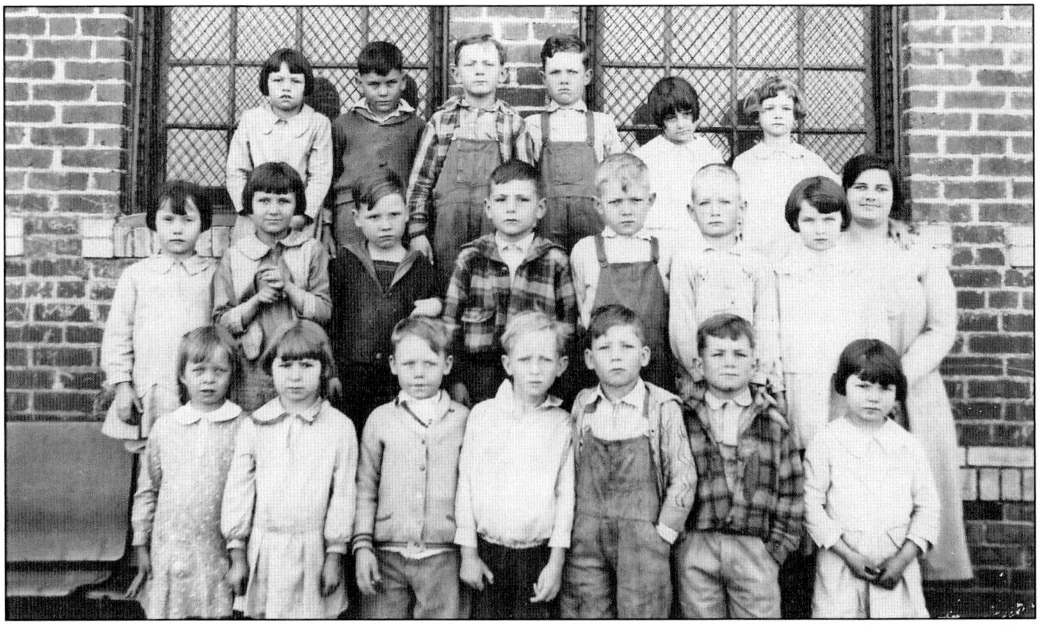

The first-grade children of Pecan Gap School in 1927 were, from left to right, (front row) Billie Jean Davis, Annie Crawford, Marshall Pickard, Leonard Jackson, Isaac Lanham, J. M. Moody, and unidentified; (second row) Joanna Hollins, two unidentified, Robert Morgan, Frank Adams, J. V. Reno, Marie Wooten, and Ione Hudson (teacher); (third row) Barbara Hancock, ? Clements, unidentified, James Adams, Adaline Burks, and Jimmie Hall. (Courtesy of Nan Olson Beeler.)

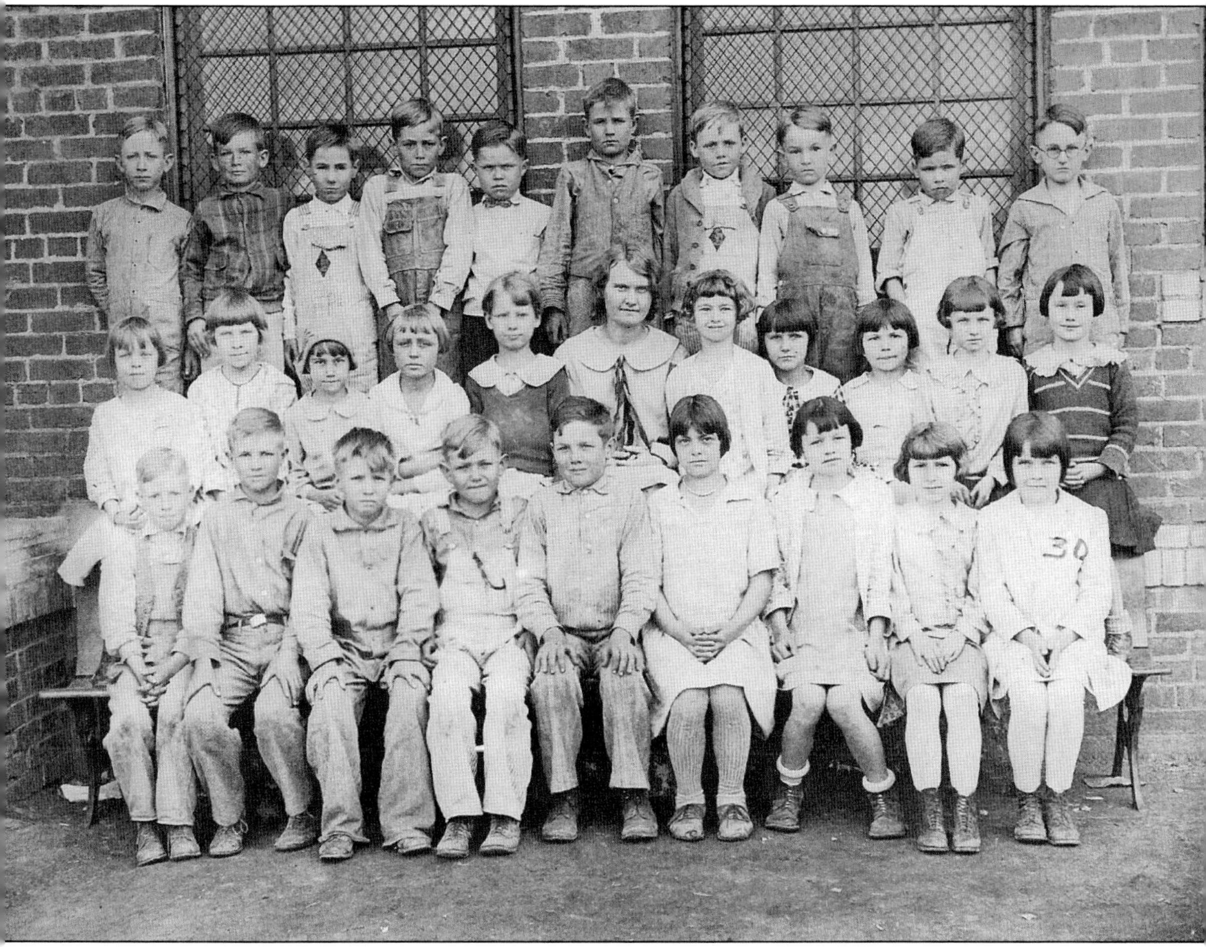

The third-grade Pecan Gap School students about 1929 were, from left to right, (first row) four unidentified, Buddy Adams, and four unidentified; (second row) Billie Davis, unidentified, Edith Myers, Pauline Miller, unidentified, Coye Young (teacher), Jimmy Hall, two unidentified, Marie Wooten, and JoAnna Hollins; (third row) Leonard Jackson, J. V. Reno, Odell Scoggins, unidentified, Billy Hollins, unidentified, Marshall Pickard, Eldon Bratton, Sam Merrill, and Billy Edwards. (Courtesy of Nan Olson Beeler.)

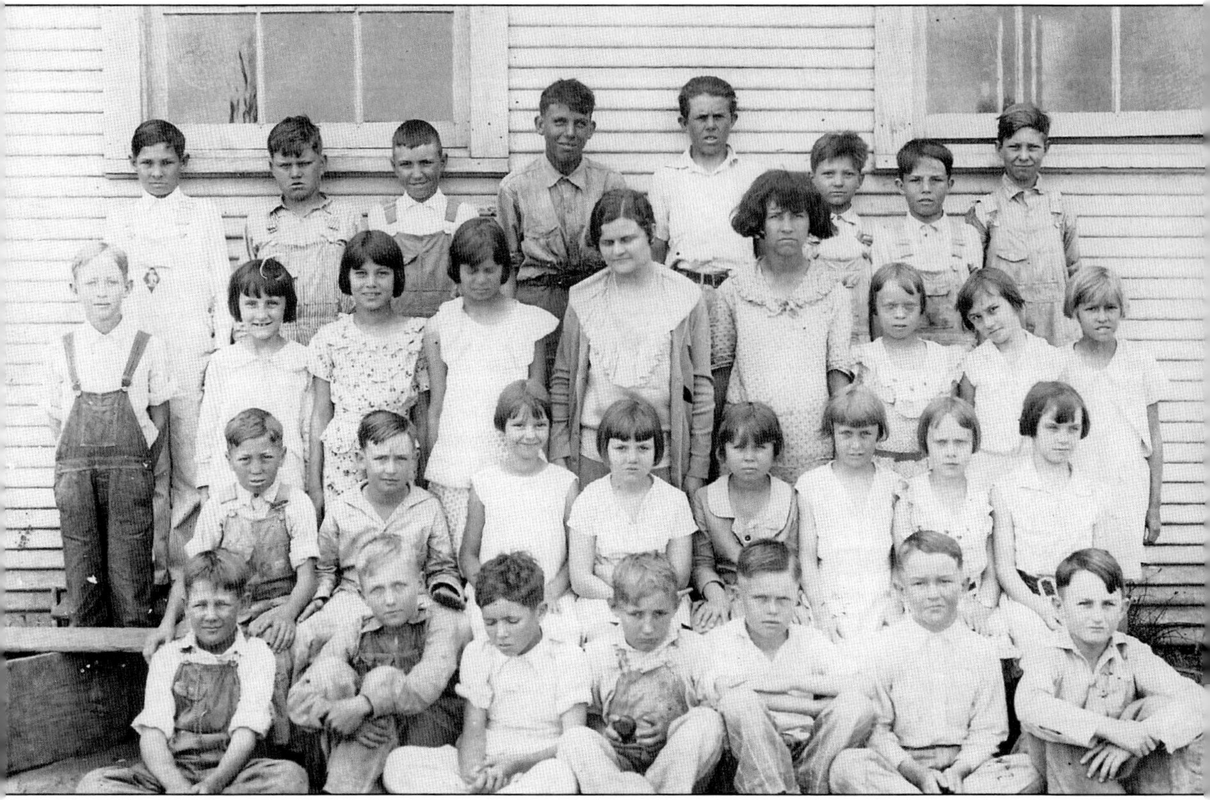

The fourth and fifth grades of Pecan Gap School in 1932 included, from left to right, (first row) Wayne Sockwell, Thomas Phillips, Sam Merrill, Herbert Langston, Billy Hollins, Eldon Bratton, and Billy Edwards; (second row) John Garner, Kyle McFerrin, Annie Albert, Vernell Gray, Dorothy Campbell, Clara Grady, Duane Davis, and Alice Fleming; (third row) Leonard Jackson, Imogene Norris, Virginia Campbell, Glenna Grady, Jewel Foster (teacher), Ada Brazer, Billie Davis, Edith Myers, and Tommie Reynolds; (fourth row) Ralph Richardson, Melvin White, unidentified, Erman McNutt, Aubrey Evans, Jimmy Rhodes, Lawrence Rittenberry, and John Rhodes. (Courtesy of Nan Olson Beeler.)

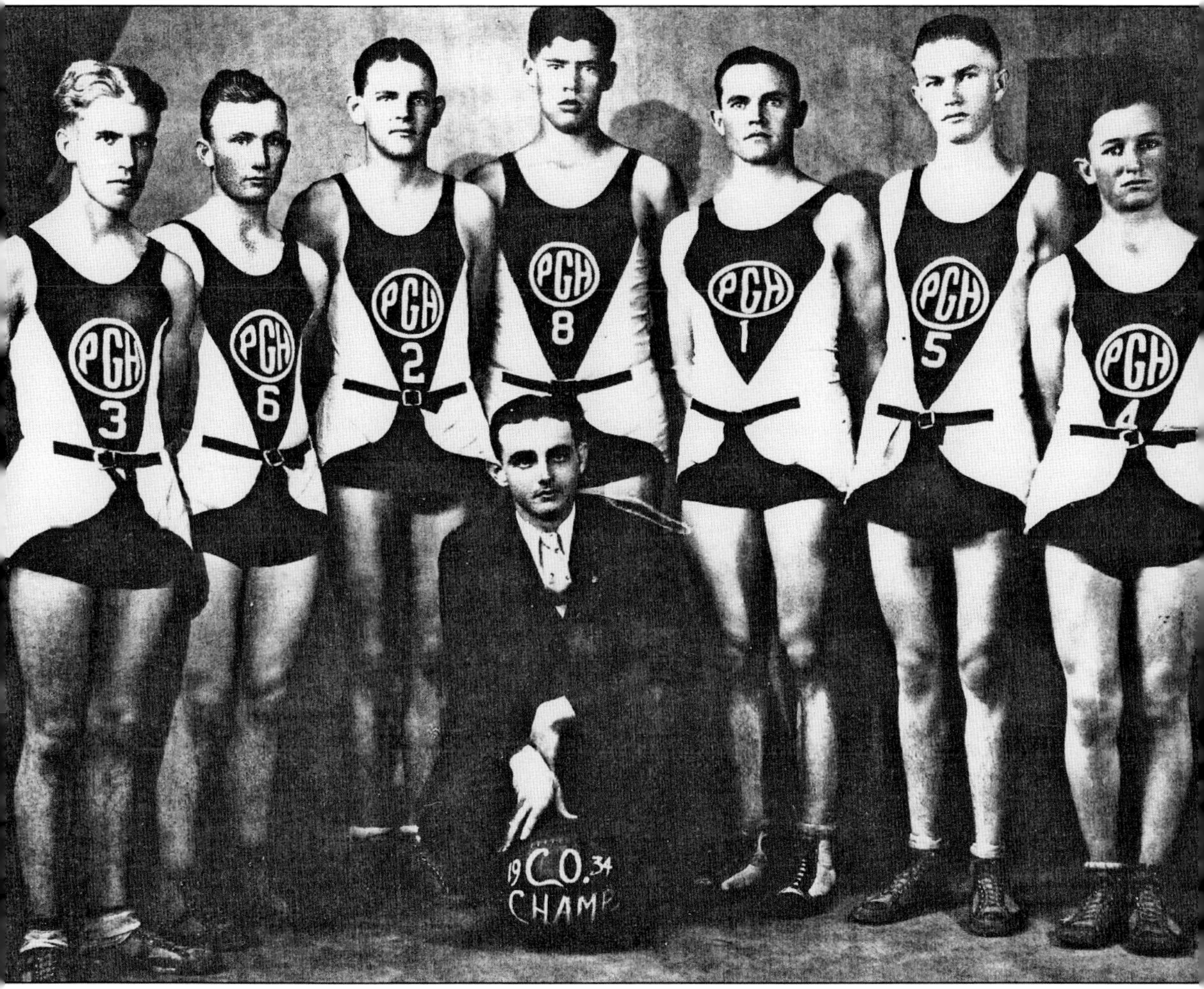

In 1934, the Pecan Gap Panthers won the Delta County Basketball Championship. The school did not have a gym, and their court was outdoors with limed lines. The team was coached by Durwood Fleming, and the team members were, from left to right, R. G. Myers, Harold Sayles, Edwin Fleming, Jack Lowery, Sam Bryant, Alfred McNutt, and Jamie Miller. (Courtesy of Pecan Gap Methodist Church.)

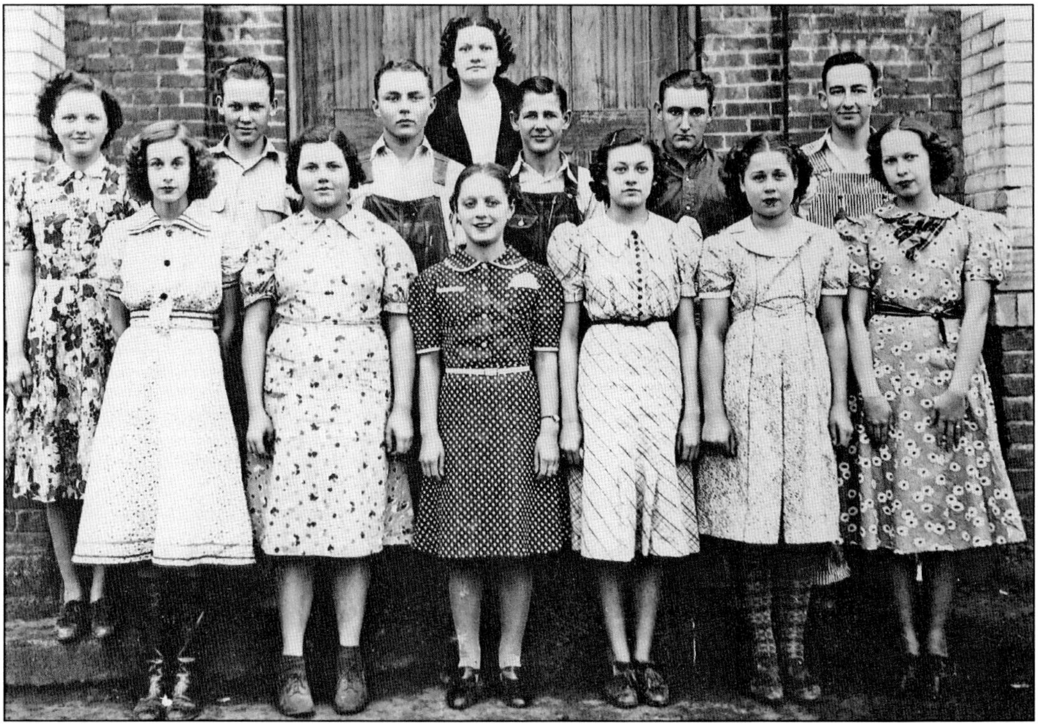

The ninth grade at Pecan Gap School in 1938 included, from left to right, (first row) Clara Grady, Vennell Gray, Clairine Cummings, Geraldine Price, Dorothy Campbell, and Duane Davis; (second row) Francyle Hall, James Liles, Brooks Fife, Wayne Sockwell, Herbert Langston, and Kyle McFerrin. Ophelia Reid, the class sponsor, is shown behind the students. (Courtesy of Nan Olson Beeler.)

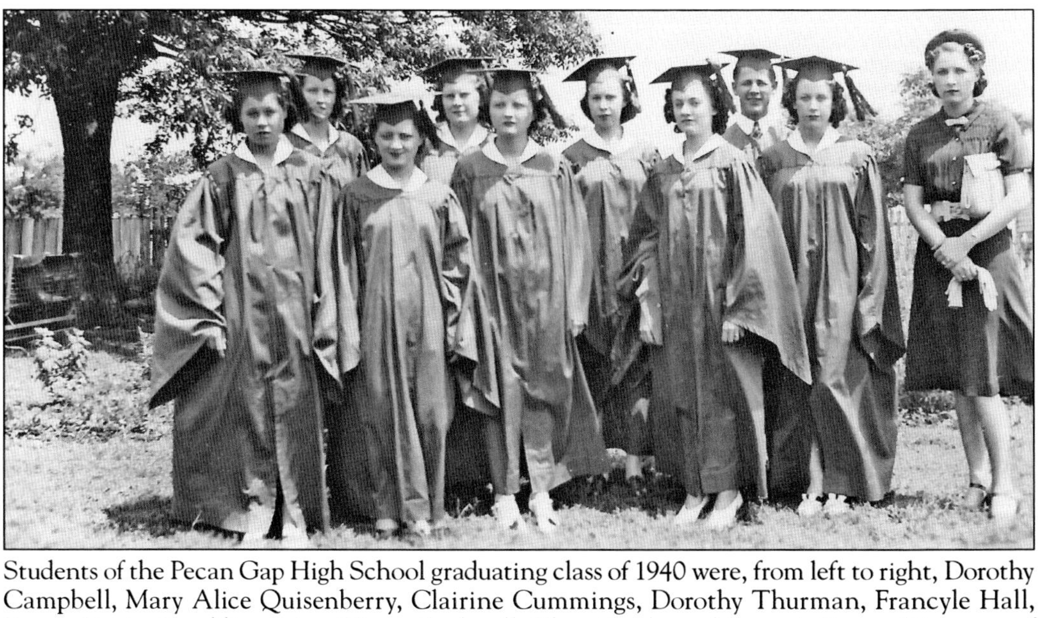

Students of the Pecan Gap High School graduating class of 1940 were, from left to right, Dorothy Campbell, Mary Alice Quisenberry, Clairine Cummings, Dorothy Thurman, Francyle Hall, Duane Davis, Geraldine Price, Wayne Sockwell, Clara Gardy, and Sammie Boyce. (Courtesy of Nan Olson Beeler.)

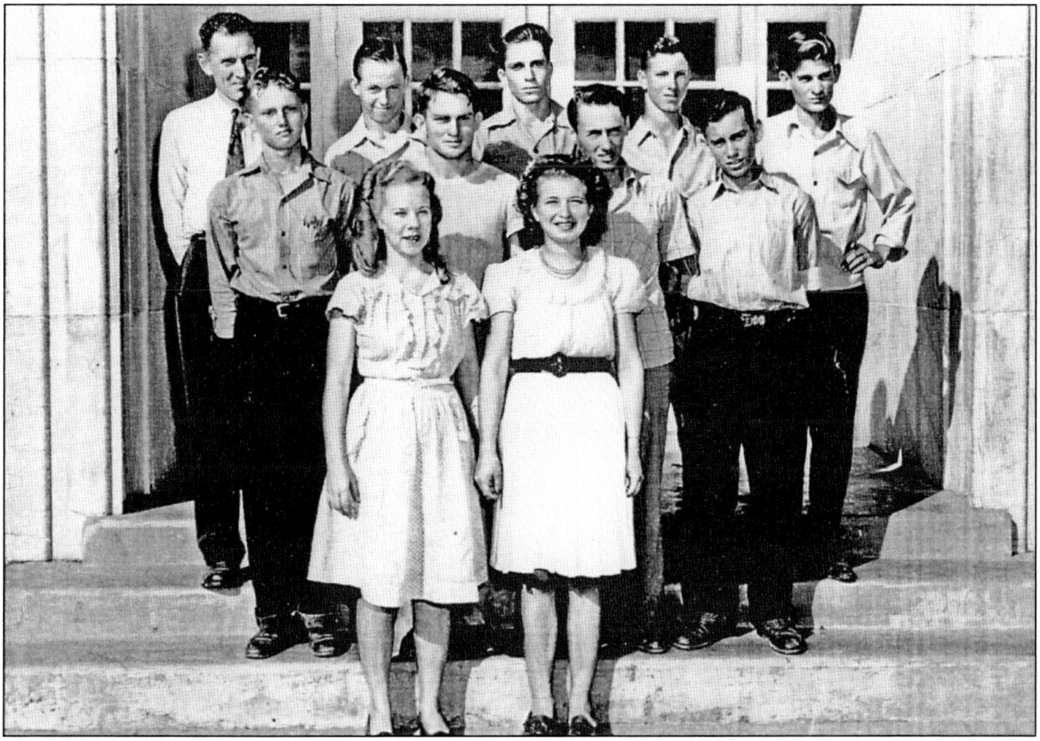

The 1947 senior class of Pecan Gap featured, from left to right, (first row) Faye Rhodes and Mary Kent; (second row) Roy Brooks, Johnny Rittenberry, Harry Scoggins, and Harold Bartlett; (third row) Harley Reeves, Joe Pickard, James Leathers, Raymond Williams, and John Rushing. (Courtesy of Sharline Freeman.)

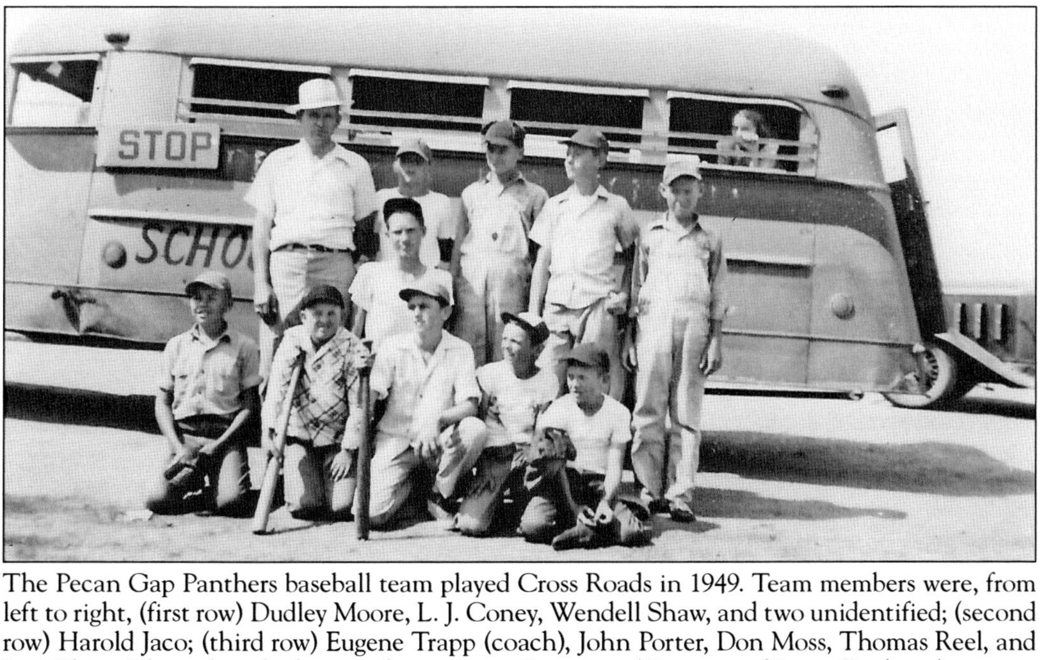

The Pecan Gap Panthers baseball team played Cross Roads in 1949. Team members were, from left to right, (first row) Dudley Moore, L. J. Coney, Wendell Shaw, and two unidentified; (second row) Harold Jaco; (third row) Eugene Trapp (coach), John Porter, Don Moss, Thomas Reel, and Joe White. The girl in the bus window is Betty Scoggins. (Courtesy of Peggy Durham.)

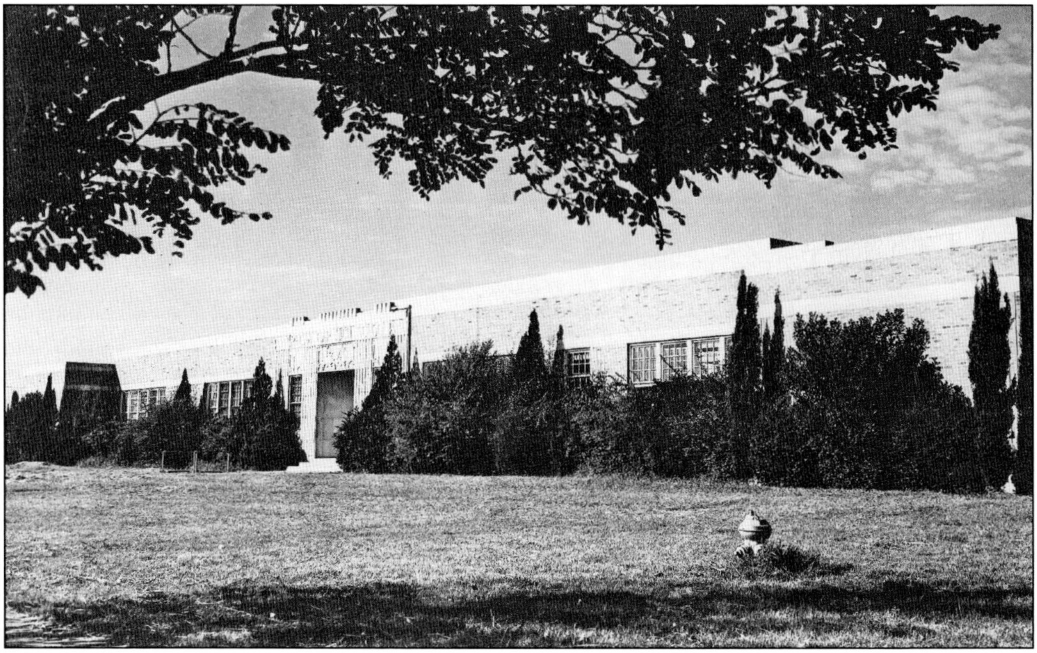

Pictured above, Pecan Gap stayed in its own district in the building constructed about 1937. In 1970, Pecan Gap joined with other small schools in Fannin County and became the Fannindel Independent School District. Below, the downtown Pecan Gap street scene shows a thriving community with many businesses, and children were able to ride their bicycles on Main Street. (Both, courtesy of Peggy Durham.)

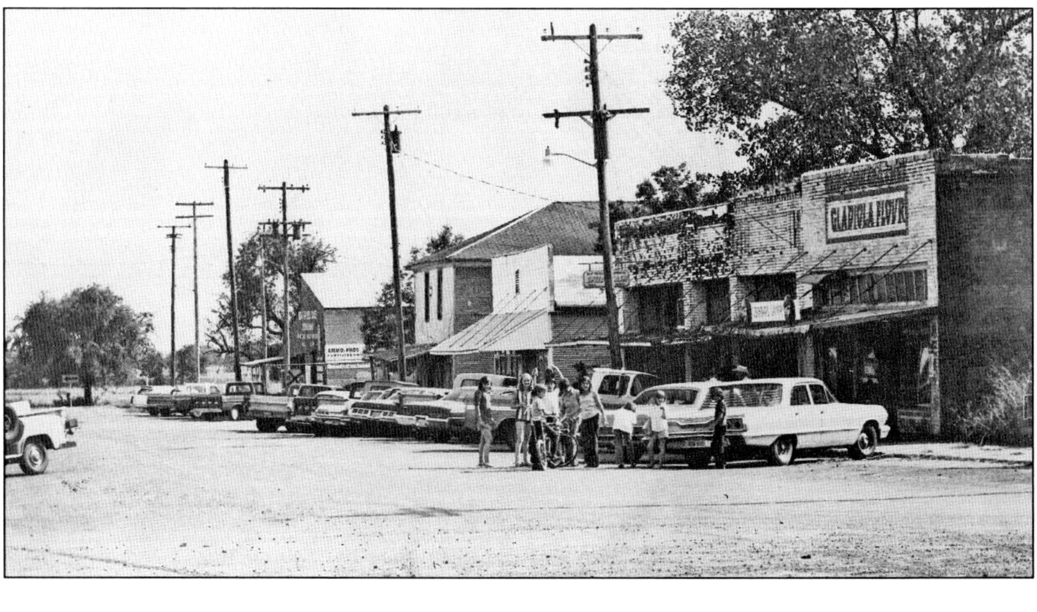

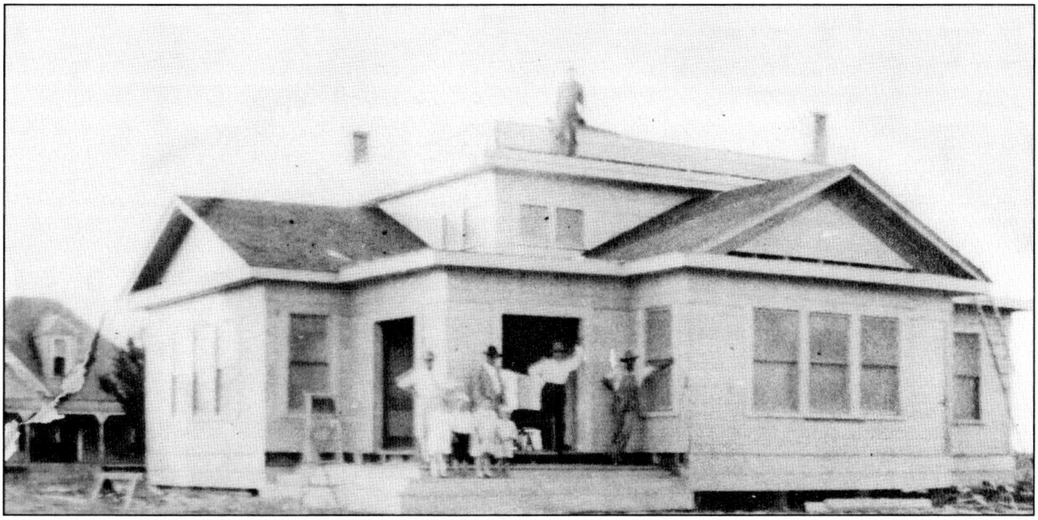

The Pecan Gap Baptist Church, above, was organized in 1885. To accommodate its growth, a new building was constructed in 1930. Below, the congregation celebrated the church's 100th anniversary in 1985. (Both, courtesy of Peggy Durham.)

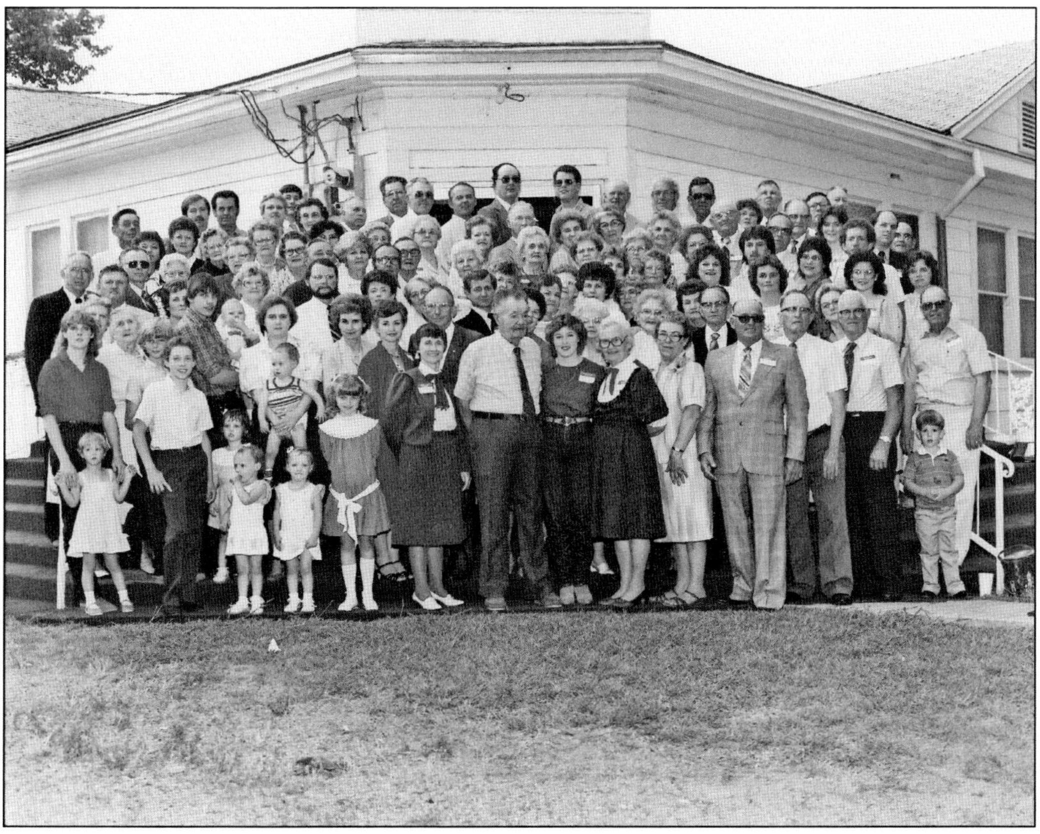

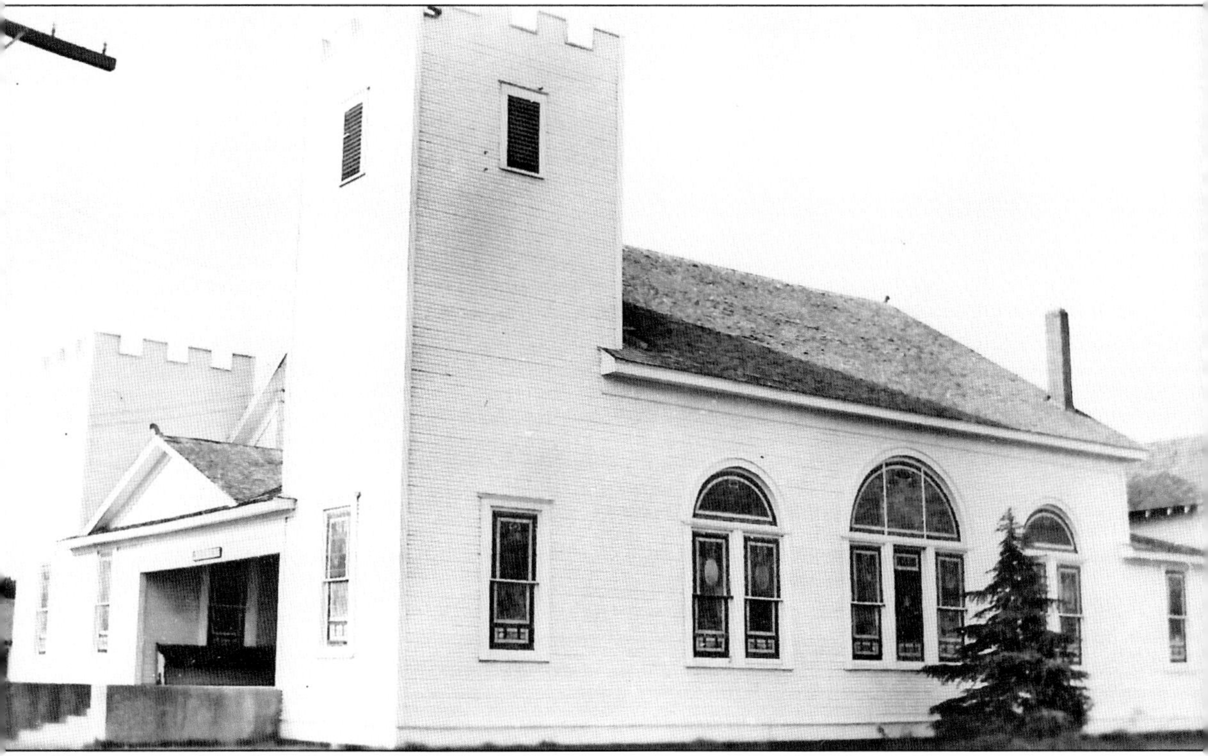

The Pecan Gap Methodist Church was begun about 1883 and became a part of the Methodist Episcopal Church, South. The picture shows the second building, which was constructed in 1918. The church sanctuary and the surrounding rooms are graced with 24 beautiful stained-glass windows. The church, still in operation, has been an important part of Pecan Gap. (Courtesy of Nan Olson Beeler.)

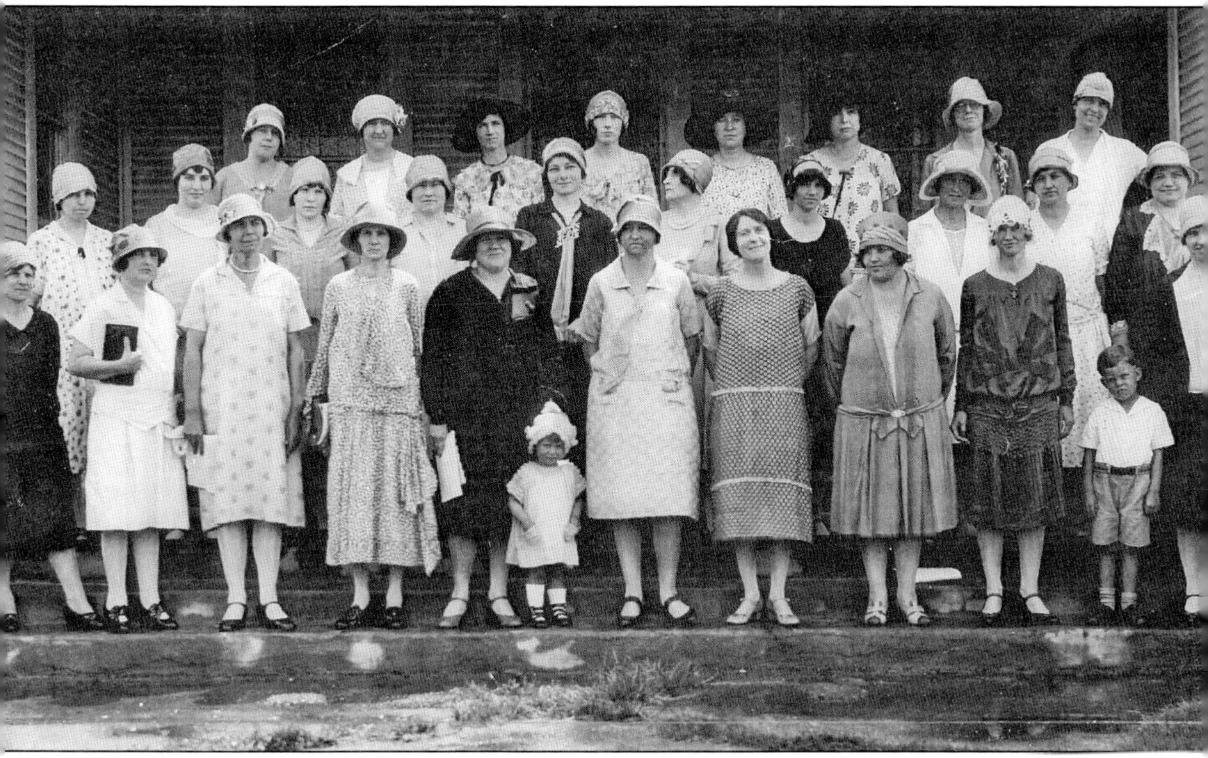

The Wide Awake Wesley Class of the Pecan Gap Methodist Church is shown on August 3, 1928. From left to right are (first row) Mamie James, Fannie Muncy, Pearl Woods, Josie James, Ethel and Anne Yeager, Myrt Houston, Bertha Pickard, Doris Thomas, Mattie Walker, Charles Garrett, and Alma Wooten; (second row) Laura Pickard, Roselle Crawford, Mae Leeman, Maggie Taylor, Laura Miller, Kate Morgan, Bertha Brooks, Ira McCrary, Pauline Crawford, and Mrs. C. B. Garrett; (third row) Mamie Bartlett, Ella Adams, Floy Houchin, Ruth McFerrin, Nannie Garrison, Grace Whittenburg, Lena James, and Rowena Roderick. (Courtesy of Nan Olson Beeler.)

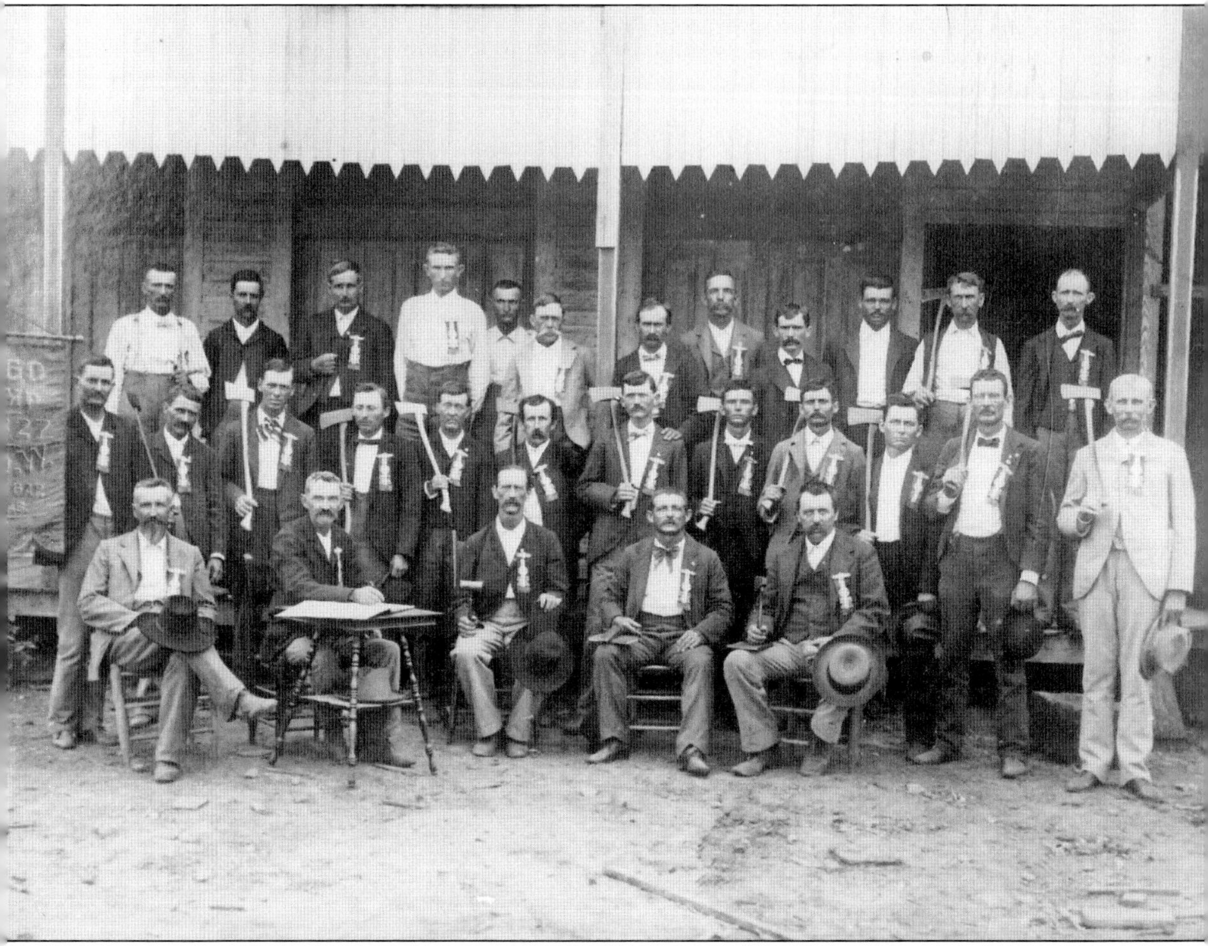

The Woodmen of the World was really an insurance company that sponsored all types of activities in the early part of the 20th century. As part of their policy, members could qualify for a tombstone that was delivered and unveiled after the person died. These stones can still be seen in area cemeteries. This Pecan Gap–area group gathered for a picture. Those pictured here are, from left to right, (first row) W. G. Morgan, Green Taylor, Rubin Davis, Rolly Humphries, and Aaron McDaniel; (second row) James Newman, John Phillips, Sidney McDaniel, Tom Crowson, Jesse Cother, James Houchin, Gustaves Parnell, Avery Phillips, James Phillips, L. M. Yeager, Ed Humphries, and W. A. Cockrell; (third row) Samuel Miller, John Scoggins, unidentified, John Shelley, Charles Miller, Ed Pickard, Dr. W. C. Rountree, J. M. Scoggins, Walter Merrill, John Scoggins, F. Miller, and W. F. Snowden. (Courtesy of Sharline Freeman.)

Three

The South Side

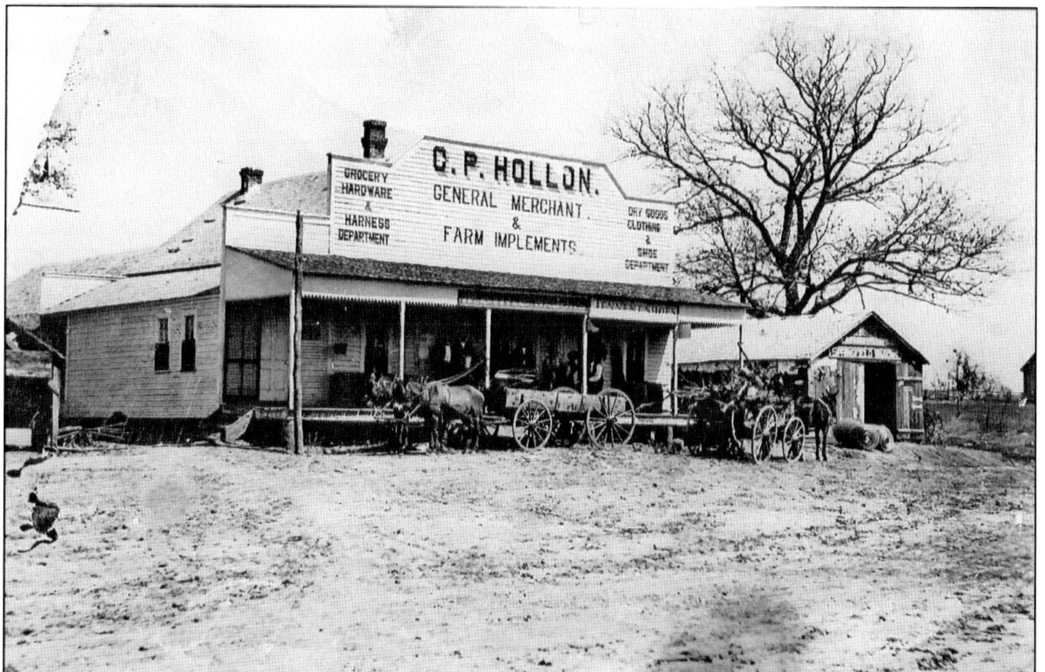

The Gough area was settled in the 1860s and 1870s. At its peak, it had a post office, general stores, a blacksmith, a carpenter, and physicians. The C. P. Hollon general store sold everything from groceries to farm implements. (Courtesy of Missouri Arnold.)

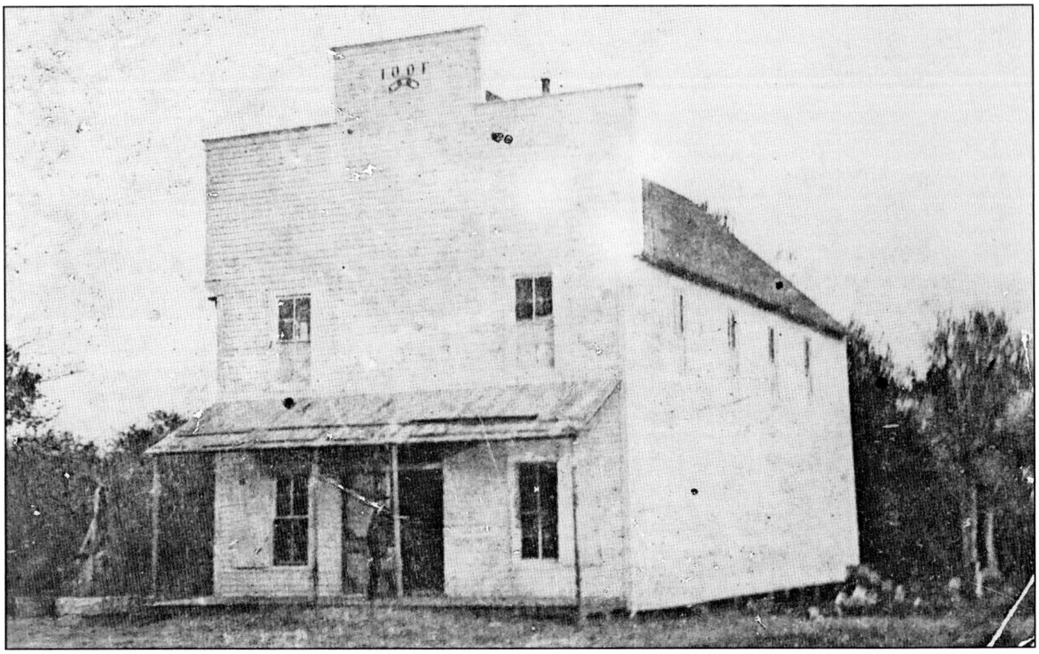

The picture above shows the Gough IOOF Lodge Hall, which housed a drugstore on the first floor during its heyday. In the picture below, the 1905 Gough-Klondike IOOF Lodge members are, from left to right, (first row) R. P. Hamilton, unidentified, W. M. Henderson, Buck Lay, J. D. Anderson, Dub Carrington, Will Little, Tom Tolbert, Arch Gilmore, and J. C. Newkirk; (second row) Moses Kirkpatrick, Jim Arnold, Tom Cregg, John Bailey, W. L. Stephenson, Frank Clawson, unidentified, Walter Stooksberry, ? Davis, and Joe Byers; (third row) W. F. Whiteside, unidentified, W. T. Potter, unidentified, W. F. Workman, unidentified, George Robinson, and unidentified. (Both, courtesy of Missouri Arnold.)

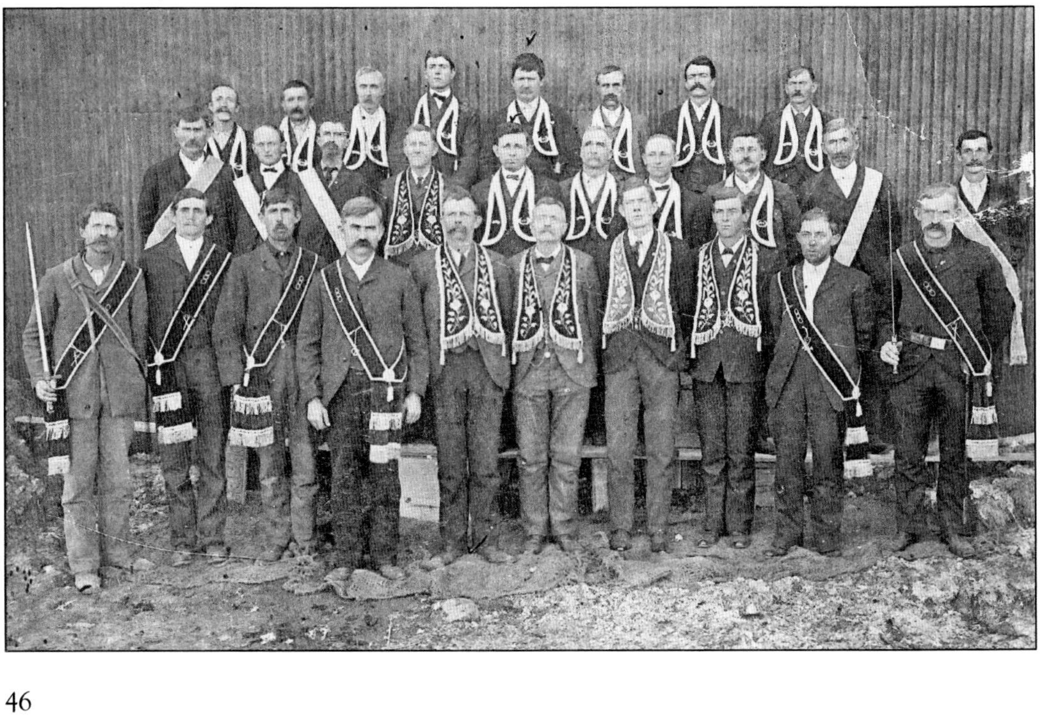

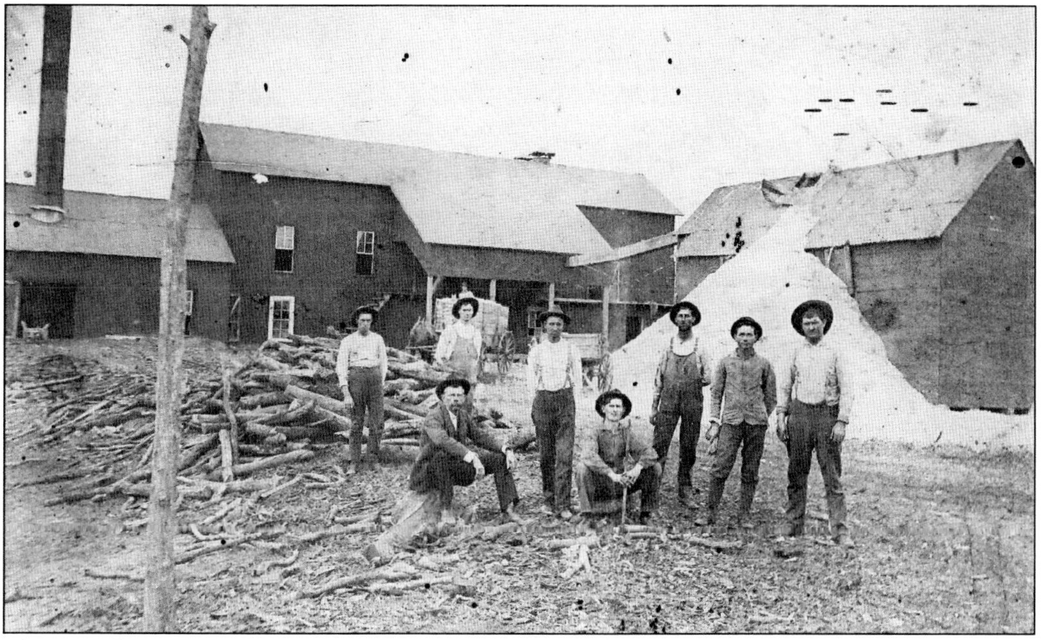

The Gough community was settled in the 1880s and named for an early minister. By 1890, the community had about 50 residents, and this picture is thought to be the Hollon and Bailey Mill and Gin. The 1890 records indicate that there were three doctors, a blacksmith, and a carpenter. When the railroad failed to come through Gough, this community, like others, declined. (Courtesy of Missouri Arnold.)

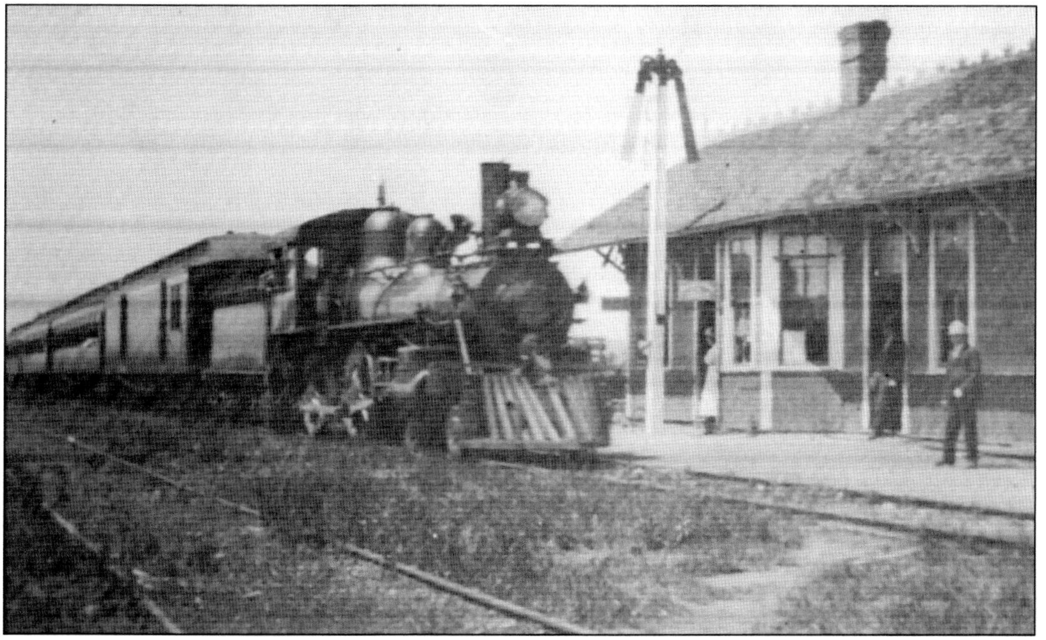

Klondike, originally called Pleasant Grove, incorporated and named the post office after the Alaskan gold rush site. John Hunt donated land for the cemetery in 1852, and the Texas-Midland Railroad began its run through town in 1897. The Methodist church and school used the same building for several years. This picture is of the train depot. (Courtesy of Cindy Anderson.)

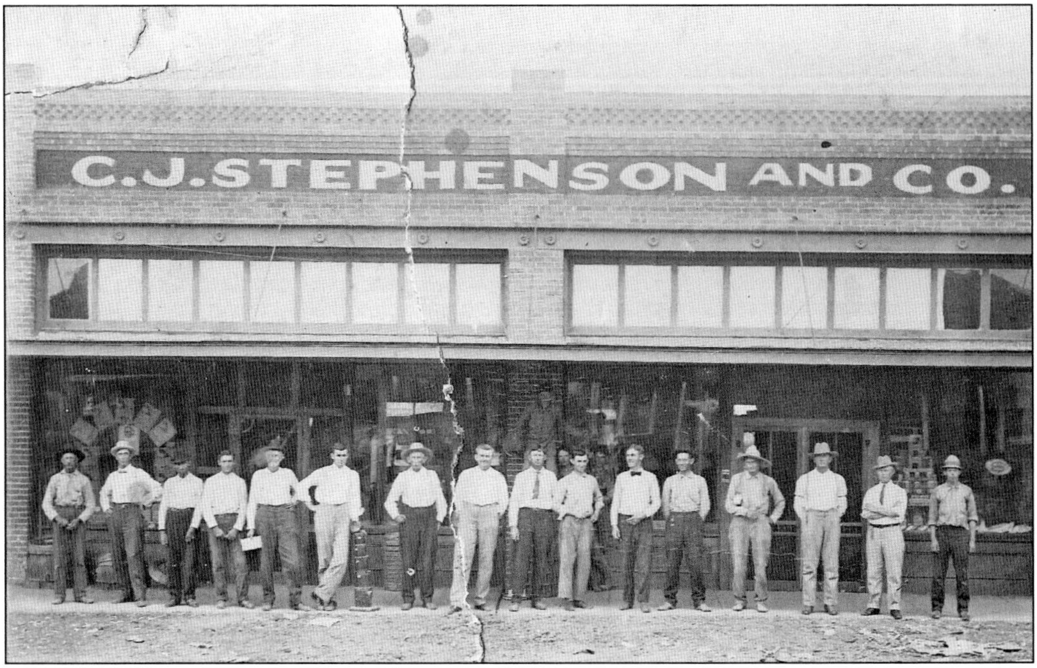

C. J. Stephenson and Company of Klondike was a large dry goods business on one side with a grocery store on the other side. Local men were, left to right, D. R. Rainey, Dr. William Forrester, ? Edwards, Archie Barrett, unidentified, ? Wynn, unidentified, C. J. Stephenson, C. Rainey, ? Parks, Grover Wynn, Frank Wilson, Owen Martin, H. P. Martin, Walter Houchin, and Bob Gant. (Courtesy of Kathy Thomas.)

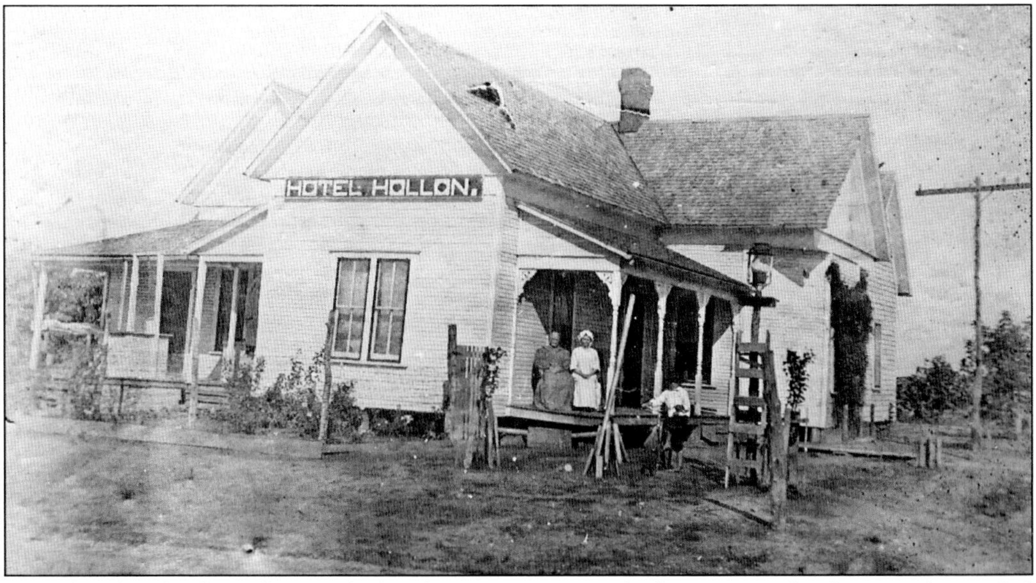

Daniel and Melinda Hollon, with daughter Mattie, owned a home near the depot and provided hotel services to businessmen stopping in Klondike. They moved their general merchandise store from the Gough community to Klondike after the railroad was built. The town had a telegraph office, three doctors, the First State Bank with J. J. Hunt as president, and two large cotton gins. (Courtesy of Delta County Library.)

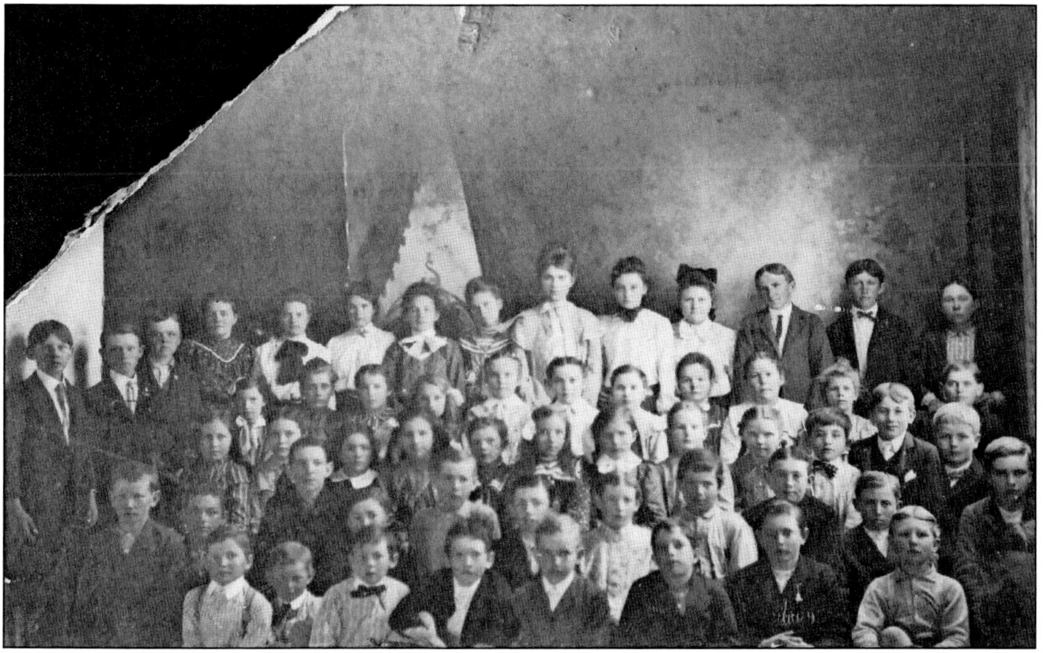

The students above were probably the first to attend the new two-story brick school built in Klondike about 1908. They are unidentified except for one or two, who establish the date. Below, the Klondike School in 1931–1932 included children from the following families: Alley, Baxley, Blundell, Carroll, Chumbley, Dalton, Davis, Dodd, Edwards, Gant, Gantt, Garrett, Gough, Hollon, Hunt, Jackson, Kyle, Little, Looney, Martin, McBride, McClung, McGee, Moore, Nelson, Patterson, Perkins, Pratt, Rainey, Reynolds, Robnett, Scott, Smith, Stringer, Stunkard, Sweat, Trevilion, Ward, Webster, Wells, Winters, and Wynn. Names may be obtained at the Delta County Public Library. (Above, courtesy of Patterson Museum; below, courtesy of Doris Alley.)

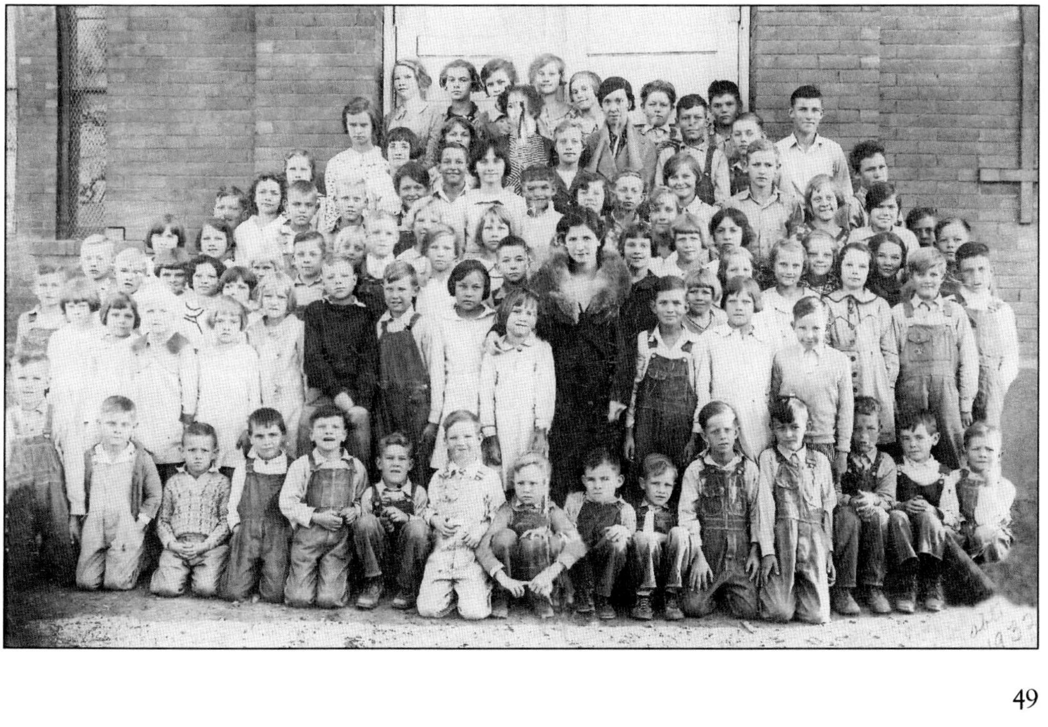

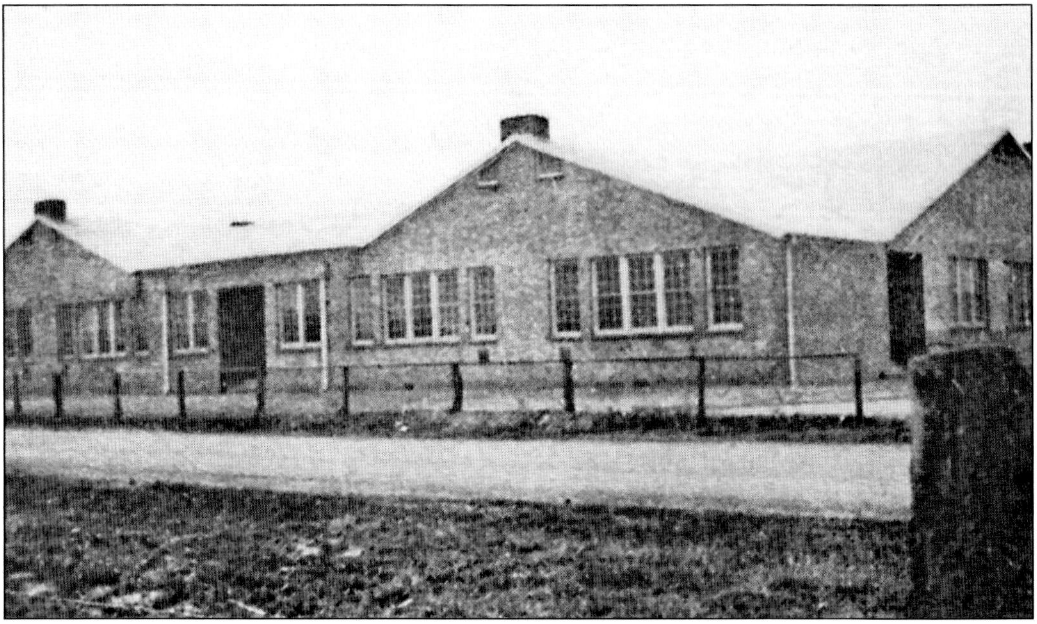

John Trevilion donated land in Klondike for the two-story school about 1908. It was torn down in 1938, and a one-story school with a basement was built on the same location. This building burned in December 1944, and the students completed the year in various structures in Klondike. The picture is from the last yearbook. (Courtesy of Delta County Library.)

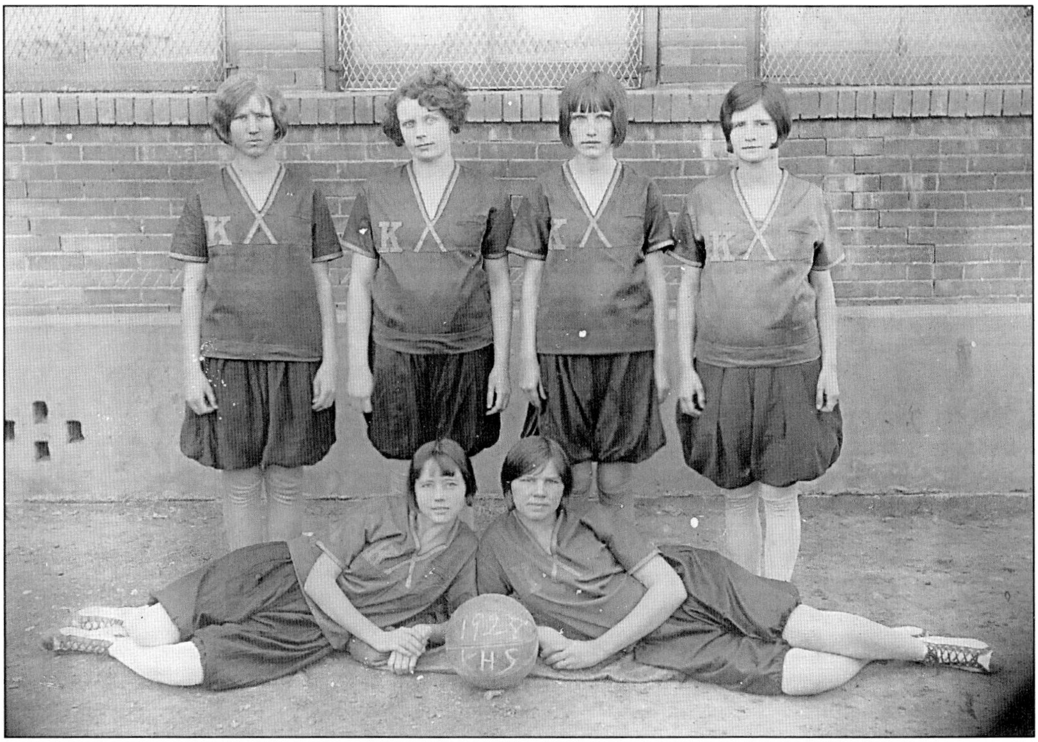

The individuals on the 1928 Klondike girls' basketball team are unidentified, but the uniforms were sure to draw a big crowd. (Courtesy of Kay Robertson.)

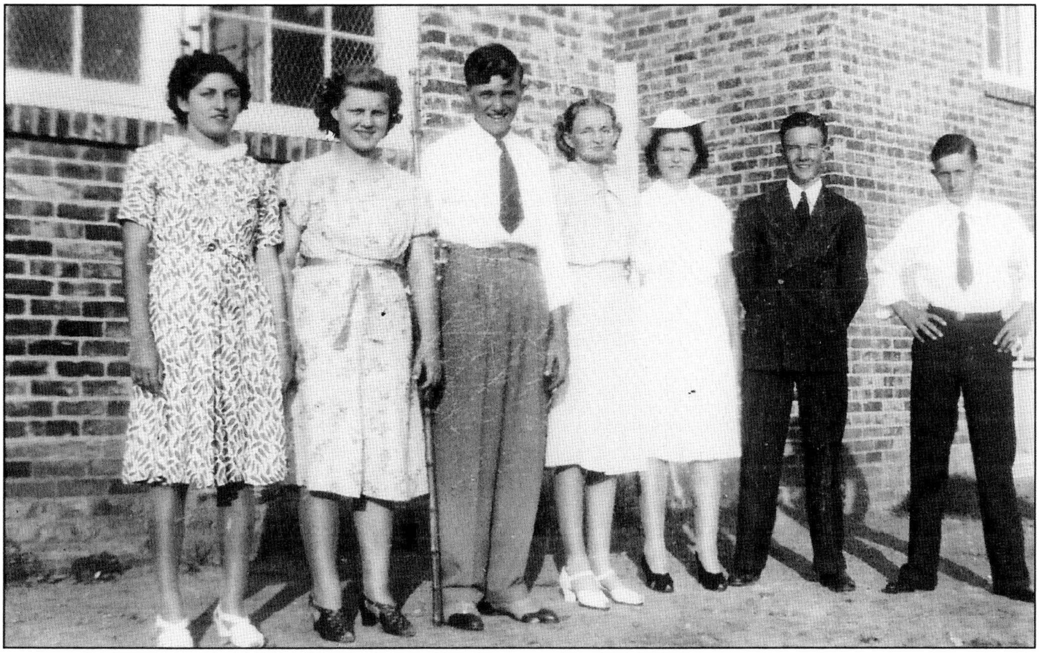

Members of the Klondike High School graduating class of 1939 were, from left to right, Marzee Stone, Audrey Faye Essary, D. M. Holcomb, Arretta Smith, Erma Grace Frazor, Bill Hatcher, and Billie Jim Rainey. Not pictured is Mary Trevilion. (Courtesy of Jerry Wood.)

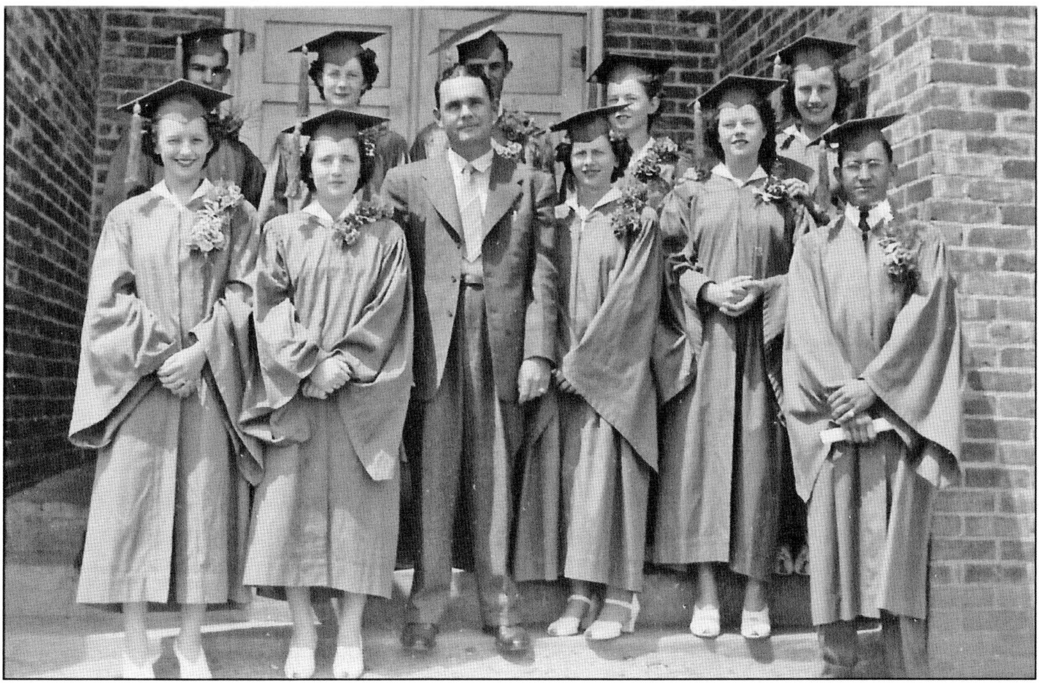

The Klondike High School graduating class of 1940 was, from left to right, (first row) Odessa Day, Margaret Patterson, Edna Jo Rainey, unidentified, and Rollin Winters; (second row) Grover Hollon, Tommy Jean Gillean, Nolan Lovell, Laverne Moore , and Val Jean Jackson. Supt. Morris Allen is in the middle of the first row. (Courtesy of the Trevilion family.)

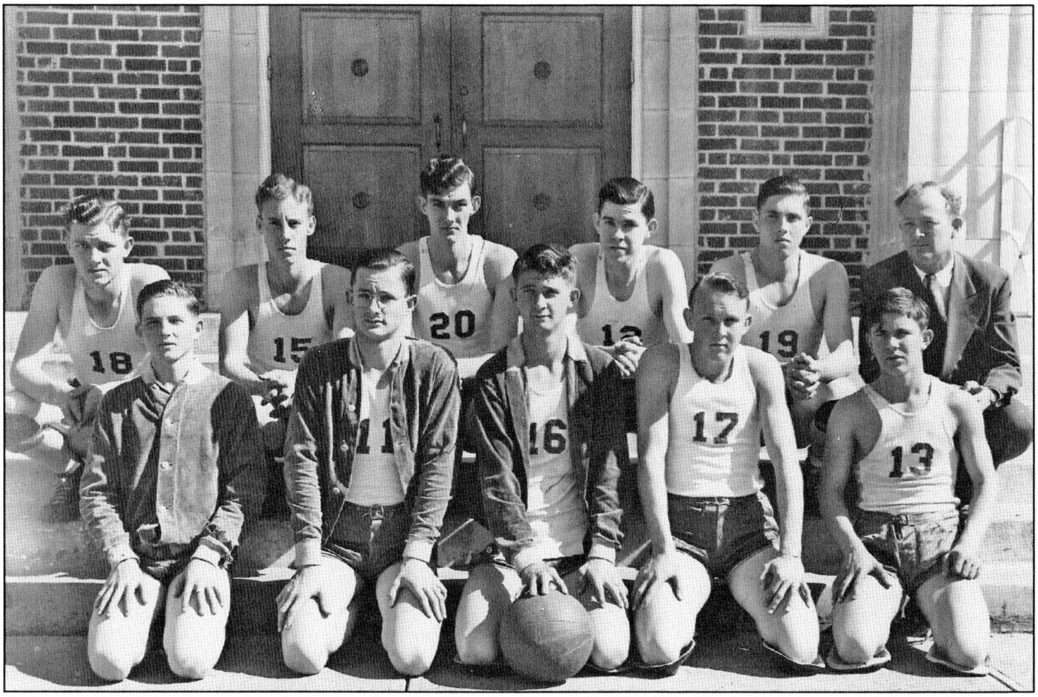

The boys of the last basketball team of Klondike, 1944–1945, are, from left to right, (first row) Lahoy Poteet, Cloyce Anderson, Dwight Martin, James Stephens, and Earle Hornsby; (second row) Billy Clyde Essary, Bennie Byers, Miller Pratt, Ray Moore, Dalton Poteet, and John Porter (coach). (Courtesy of Jowayne and Freda Poteet Wilson.)

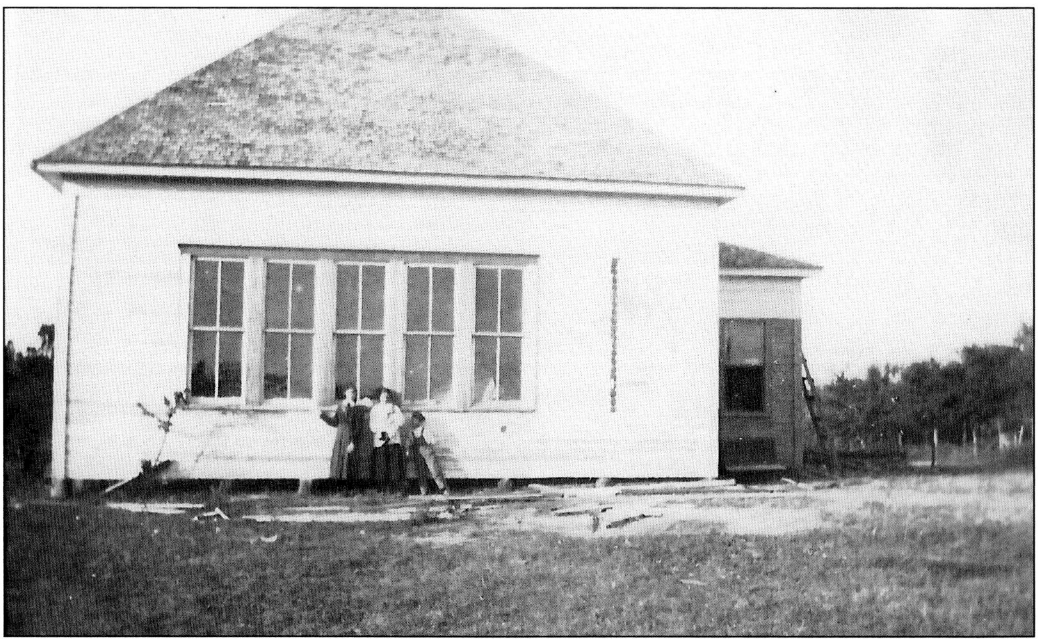

West Delta School District was formed in the fall of 1945 by joining the Shiloh and Klondike schools; it consolidated with the Cooper School District in 1960. This photograph shows the early high school. Other buildings were added later. (Courtesy of Delta County Library.)

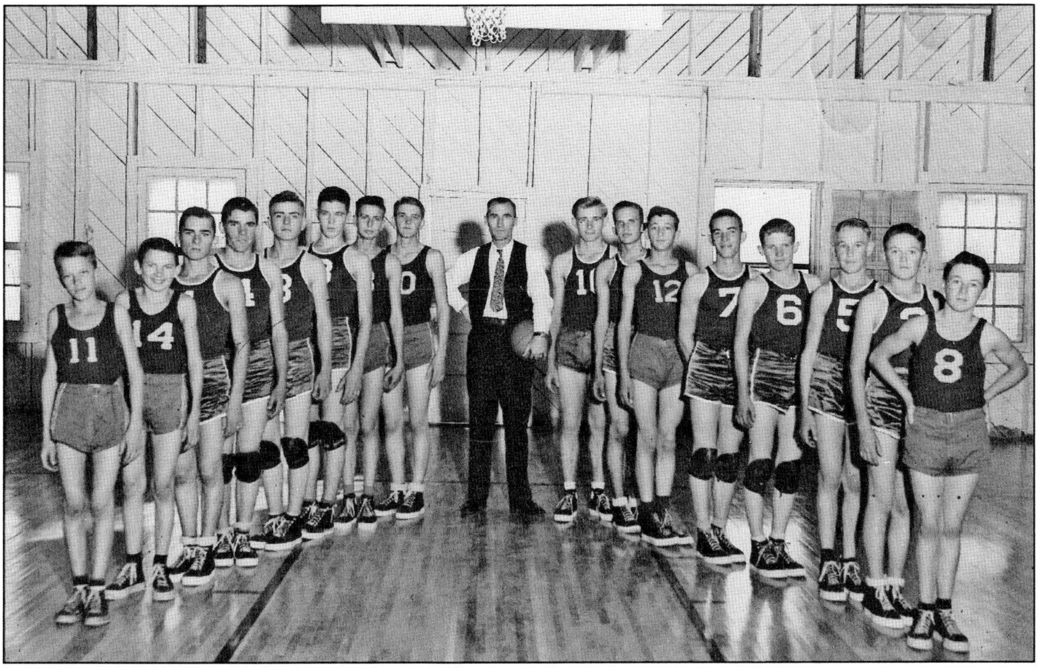

The West Delta 1949 boys' basketball team was, from left to right, Clyde Martin, Dan Rhodes, Jimmy Arnold, Jimmy McBride, Glen Sloan, Don Nelson, Glendon Essary, Gaston Dodd, R. C. Mills (coach), Jowayne Wilson, Hubert Wickersham, Joe Neal Click, Gerald Moore, Charles Glen Gervers, Clarence Doolin, Harold Moore, and Billy Wayne Thomas. (Courtesy of Jowayne and Freda Poteet Wilson.)

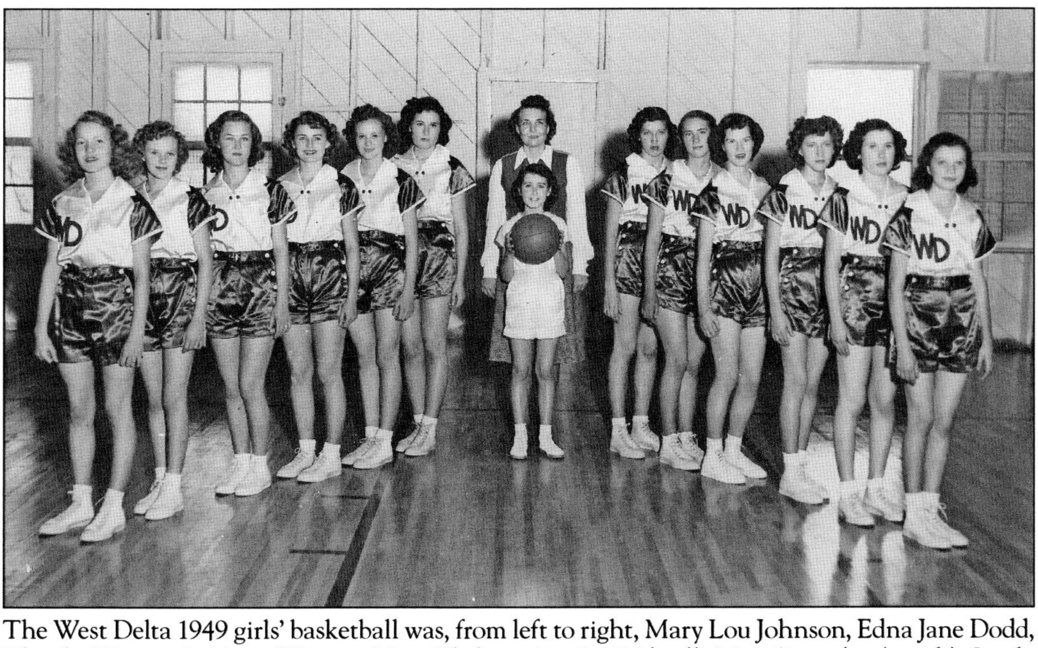

The West Delta 1949 girls' basketball was, from left to right, Mary Lou Johnson, Edna Jane Dodd, Thieda Weems, Jo Ann Weems, Veta Thilson, Louise Tidwell, Mrs. Spangler (coach), Loula Tidwell (mascot), Dain Nelson, Ann Brooks, Iris Chancellor, Clara Martin, Nelda Tidwell, and Betty Stunkard. (Courtesy of Jowayne and Freda Poteet Wilson.)

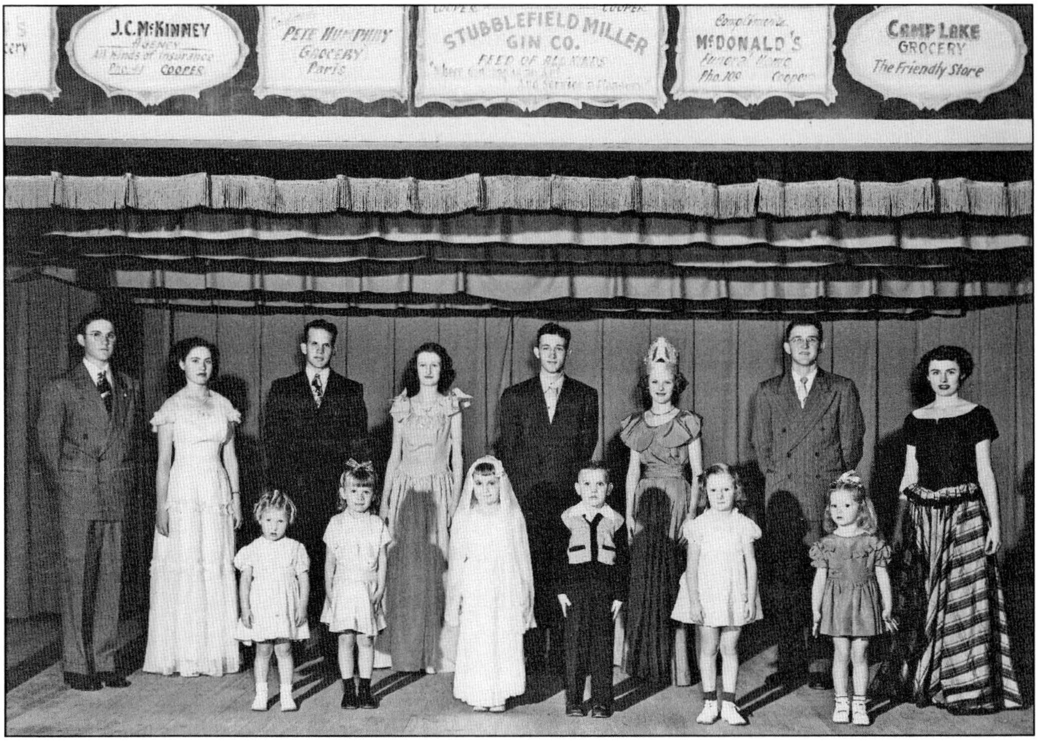

Note the advertisements above the stage of the West Delta auditorium at the 1949 Harvest Court. Students are, from left to right, (first row) Juhree Moore, Elizabeth Gerbets, Suzanne Click, James B. Hunt, Brenda Hunt, and Lula McCombs; (second row) Harold Moore, Freda Poteet, Hubert Wickersham, Nelia Humphries, Joe Neal Click, Edna Dodd, Gaston Dodd, and Jo Ann Weems. (Courtesy of Jowayne and Freda Poteet Wilson.)

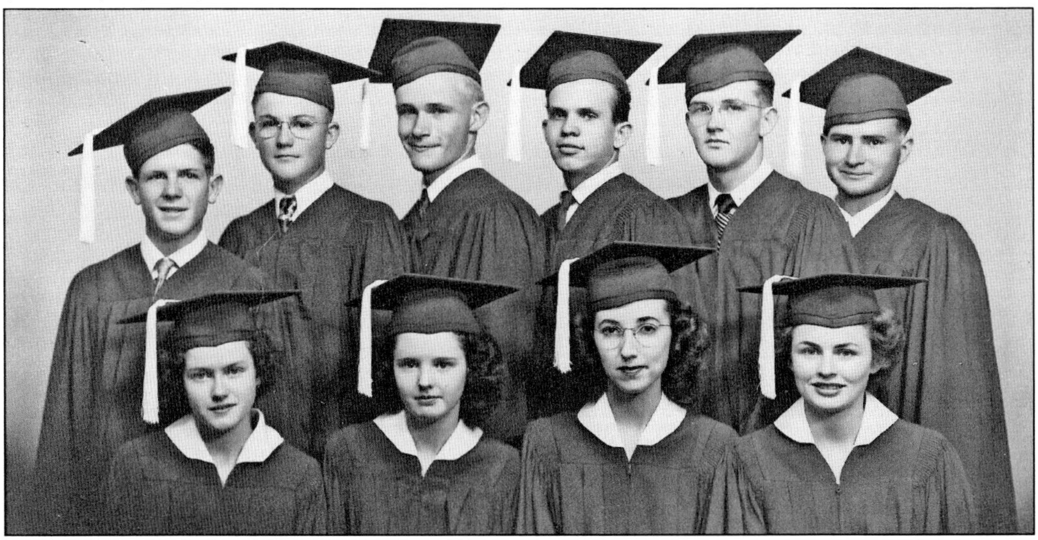

The 1950 seniors of West Delta High School were, from left to right, (first row) Patsy Phillips, Louise James, Reba Ray, and Jo Ann Weems; (second row) Wadie Moore, Harold Moore, Jowayne Wilson, Hubert Wickersham, Gaston Dodd, and Gene McCannon. (Courtesy of Jowayne and Freda Poteet Wilson.)

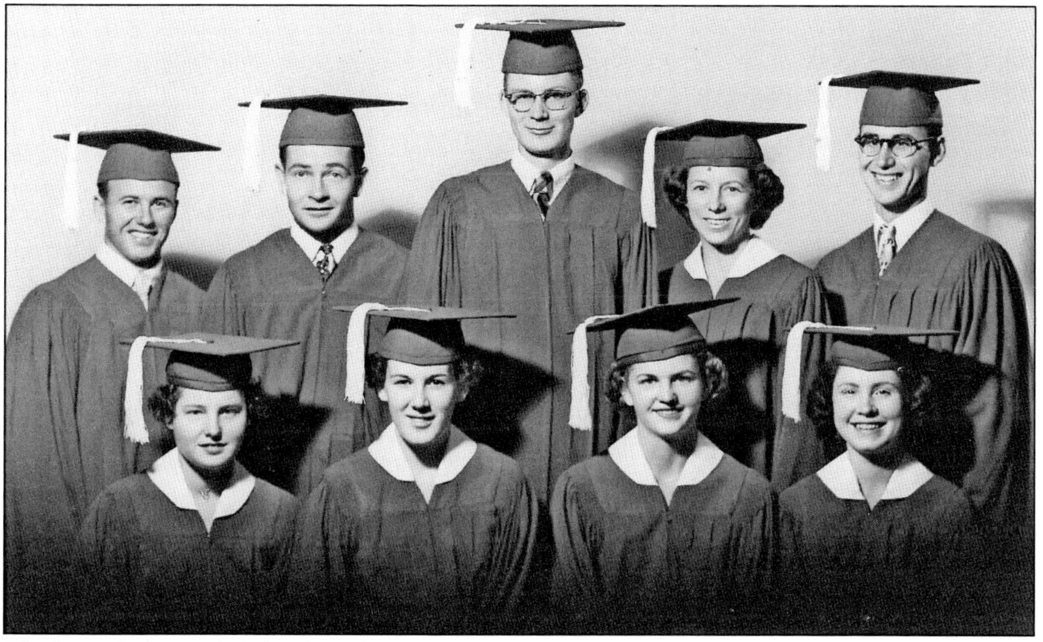

The West Delta High School graduates of 1953 were, from left to right, (first row) Rosa Lee James, Peggy Tidwell, Mary Wallace, and Freda Poteet; (second row) Coy Cotton, Charles Henry Sweat, Earl Welch, Marie Gant, and George Cummings. (Courtesy of Jowayne and Freda Poteet Wilson.)

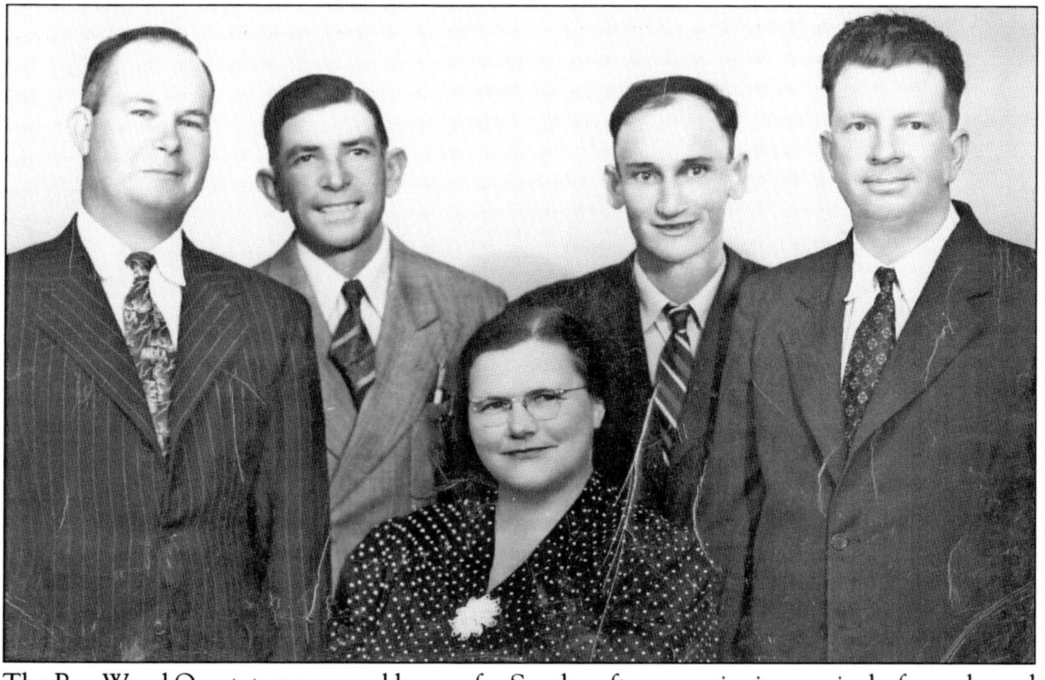

The Ray Wood Quartet sang gospel hymns for Sunday afternoon singing, revivals, funerals, and other events. The group sang on a radio program that was broadcast on Sunday mornings from the Odd Fellows building on the square. The members of the quartet, from left to right, were David Clark, Ray O. Wood, Woodrow Dodson, Clyde Robnett, and Valta Robnett, the pianist. The Robnetts lived in Klondike. (Courtesy of Peggy Hadaway.)

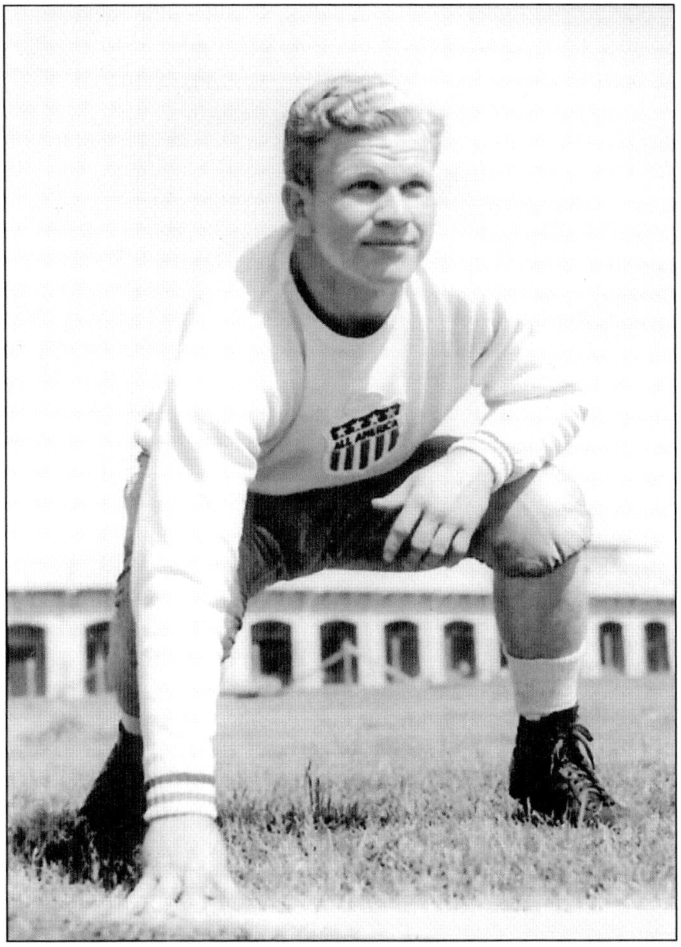

Marshall Robnett was born, raised, and buried in Klondike, but he graduated from Cooper High School. He attended East Texas State Teachers College before entering Texas A&M College at Bryan and played on the football team that won the Southwest Conference title in 1939. He majored in physical education, hoping to become a coach, but never finished the degree. In 1941, he played center for the Chicago Cardinals football team and was named Rookie of the Year. He then entered military service; after one year, an injured knee led to a medical discharge. He rejoined the Cardinals and played two more years before he ended his football career. In 1969, he was elected to the Texas A&M Athletic Hall of Fame. Below is the team picture for the Texas Aggies showing Marshall, No. 43, in the second row. (Both, courtesy of Texas A&M yearbook.)

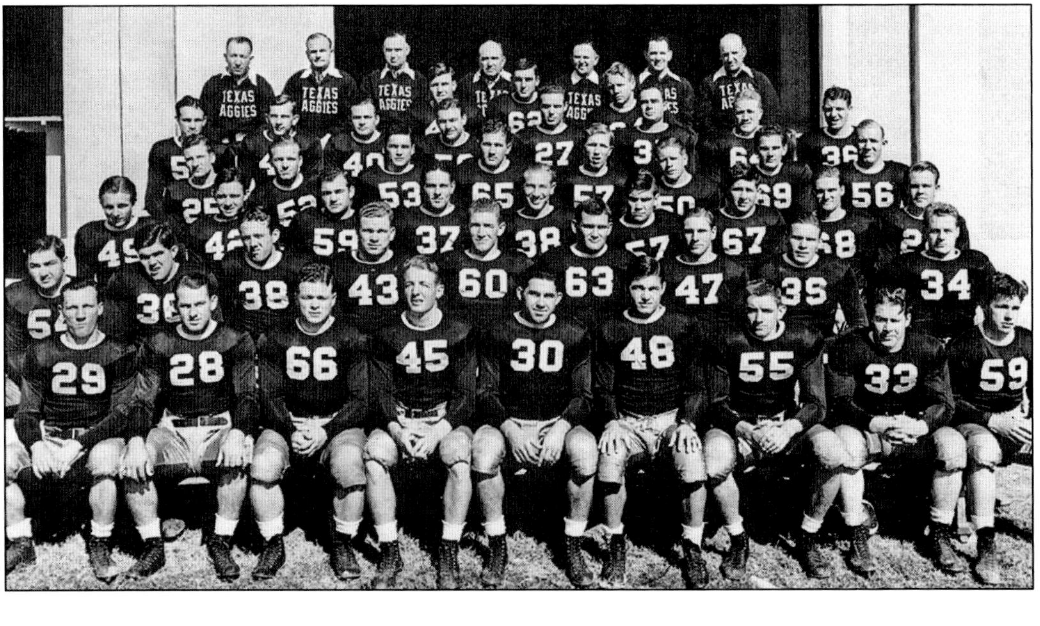

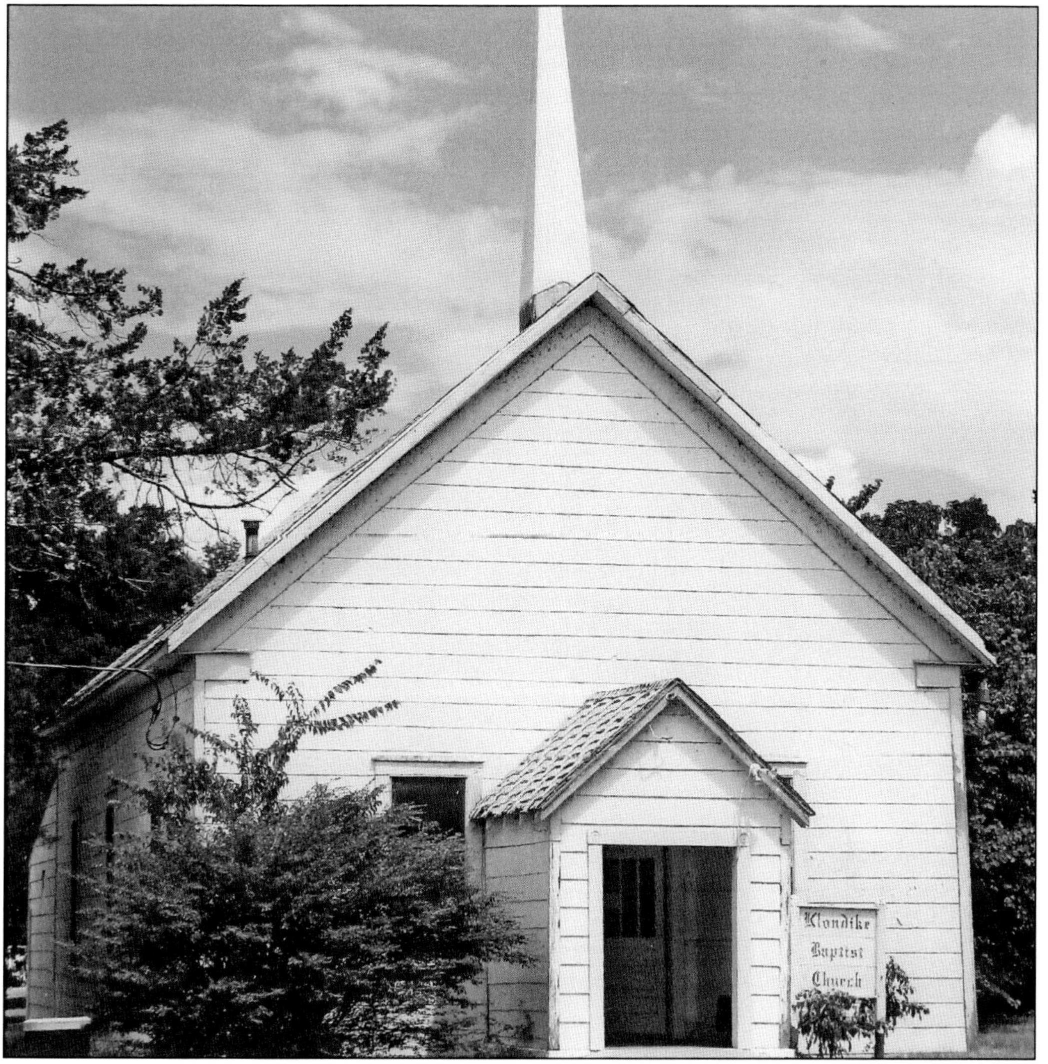

The Klondike Baptist Church was organized in 1897. The congregation met in the Klondike Methodist Church building until they could get their church constructed in 1901. The church did not have a baptistry until after 1982, so they used local stock tanks for the baptismal ceremonies. The first building was remodeled in 1982, and in 2000, a new church was constructed a few yards east of this structure. The Klondike Baptist Church celebrated its centennial anniversary in 1997. (Courtesy of Klondike Baptist Church.)

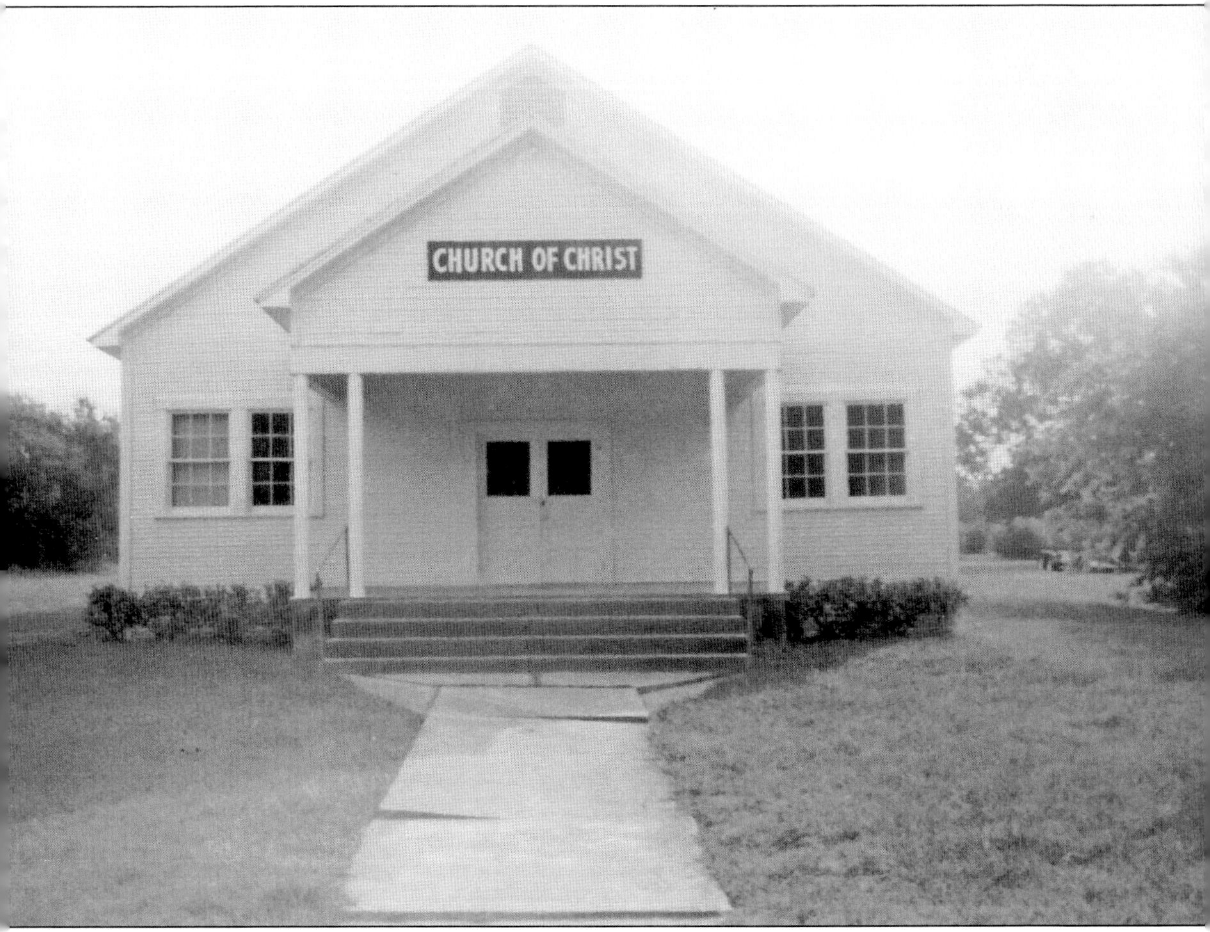

The Klondike Church of Christ was organized about 1900 by the Robert Hooten family. The first church building and tabernacle were located on County Road 2032 one block north of Farm Road 1528. In 1943, land was donated by Flav McBride at Farm Road 1528 and County Road 2023, and a new building was built by John McCombs and other members of the congregation. At that time attendance, was 80 to 100 every Sunday. Church is still held every Sunday morning. (Courtesy of Klondike Church of Christ.)

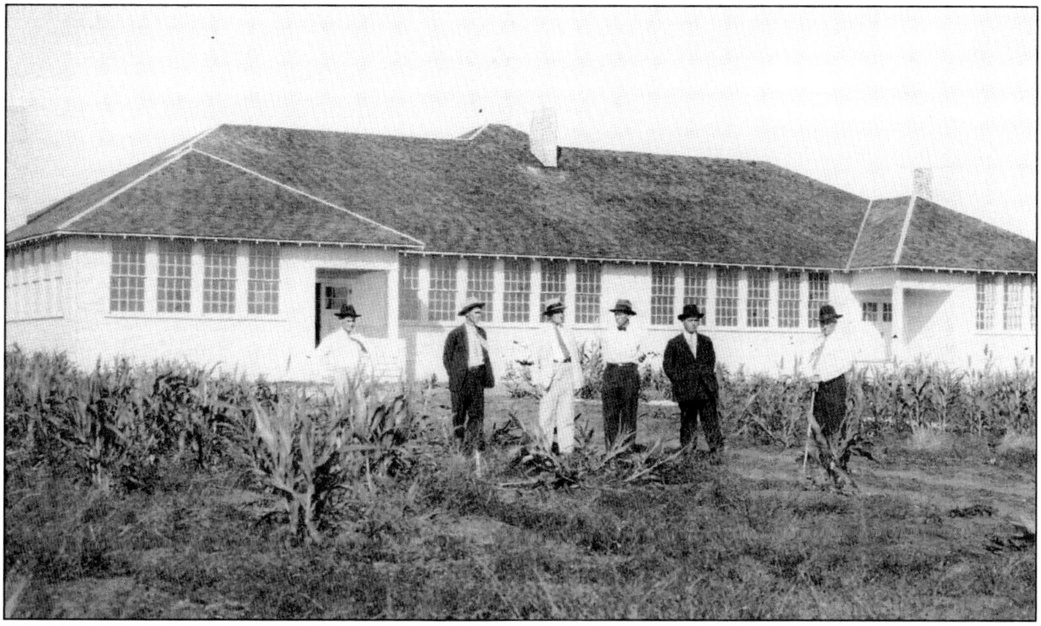

J. W. Yowell opened a general merchandise store in the early 1880s on the stage line from Pecan Gap to Commerce on the Delta-Hunt county line. A community developed there around churches and the school. A new building in the cornfield is shown above in 1928. (Courtesy of Kay Glaspie.)

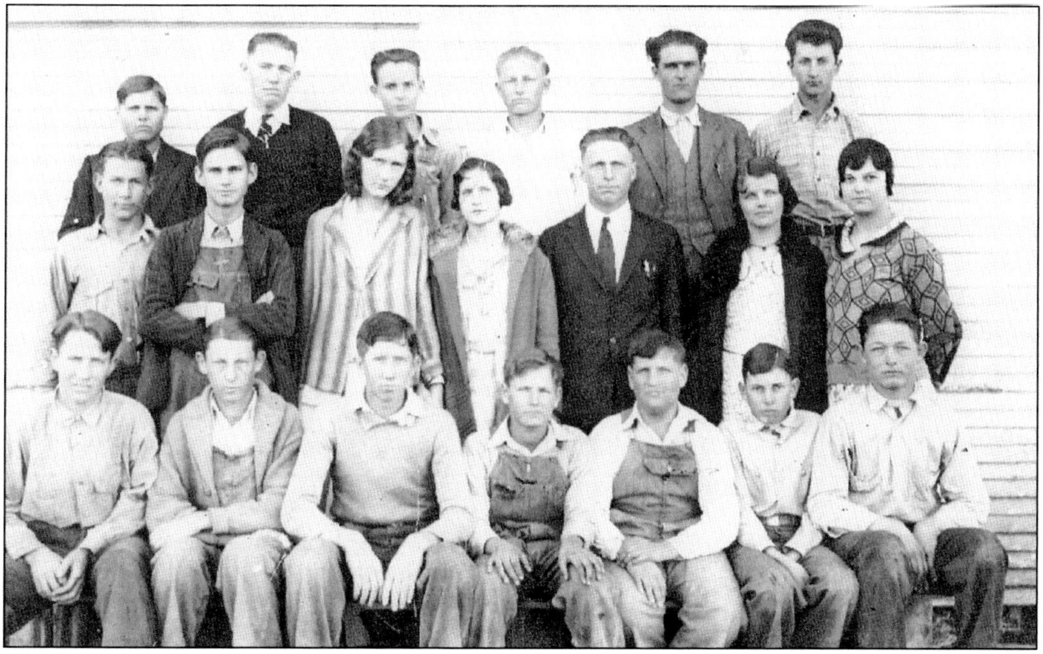

The class of 1936 at Yowell included, from left to right, (first row) Margro Patterson, Stanley Strickland, W. B. Smith, B. F. Presley, Gay Humphries, Harold Shaw, and Ray Ellis; (second row) Eddie Bryant, Oliver Carver, Aline Phillips, Opal Presley, W. C. Irons (teacher), Anadarkas Attlesey, and Pauline Ellis; (third row) Marcel Anderson, H. B. Johnson, Willie Joe Burrough, Buster Coney, Thurman Ellis, and Tyson Hill. (Courtesy of Kay Glaspie.)

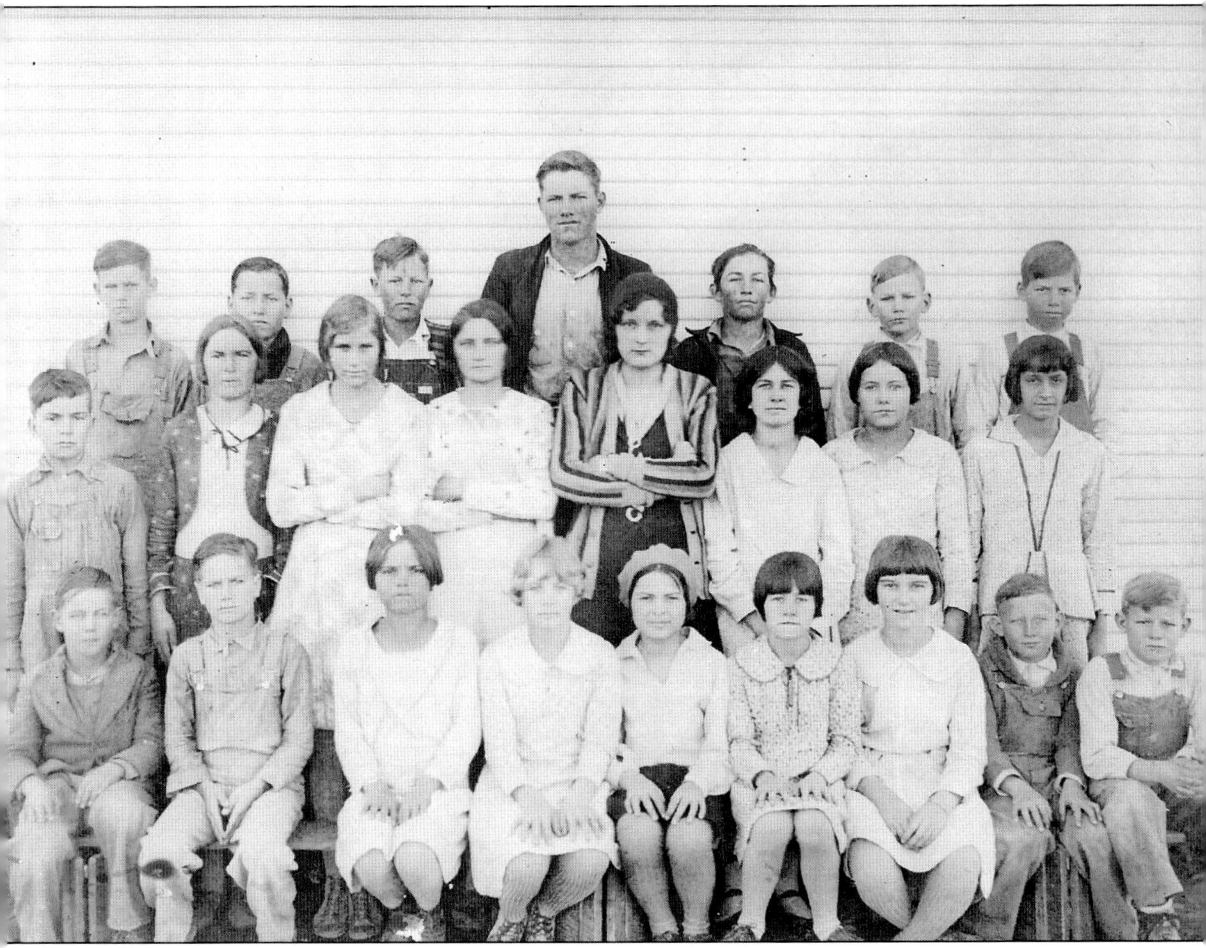

One of the earlier schools in the county, the Antioch School was started about 1879, and it continued to operate until 1950, when the district was divided between Pecan Gap and Cooper. In 1932, the students were, from left to right, (first row) Weldon Cross, R. W. McVay, ? Reasson, Laroice Ballentine, Gaynell Thomson, Laura Atterberry, Velma Millard, Luther McCullough, and Francis Garrison; (second row) Homer Lee, Lucille Reasson, Kathryn McVay, Maudell McCullough, Fay Wheeler (teacher), Irene Tatum, Louise Ballentine, and Waldean Lee; (third row) Roy Holcomb, Mecado Moore, Jack Arnold, unidentified, Leon Tatum, V. L. Garrison, and Boyce Bailey. (Courtesy of Leo and Dorothy Millard.)

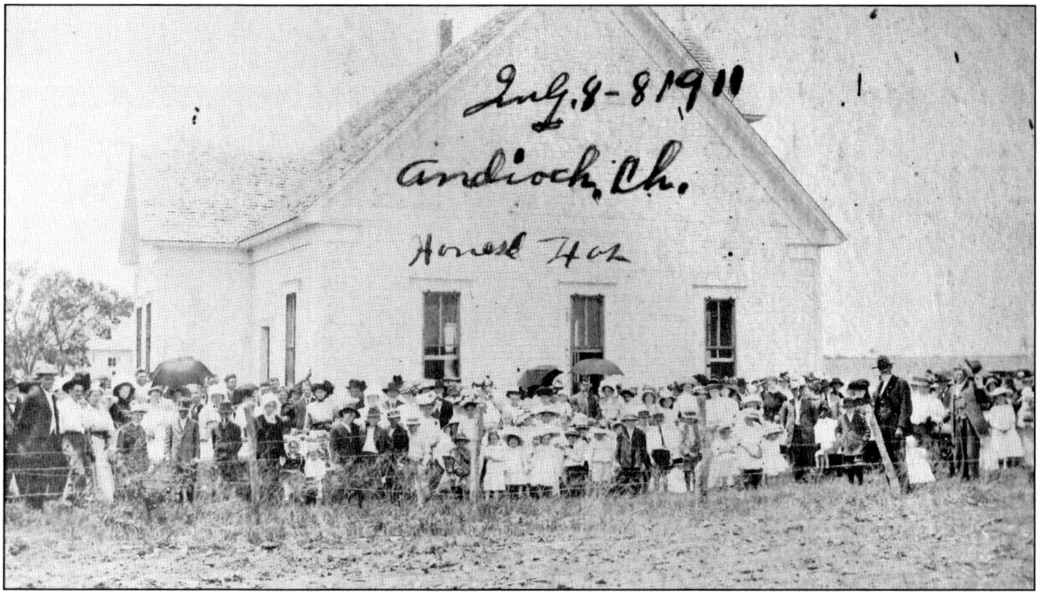

The Antioch area was settled by 1849, when the title to land for the Antioch Cemetery was obtained. Cotton was an important crop in the early years, but honey became the major product after Charles "Honey" Smith began the industry in 1850. An Antioch school opened in 1879; classes met in the local Baptist church. The congregation appears in a July 1911 picture. (Courtesy of Patterson Museum.)

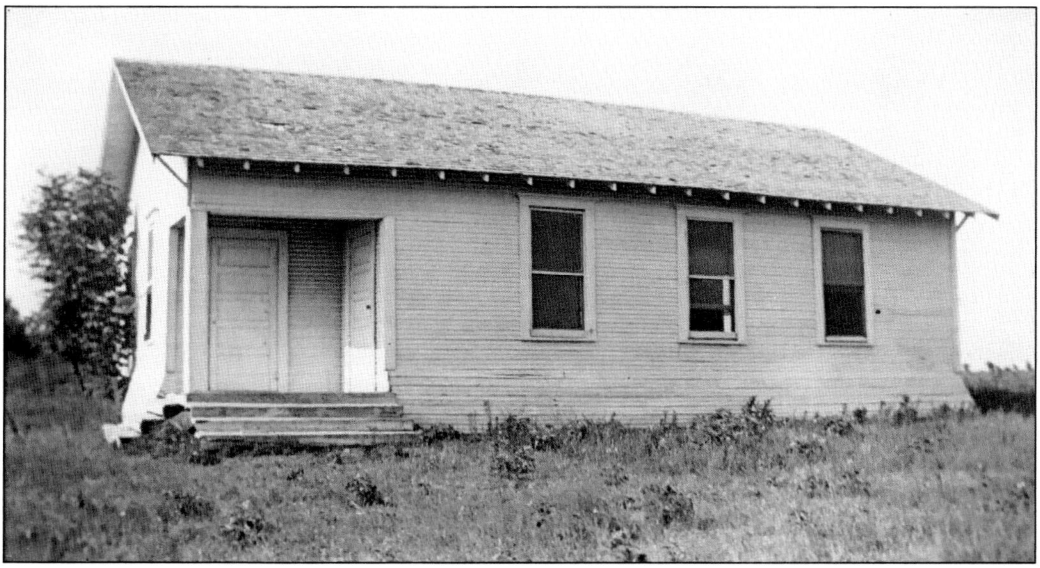

This Baptist church was located in the Doctors Creek community northwest of Cooper and south of Price at the intersection of two dirt roads. In 1882, a school was established, and it closed in 1949. (Courtesy of Faye Lancaster.)

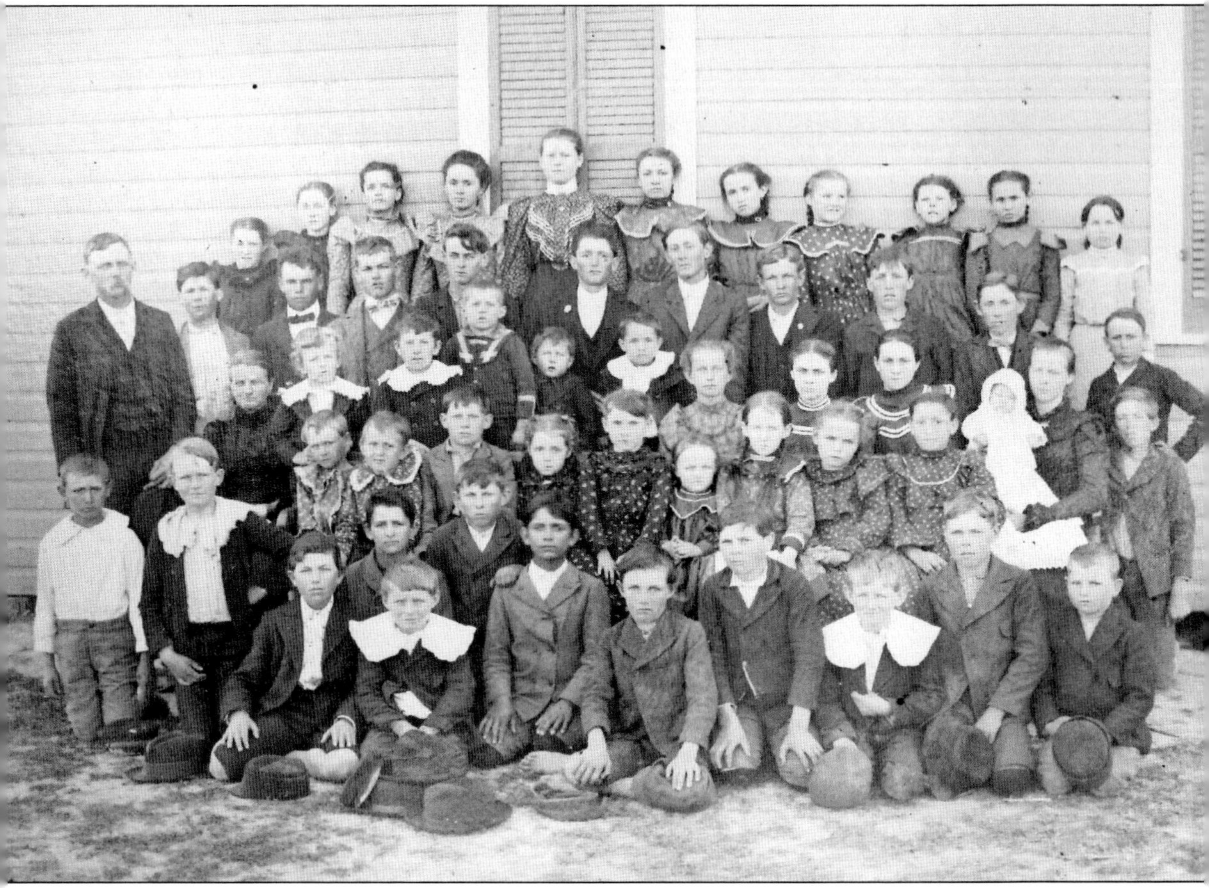

Long Taw developed in the 1850s, when freighters hauling cotton, vegetables, and livestock to market stopped for water on the Bonham–Jefferson Road. The drivers said it was a long tow ("long taw") or distance from water at the South Sulphur River crossing to this point. The students in school in 1898 were, from left to right, (first row) Ezelle Hooten, John Oyler, Earl Aston, Will Blankenship, Henry Oyler, Frank Fulton, John Nelson, Tommy Aston, Harry Hardy, and Johnny Hooten; (second row) Grady Fisher, Arlie Fisher, Clifton Fisher, Buck Rattan, Buck Blankenship, Susie Winchell, Edith Winchell, Rowena Miller (visitor), Una Good, Clyde Hardy, and Sallie Oyler; (third row) Mrs. Martin Sheffy (visitor), Dedrick Sheffy, Alta Poteet, Autrey Blankenship, Travis Blankenship, Frank Oyler, Myrtle Aston, Lillie Miller, Evanda Miller, Mrs. Hugh Wattenbarger with baby (visitor), and Clarence Fulton; (fourth row) Lawrence Miller (teacher), Walter Nelson, Ben Hardy, Joe Travis, Bess Aston, Charlie Oyler, Oscar Fisher, Charlie Sissel, John Fulton, Carl Winchell, and Ed Sissel; (fifth row) ? Winchell, ? Winchell, Carrie Oyler, Della Oyler, Effie Griffith, Annie Sissel, Ealie Rattan, Sue Travis, Eva Nelson, Minnie Fisher, and Effie Hooten. (Courtesy of Patterson Museum.)

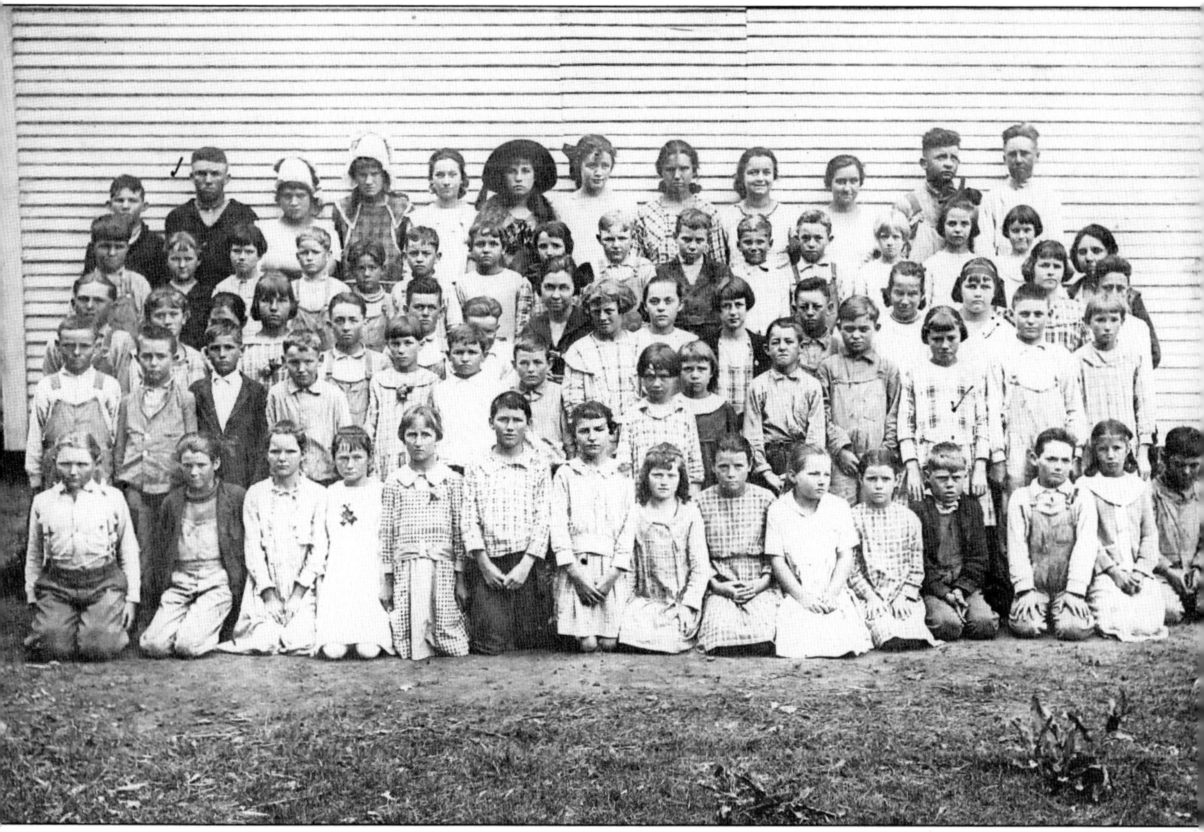

Shiloh taught students in the combined church, schoolhouse, and community center by 1847. The students and teachers of 1922 were, from left to right, (first row) Cullen Wood, Wade Moore, unidentified, Orval Miller, Lois Winchester, unidentified, Pauline Stringer, four unidentified, Seaman Nelson, unidentified, Lorene Stringer, and unidentified; (second row) Howard Stunkard, Floyd Ray, three unidentified, Fred Moore, Prentice McCombs, Willie Jess Martin, Velma Stunkard, Eval Matin, Hermon Nelson, Pauline Martin, Eldon Stringer, and Carley Reynolds; (third row) four unidentified, Florene Winchester, Elbert Robnett, Bennie Wood, Obie Moore, Janice Culner (teacher), Bess Martin, Rosa Johnson Rowena McCombs, Obie Martin, unidentified, Metie Lee Hooten, Ocie Moore, Ross Stooksberry, and Mrs. Bridges; (fourth row) Dalton Nelson, unidentified, Minnie Lee Wood, ? Reynolds, Roy Lee Moore, unidentified, Winnie Johnson, Winnie Ray, Earl Wood, Joe Bailey Brack, unidentified, Clayton Johnson, Sudie Robnett, and two unidentified; (fifth row) Carl Lee Brack, Glen Brack, Ouida Martin, Effie Harris, Effie Robnett, Velma Randall, Lorraine England (teacher), Bertha Stringer, Mattie Moore, Docia Moore, Russell Stooksberry, and unidentified. (Courtesy of Pattie Brack Pettigrew.)

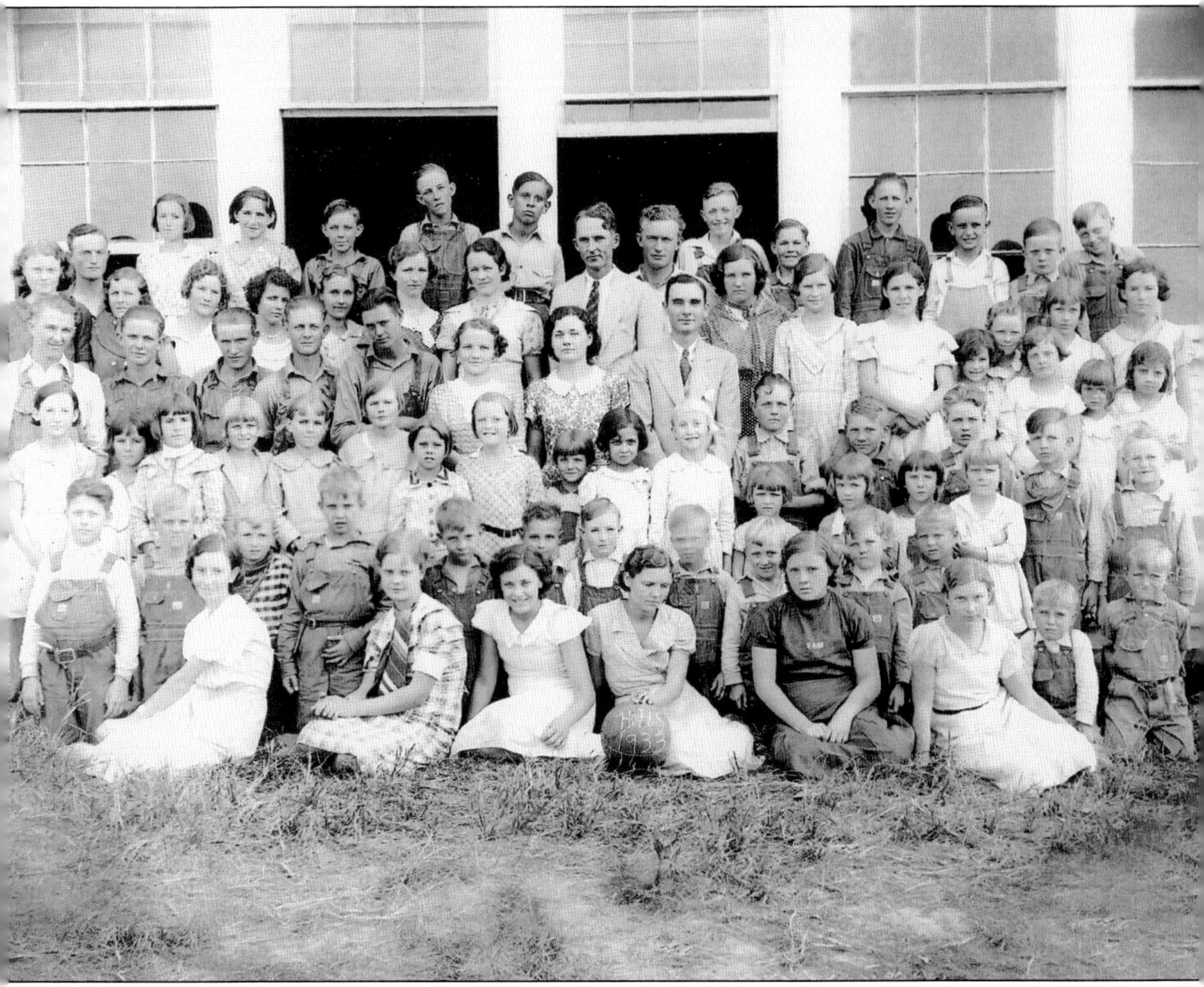

This Horton school photograph from 1933 shows the girls' basketball team in the first row. From left to right are (first row) Marie Jones, Juanita Sandidge, Carlene Robinson, Lovela Moore, Berniece McCurdy, and Kathryn Spring; (second row) J. M. Spring, Marlos Smith, ? Kelly, unidentified, ? Sandidge, unidentified, ? Webb, Derrald Moore, A. J. Smith, Bobby Shipp, unidentified, Raymond Robinson, and John Turner; (third row) ? Webb, unidentified, ? Redmond, Ruth Smith, Oralee Turner, unidentified, Addlyeen Moore, unidentified, ? Robinson, Wynelle Jones, Imajean Hensley, Cecil Shipp Jr., Deon Wilburn, Robert Shipp, and W. C. Jones; (fourth row) Edward Gentry, Leon Sandidge, Grady Jimison, Harold Sandidge, Marvin Gilbert, Mildred Pope (teacher), Freida Lowe (teacher), Jack Pope (teacher), unidentified, Verda Sandidge, unidentified, and Mary Jones; (fifth row) Vera Banks, Francis Banks, Connie McWilliams, Flossie Garrett, Vernell Tice, Maurine Gilbert, Una Turner, Ethelene Hamilton (teacher), Nello D. Gilmore (teacher), Lena Redmond, ? Hart, Maggie Redmond, two unidentified, and Pearl Webb; (sixth row) unidentified, Ruth Abbott, Ladane Johnson, Melvin Teague, Morris Jones, Alvin Banks, Billy Hamilton, unidentified, L. V. Abbott, Edward Jones, Alan Sandidge, and Elmo Banks. (Courtesy of June Dunn.)

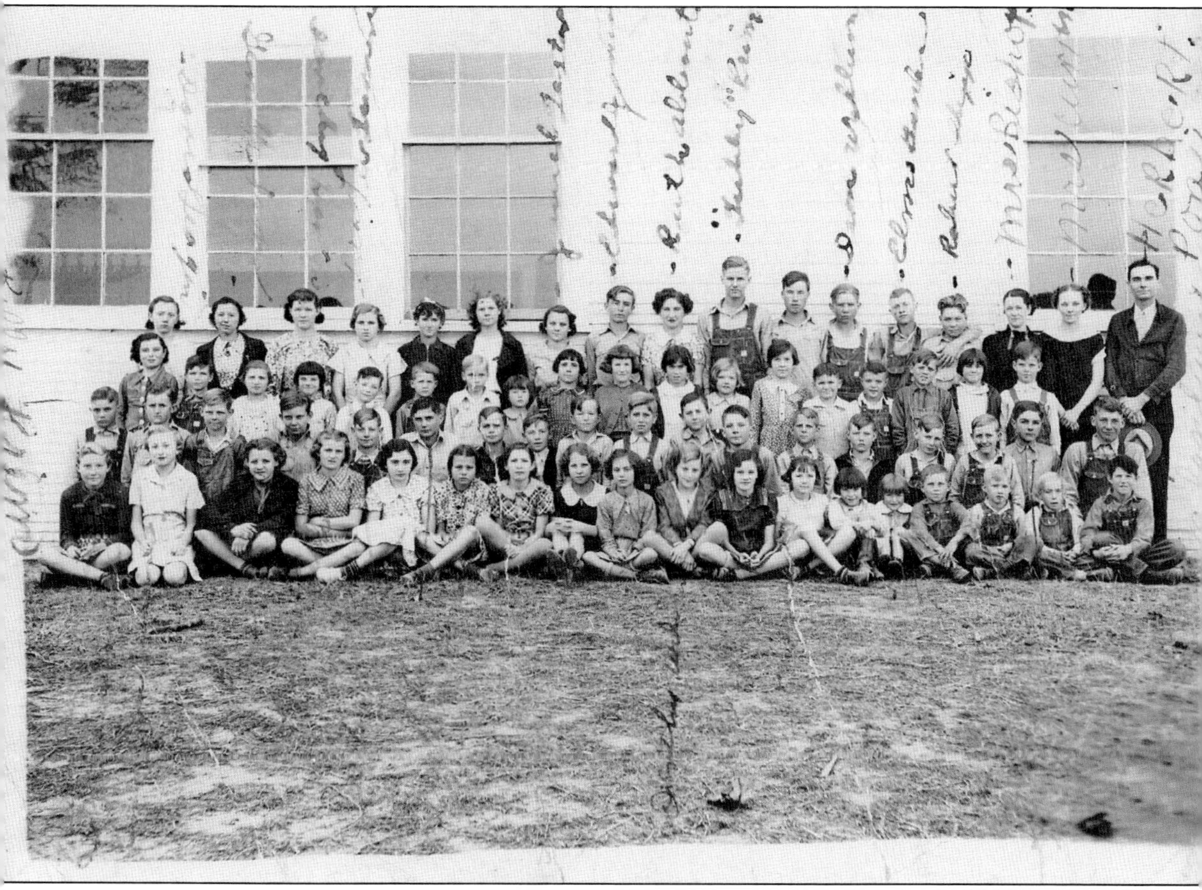

The Horton School was thought to have been established shortly after the Civil War, around 1867. The school flourished with the growth of the community, and the school was the center of community activities. In 1938, the school had about 70 students. By 1939, there were 75 residents within the community, with many other residents living in the outlying areas. (Courtesy of June Dunn.)

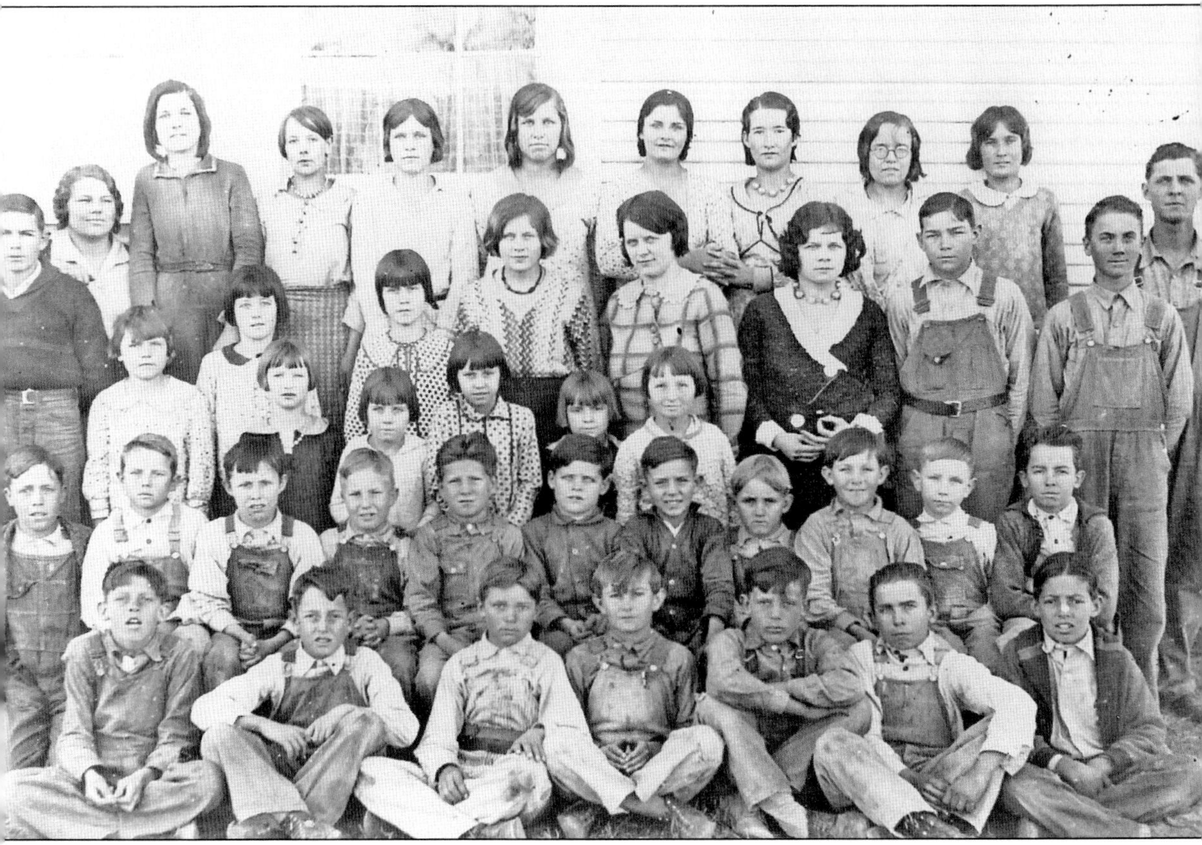

The Hickory Grove School was probably started in a private home about 1875. The area built a school and a Baptist church and started a cemetery. The class of 1929–1930 is, from left to right, (first row) Pete George, Leonard Hinsley, R. W. Foster, Cleopus Pence, C. J. Cates, Doyle Acker, and Otis Watkins; (second row) Burton Smith, J. B. Acker, H. N. Watkins, Doyle Wester, W. A. Young, Prince Boyd, George Simpson, Curtis Whitley, Cleopus Whitley, Herbert Jeter, and Ray Acker; (third row) Clara Nell Foster, Maxine Boyd, ? Cates, ? Boyd, Rava Nell Yelverton, Julia May Acker, and Elizabeth Oats; (fourth row) Myrdell Young, Laura Wood, Naomi Robinett (teacher), Myrtle Robinett (teacher), L. E. Foster, Clyde Johnson, and Logan Lair; (fifth row) Melvin Simpson, Mozelle Foster, Ellen Boyd, Rosa Lee Young, Beauton Davis, Myrtle Davis, Hazel Simpson, Fay Watkins, Crystal Watkins, and Marie Johnson. (Courtesy of Noble Acker.)

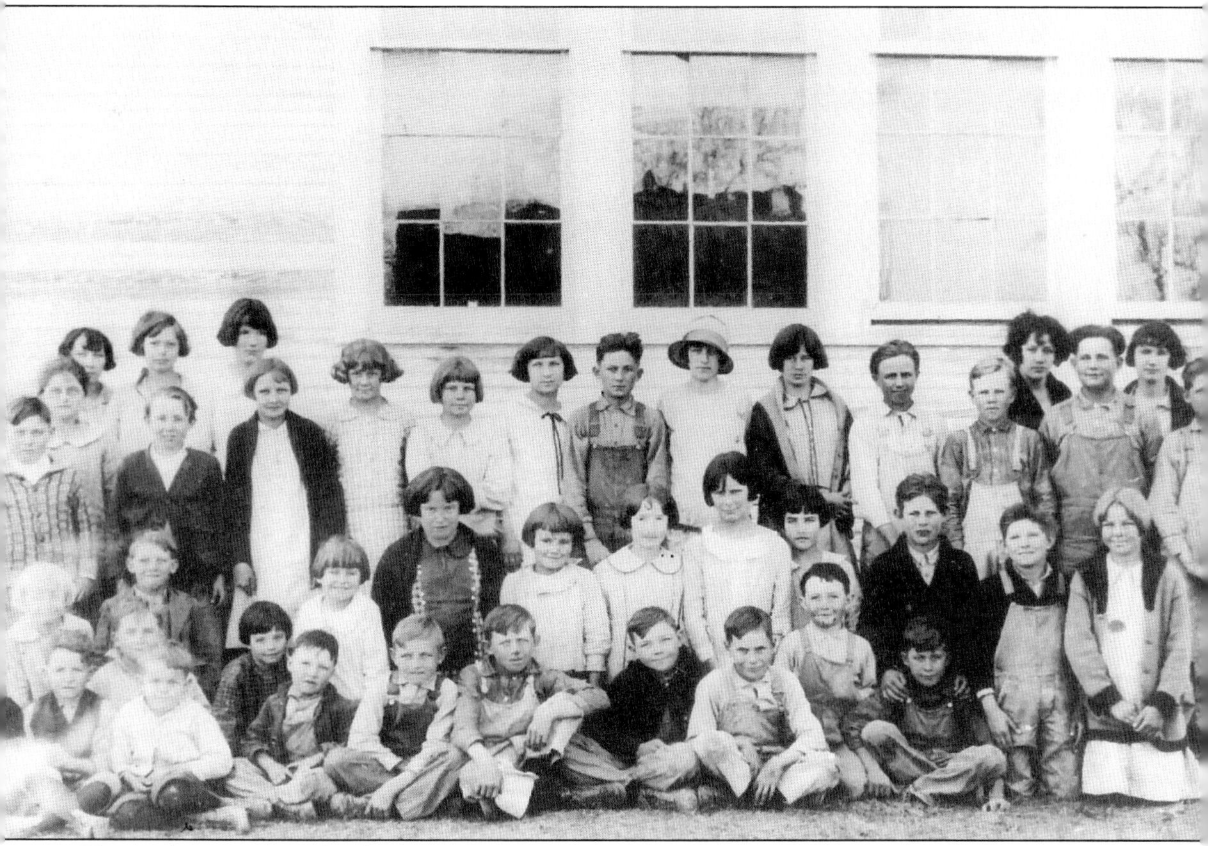

The Hickory Grove School students in 1927–1928 were, from left to right, (first row) unidentified, Ray Acker, Doyle Acker, C. W. Wickersham, ? Boyd, Zane Oates, Cleopus Whitley, Pete George, L. E. Foster, Elmer Cates, W. D. Oates, and Lewis Young; (second row) Myrdell Young, ? Yelverton, unidentified, Elaine Young, Crystle Watkins, Oleta Wickersham, Fay Watkins, Ima Cates, Ellen Boyd, Aulton George, Lee Edwards, and Mozell Foster; (third row) Jack Baker, Lisie Lair, Marvin Watkins, Vivian Patterson, Ruby Eddie, Willie Hitt, Mildred Foster, Lillie May Edwards, Lowell Young, unidentified, Lois George, Bude McFadden, Stanley McFadden, unidentified teacher, Willie Winton, ? Crumley (teacher), and Logan Lair. (Courtesy of Noble Acker.)

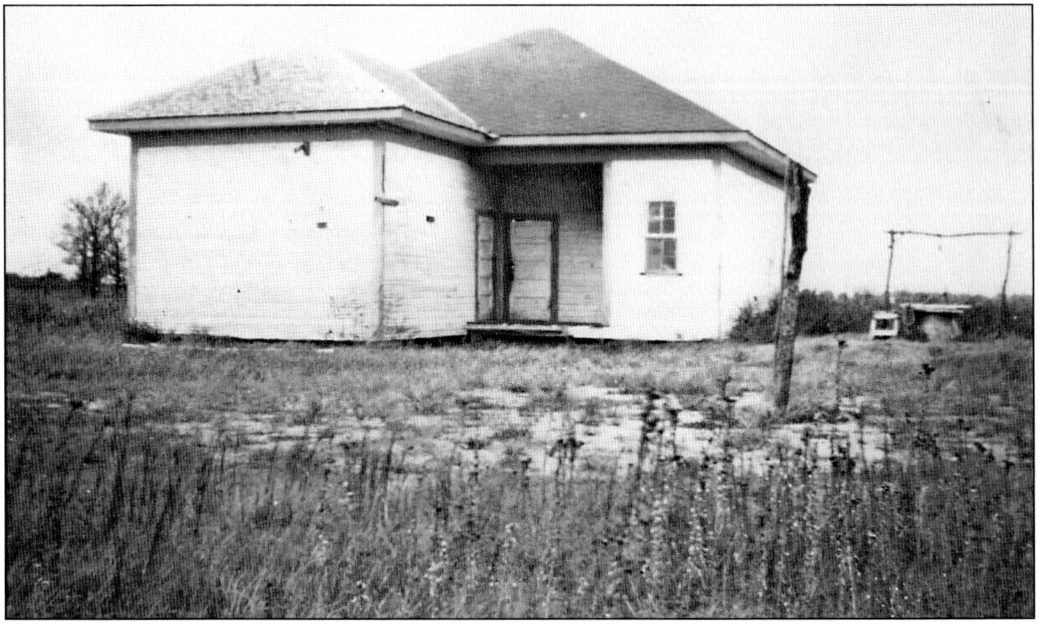

This picture of the Pecan Grove School speaks of a bygone era when rural schools dotted the countryside. Early settlers in the Granny's Neck area included the DeSpains and Sinclairs, who arrived in the 1840s. The citizens established a school near Harper's Crossing after the Civil War but later moved the school to Pecan Grove. In 1939, records indicate that there were 40 students. (Courtesy of Delta County Library.)

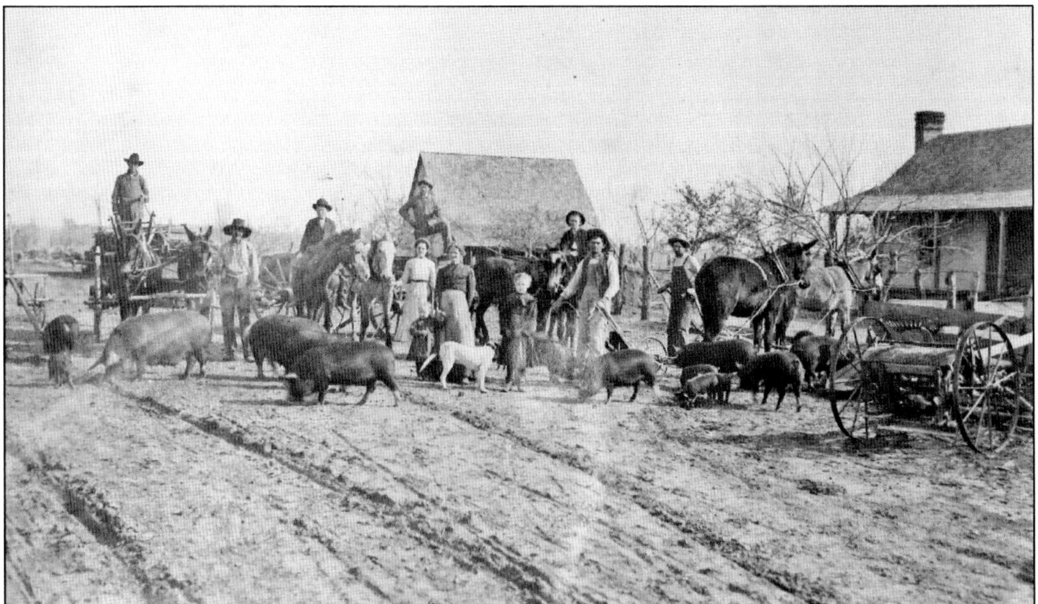

Granny's Neck or Harper's Crossing was on the Bonham–Jefferson Road at the South Sulphur River. It was settled in 1846 and became a major thoroughfare for transporting cotton. The community was named for Mary "Granny" Sinclair, who raised goats on a neck of land jutting into the river. The Talley farm above was a part of the community and a typical farm scene. (Courtesy of Patterson Museum.)

Four

The East End

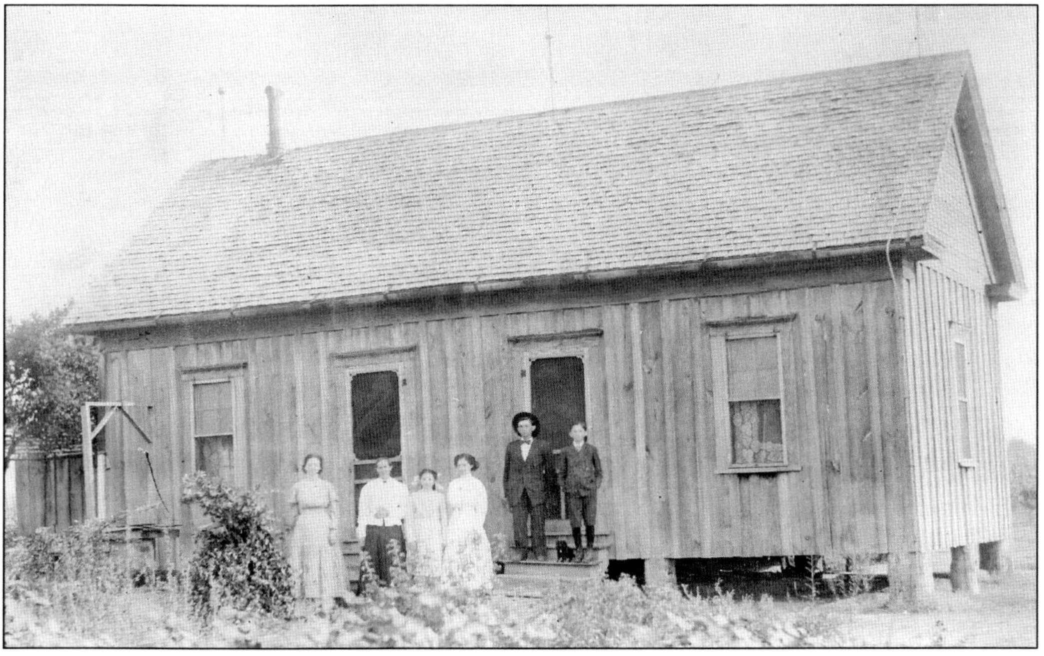

The Sarah Jenkins Taylor family home was built in 1905 west of Charleston. Front porches, a chimney, and more rooms were added to the home later as the family grew. Note the lightning rods on the top of the house, the cistern where rainwater was caught, and the smokehouse with the bois d'arc tree at the corner of the house. (Courtesy of Laura Jo Taylor.)

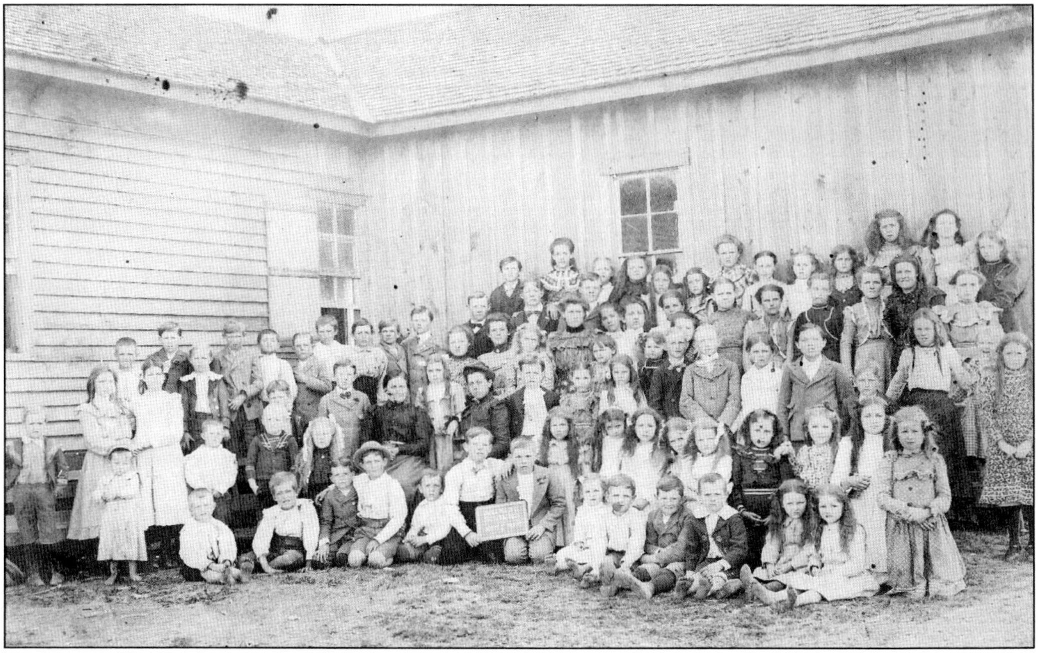

The Brushy Mound School was started in the early 1880s. About 1904, students posed for the picture above. Students pictured below at Brushy Mound in 1918 are, from left to right, (first row) Bethol Petitfils, Geraldine Woods, Blanche Harris, Estelle Young, Lazelle Campbell, Margaurite Petitfils, Randal Spradlin, Willie Gill, Nevada Moore, Hazel Jeter, and Iona Thompson; (second row) Howard Mitchell, Dow Craig, Doris Miller, Wallace Thompson, Lorene Hudson, two unidentified, Irene Whitlock, Lowell Mitchell, and Thalia Riley; (third row) Flossie Miller, Paul Hendley, Celine Petitfils, Paul Petitfils, Annie Stewart (teacher), Aubrey Culp, Abbie Craig, unidentified, and Christine Draper. (Above, courtesy of Laura Jo Taylor; below, courtesy of Daphne Story.)

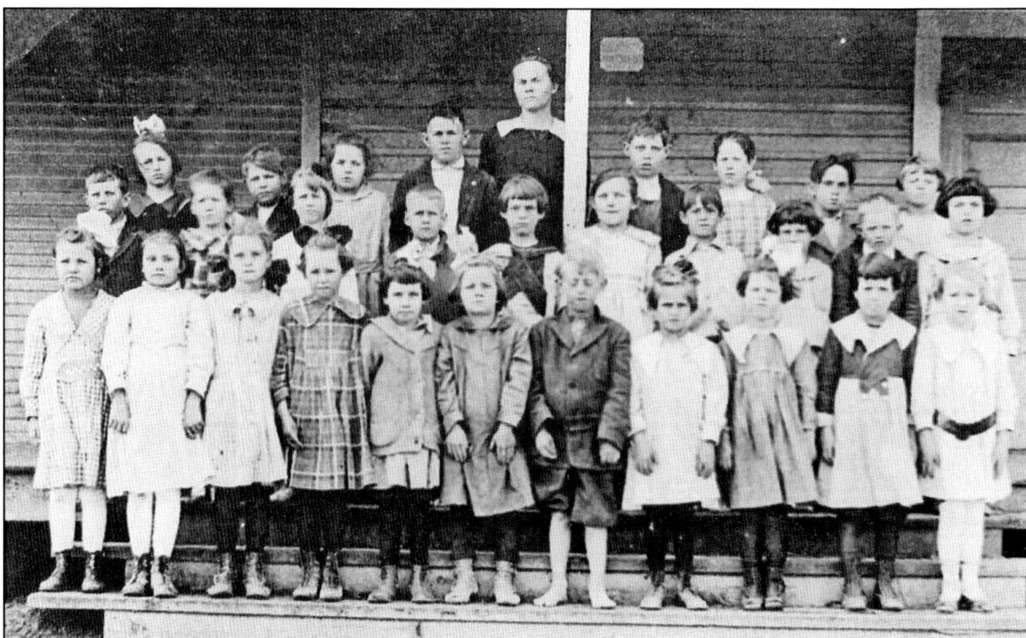

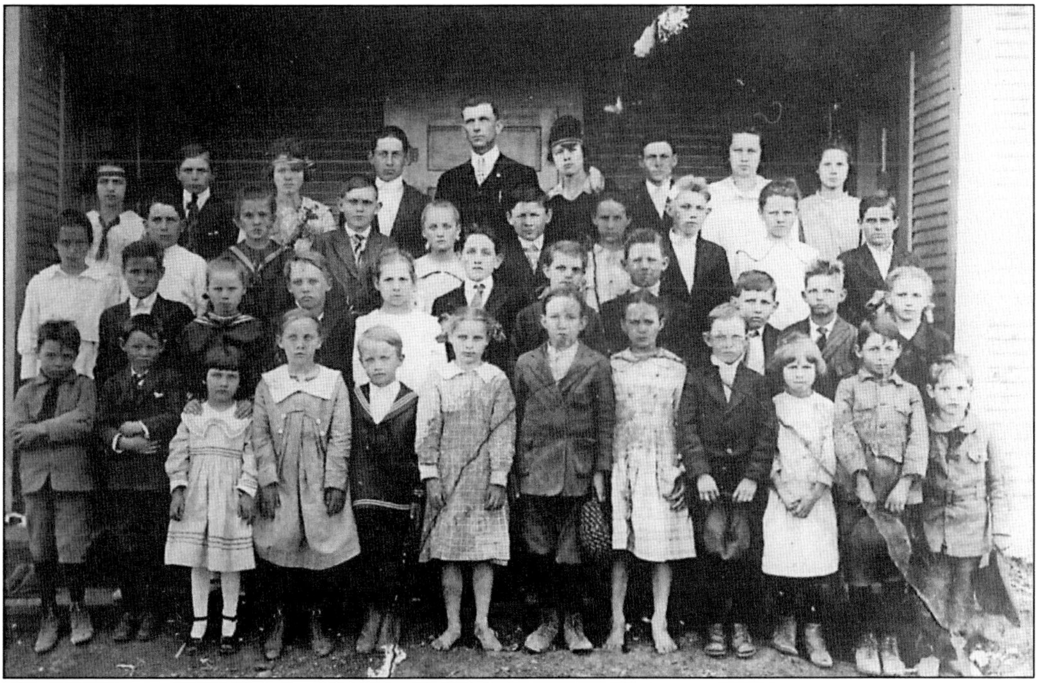

Milam was a school district only and was sometimes called Buzzard's Roost or Bugscuffle. It was established about 1910 in the middle of blackland farms. The students of 1920 were from the following families: Bulin, Clayton, Thomas, Little, Divers, Crews, Sanders, Hubbard, Chapman, Williams, Worley, and Medlin. Edmond Singleton was the teacher. (Courtesy of Daphne Story.)

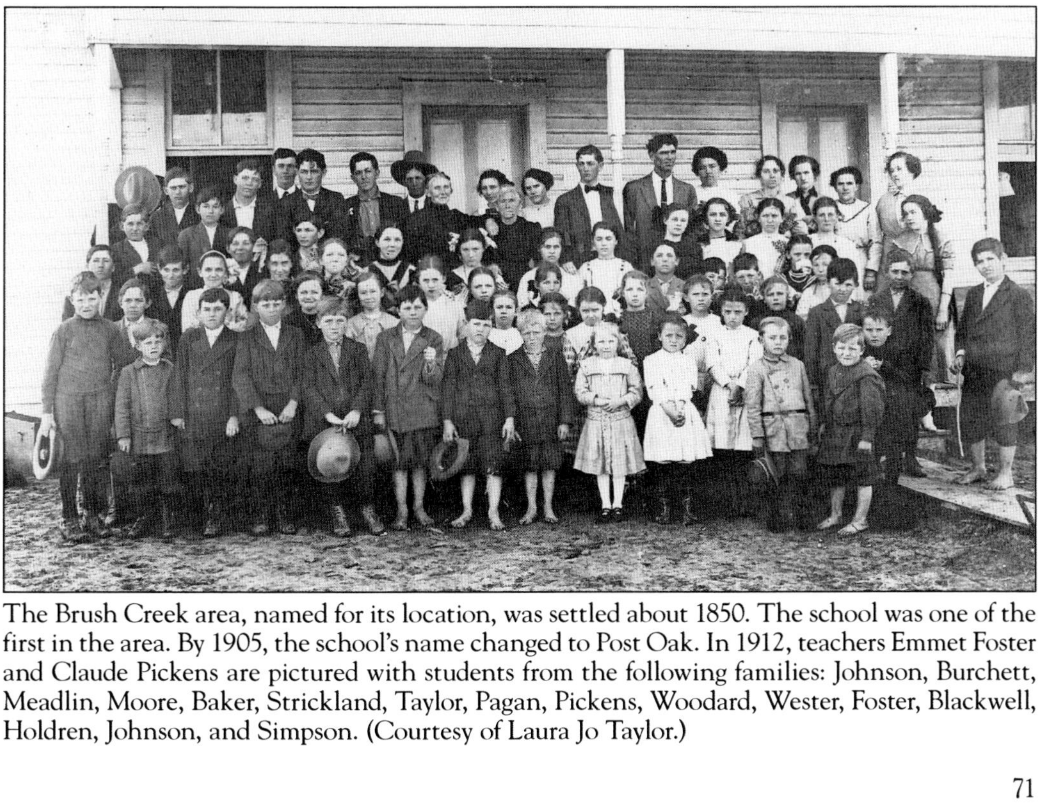

The Brush Creek area, named for its location, was settled about 1850. The school was one of the first in the area. By 1905, the school's name changed to Post Oak. In 1912, teachers Emmet Foster and Claude Pickens are pictured with students from the following families: Johnson, Burchett, Meadlin, Moore, Baker, Strickland, Taylor, Pagan, Pickens, Woodard, Wester, Foster, Blackwell, Holdren, Johnson, and Simpson. (Courtesy of Laura Jo Taylor.)

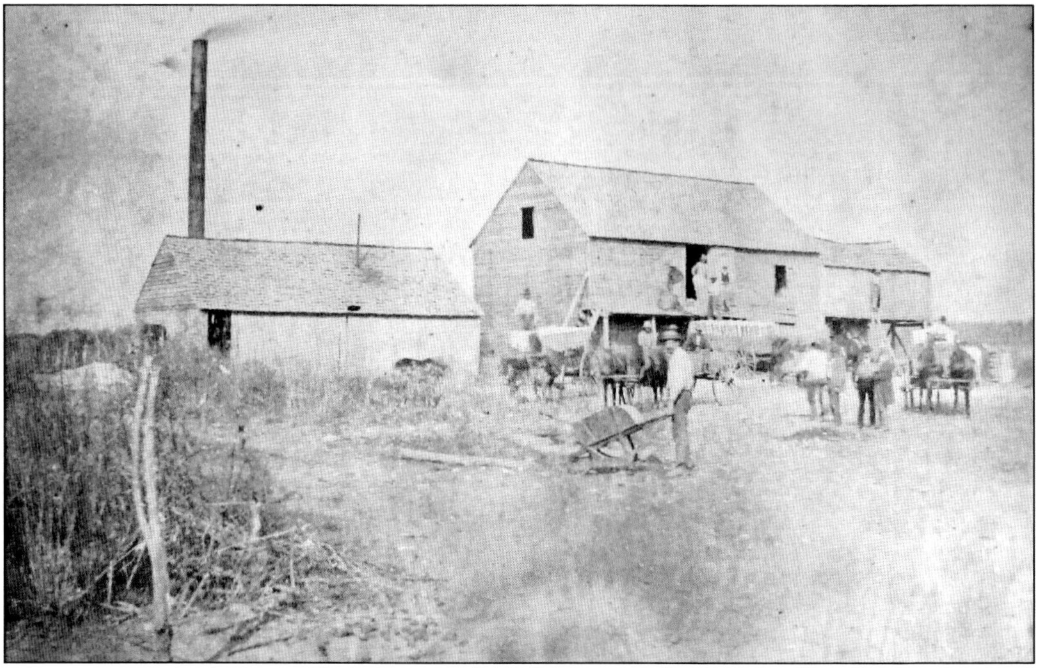

Lake Creek's first post office was called Odd's Creek, but only for six months. In 1885, it was opened under the name Lake Creek, and the community consisted of a dry goods and grocery store, a general store, a blacksmith shop, a corn mill and gin, and several churches. The Lake Creek gin, pictured above, was in operation about 1890. Below is the Presbyterian church, which was built about 1900. The church building was destroyed by a storm in 1926. (Both, courtesy of Patterson Museum.)

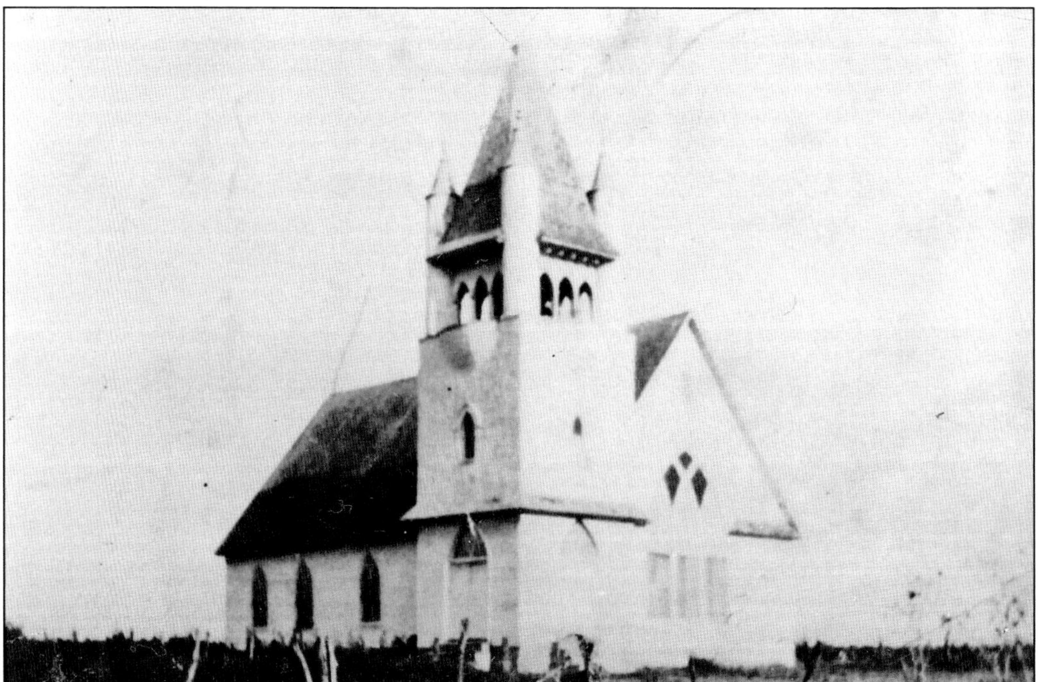

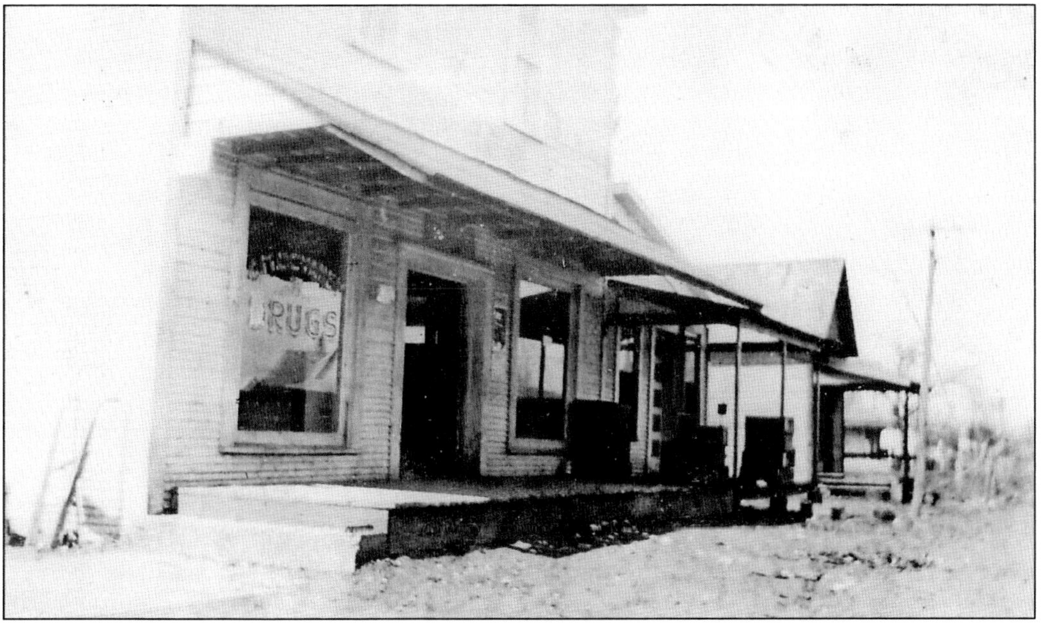

This street scene of Lake Creek about 1910 shows J. H. Devaney Drug Store and Dr. M. A. Estep's office to the far right. The All Free and Accepted Mason Lodge met on the second floor of the drugstore. (Courtesy of Patterson Museum.)

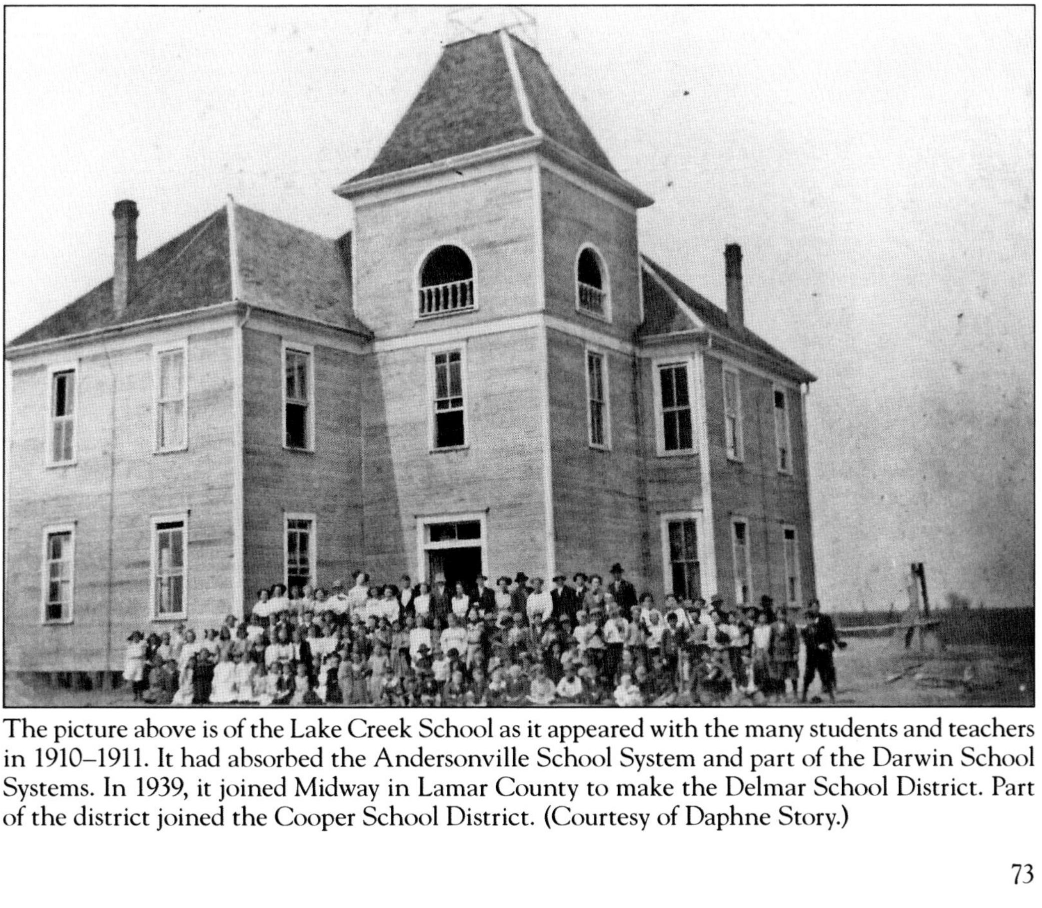

The picture above is of the Lake Creek School as it appeared with the many students and teachers in 1910–1911. It had absorbed the Andersonville School System and part of the Darwin School Systems. In 1939, it joined Midway in Lamar County to make the Delmar School District. Part of the district joined the Cooper School District. (Courtesy of Daphne Story.)

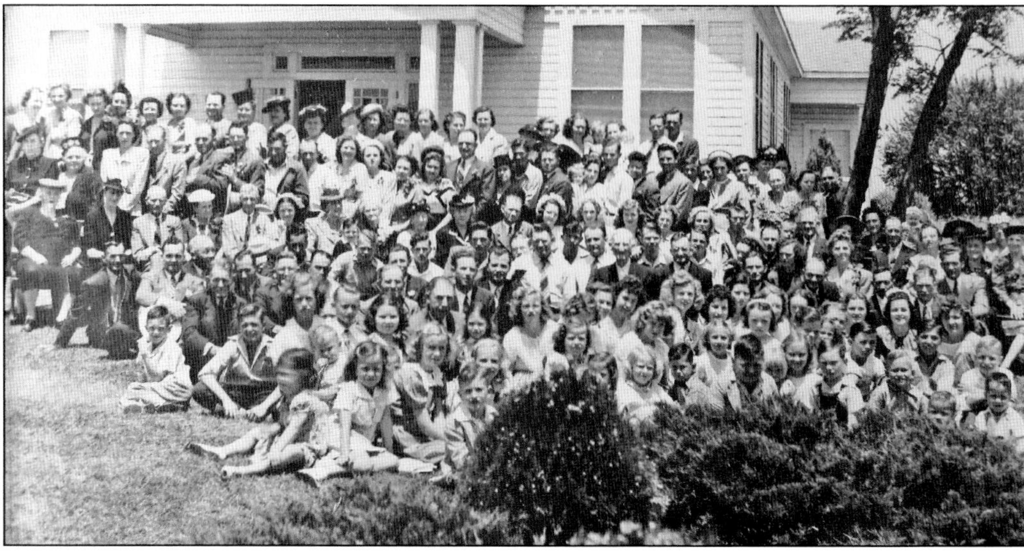

The above picture shows the celebration of the anniversary of the Lake Creek Methodist Church. There were originally two Methodist churches in the area, the Methodist Protestant and the Methodist Episcopal. The churches eventually merged. (Courtesy of Patterson Museum.)

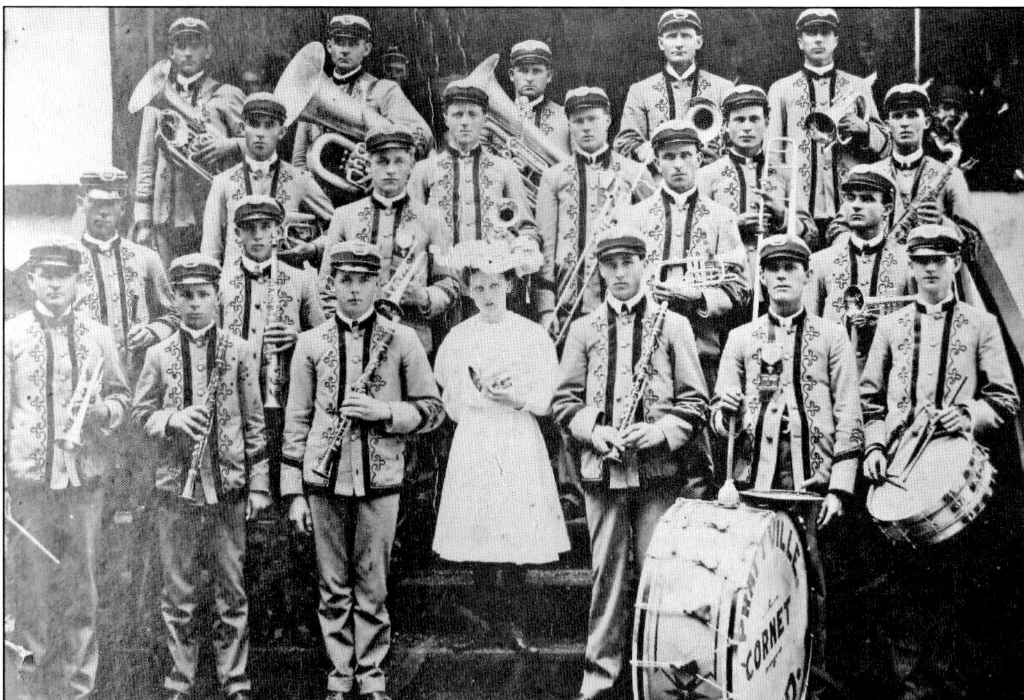

Prattville Cornet Band members are, from left to right, (first row) W. A. Thomason, Charlie McClain, Bob Stovall, Jessie Thomason, Frank Lamb, Clark Chambliss, and Ray Blevins; (second row) Elmer Thompson, Paul Lamb, Harve Wilson, Lewis Taylor, and Arch Hendrix; (third row) Alphus Beckham, Jess Pound, Hannon Pound, Hadie Lamb, and Hugh Lamb; (fourth row) Milton Thompson, W. A. Thompson, Will Pratt, Martin Crook, and Bill Mitchell. (Courtesy of Patterson Museum.)

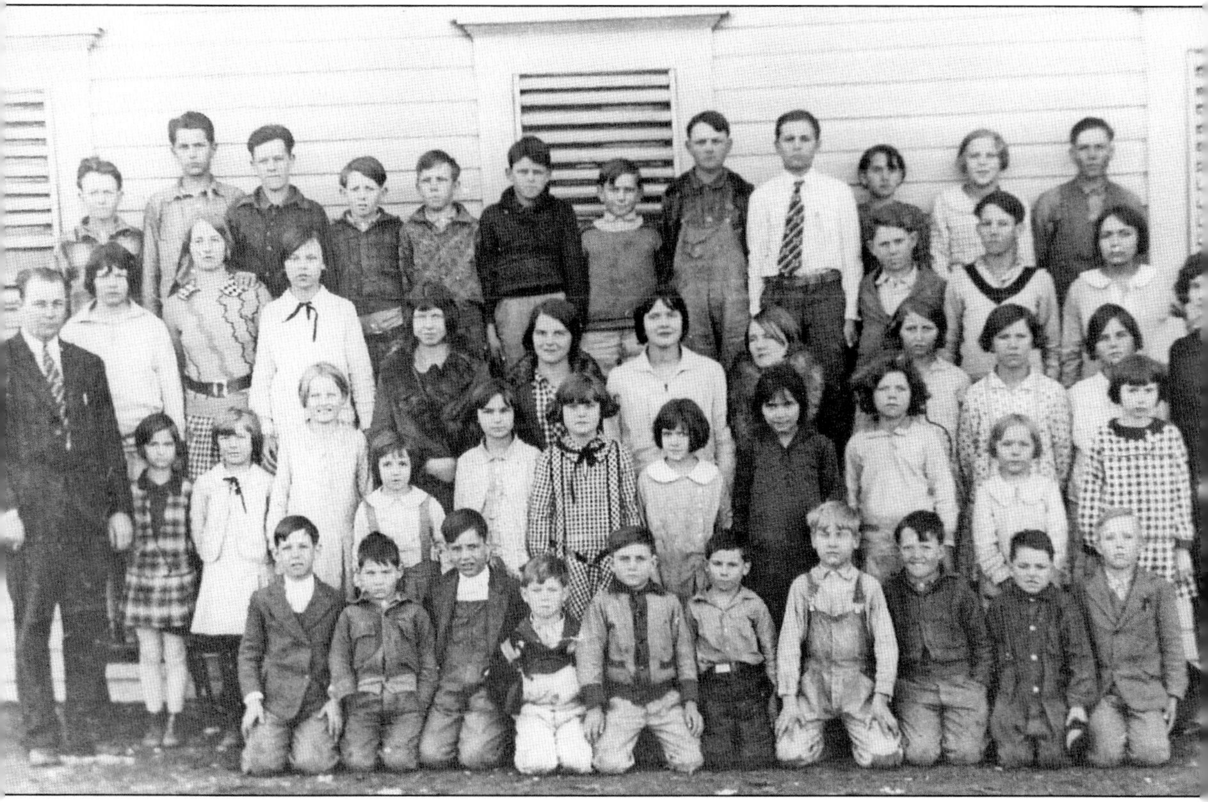

The Perkins School was located just west of the Prattville community on J. A. Perkins's land. C. C. Dunagan and J. A. Perkins were the original teachers. In 1928–1929, the teachers were Buel Jeffries and Gladys Meadlin. The students were, from left to right, (first row) Harry Nimmo, Doyce Meadlin, Jeter Nimmo, Russ Robinson, Dalton Wood, unidentified, ? Russell, and three unidentified; (second row) Estelene Gunter, unidentified, Wanda Harris, Mary Nimmo, Francis Gunter, Valta Pratt, Thelma Stewart, Edna Robinson, unidentified, and Zouela DeVaney; (third row) Aline Robinson, Hazel Meadlin, Leona Jeter, Billie Robinson, Beauton Meadlin, Frankie Mae Stewart, Rena Lovin, unidentified, Beatrice Robinson, and Juanita Jeter; (fourth row) John Robinson (third from right); (fifth row) unidentified, Elvin DeVaney, three unidentified, Eldon Stewart, Coleman Gunter, unidentified, Laverne Russell, Evelyn Harris, and Glen Wood. (Courtesy of Daphne Story.)

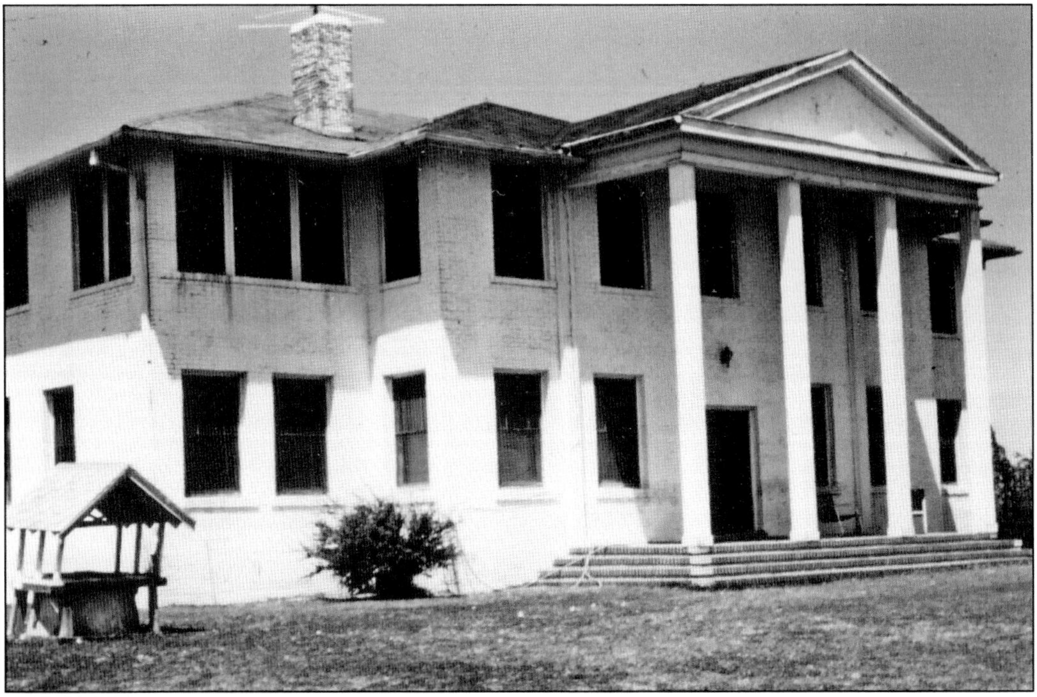

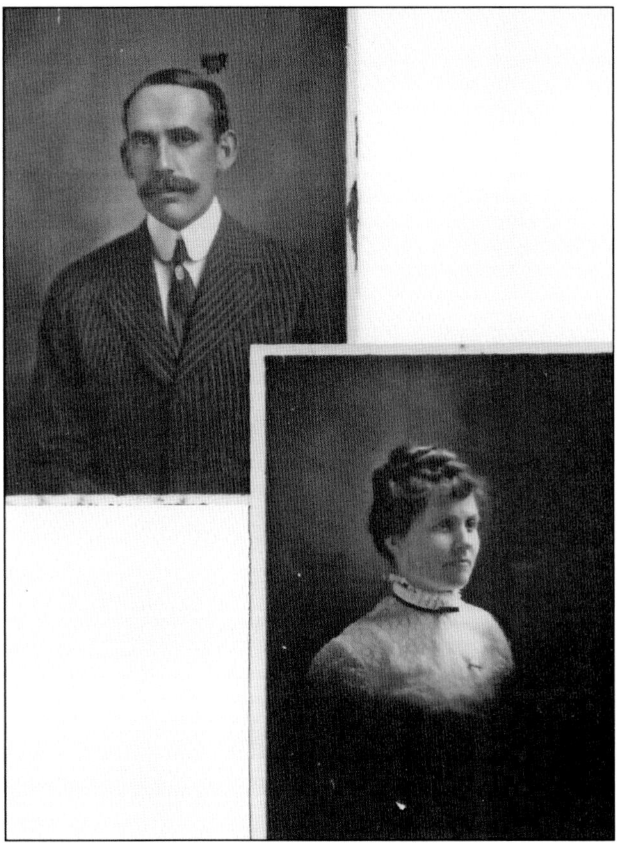

Dr. O. Y. Janes, M.D., and his wife, Evelyn, built the old home place in the middle of 2,000 acres of cotton as the original Janes Clinic and Hospital in 1920. Located in Prattville (now nonexistent), the hospital had 22 rooms. Five rooms upstairs were for patients. There was a single communal bathroom. Evelyn Janes cooked for all on the old wood stove in the downstairs kitchen. Everyone came to a large round wooden table to put food on their plates and go back to each room to eat. They moved the office to above the fire station in Cooper while building the Janes Clinic and Hospital in 1935 because, as Dr. Janes said, "Nobody wanted to be sick in the middle of a cotton patch." Their three sons (Doctors Osler, Olen, and Gaza) later practiced medicine there. (Both, courtesy of the Dr. Olen G. Janes, M.D., family.)

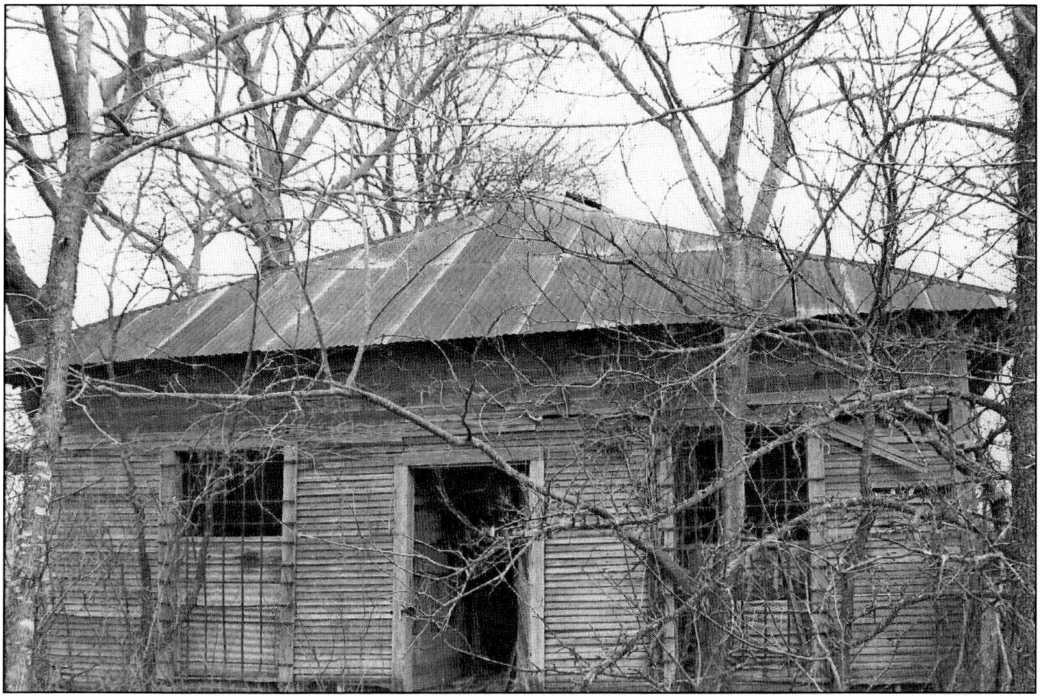

Prattville was a community established with a post office in 1881. William Pratt opened a general merchandise store, and it became a thriving community with several businesses. Pratt's vacant store, pictured above, stood for many years. Below is evidence of one of the businesses. In the later 1800s, whiskey was legally distilled in Prattville, but it could not be sold in Delta County, which was dry. The whiskey was barreled and hauled, cushioned in cottonseed, to Paris on wagons. The person who hauled it to Paris could take jars along to legally bring whiskey back. (Above, courtesy of Clara Foster Slough Museum; right, courtesy of Patterson Museum.)

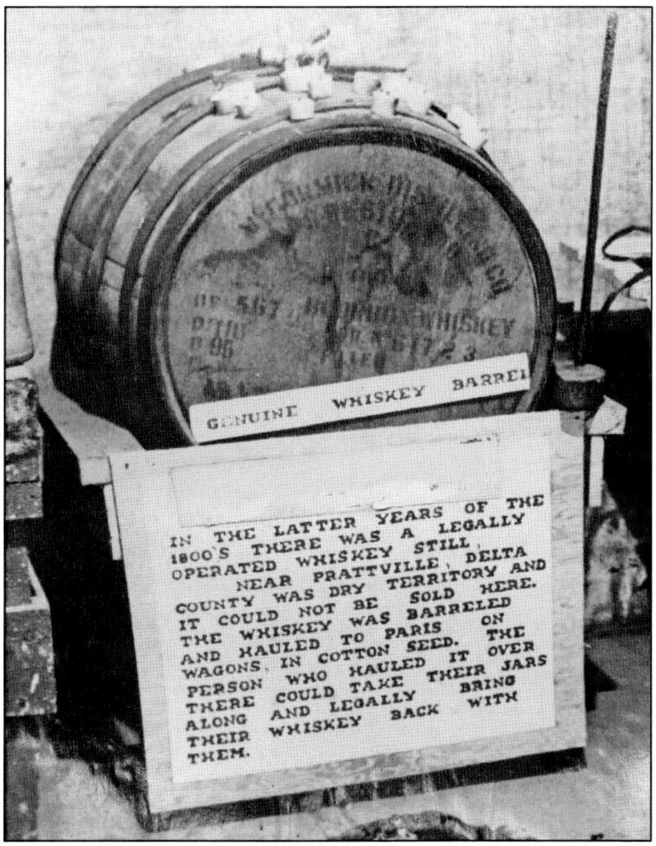

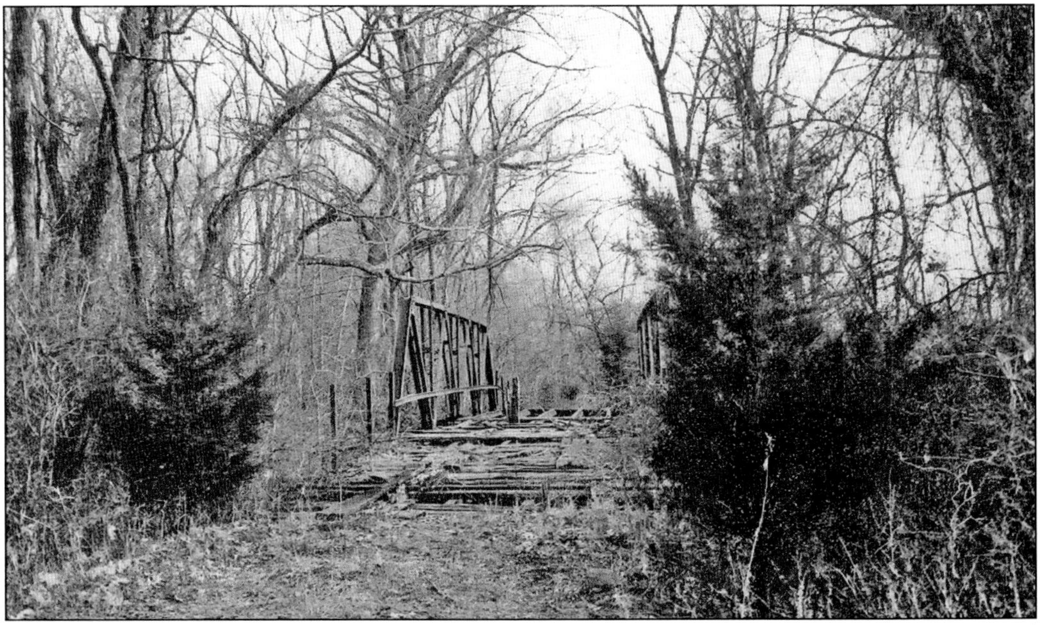

Pacio was first established as the Lone Elm School about 1890. In 1892, James Porter Mote established the post office, misspelling the Spanish word *patio*, hence Pacio. It was located on the early dirt thoroughfare from Charleston, across the North Sulphur River, to Slabtown in Lamar County. Above is a picture of the old bridge. Below is a picture of Jay Gentry in front of his store, which was a favorite stopping place for the local people passing through the area. (Above, courtesy of Clara Foster Slough Museum; below, courtesy of Shirley Smith and Katie Malone.)

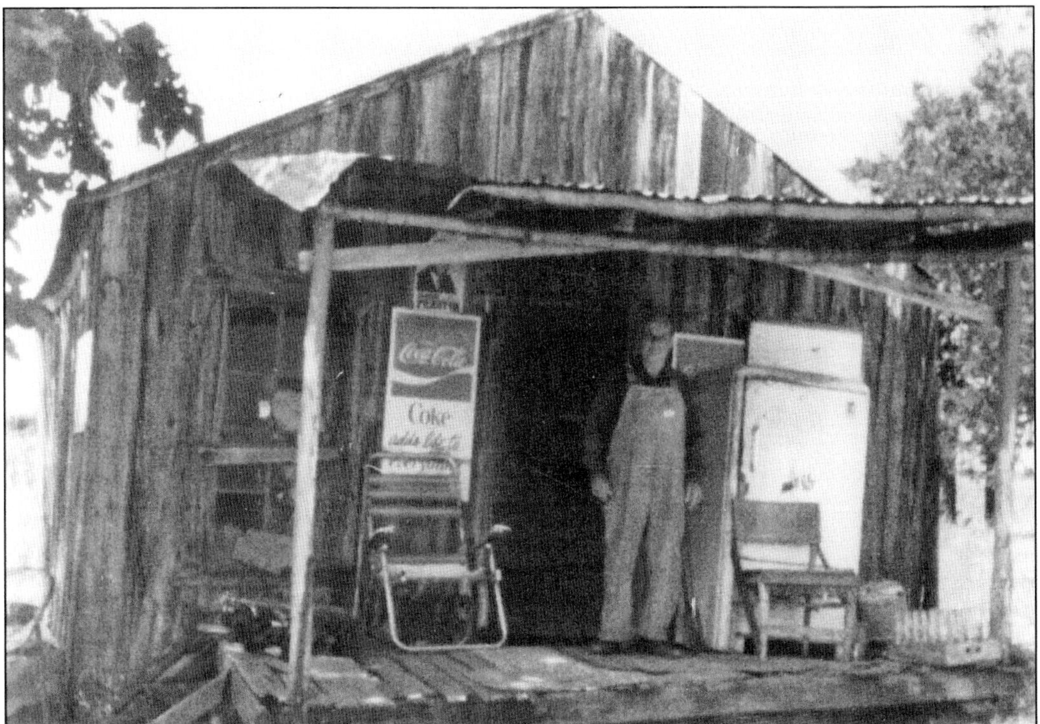

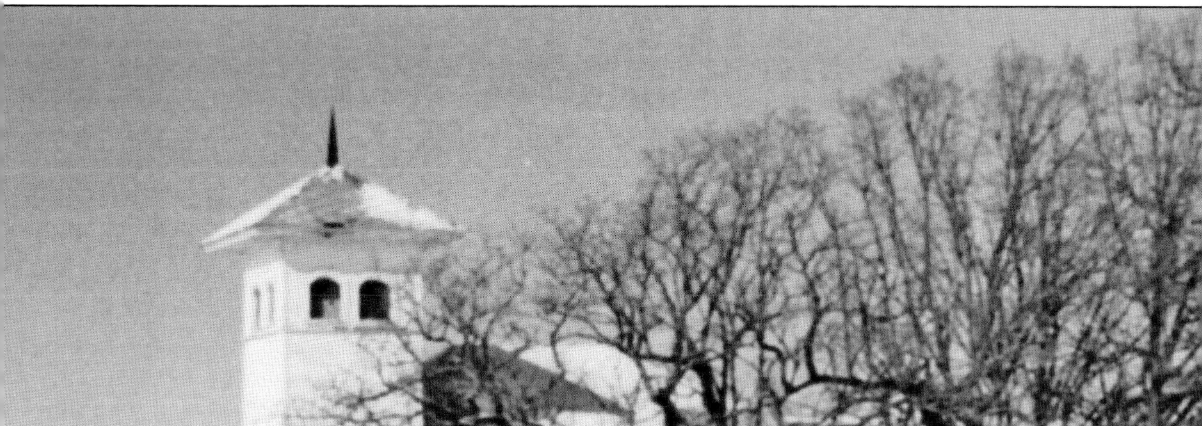

The first Charleston Methodist Church was built on the site where the county barn is today. The current church was built in 1917 with the help of community members. Many different denominations have used this facility, as at one time it was the only church in Charleston. The current congregation is active and is led by the much-loved Gary Regan, a Delta County native. (Courtesy of Jon Scott.)

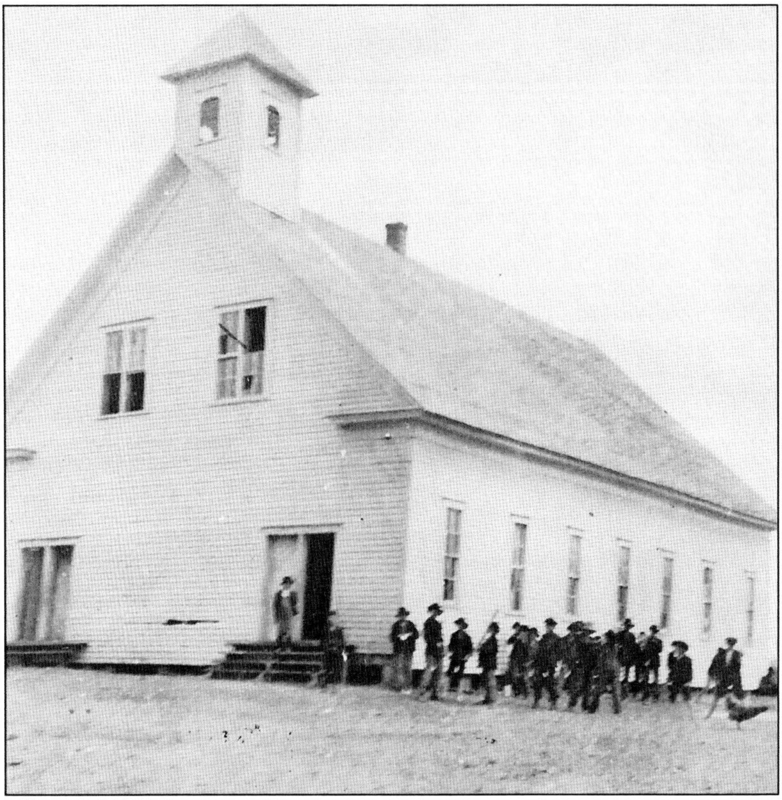

Charleston was established very early in the county's history. This is an early Charleston school called the Old College, or Street College, located across from the old Holiness Tabernacle. The picture at left shows the school before the addition, and the picture below shows the school after it was enlarged. (Left, courtesy of Delta County Library; below, courtesy of Gwen Pickering Wood.)

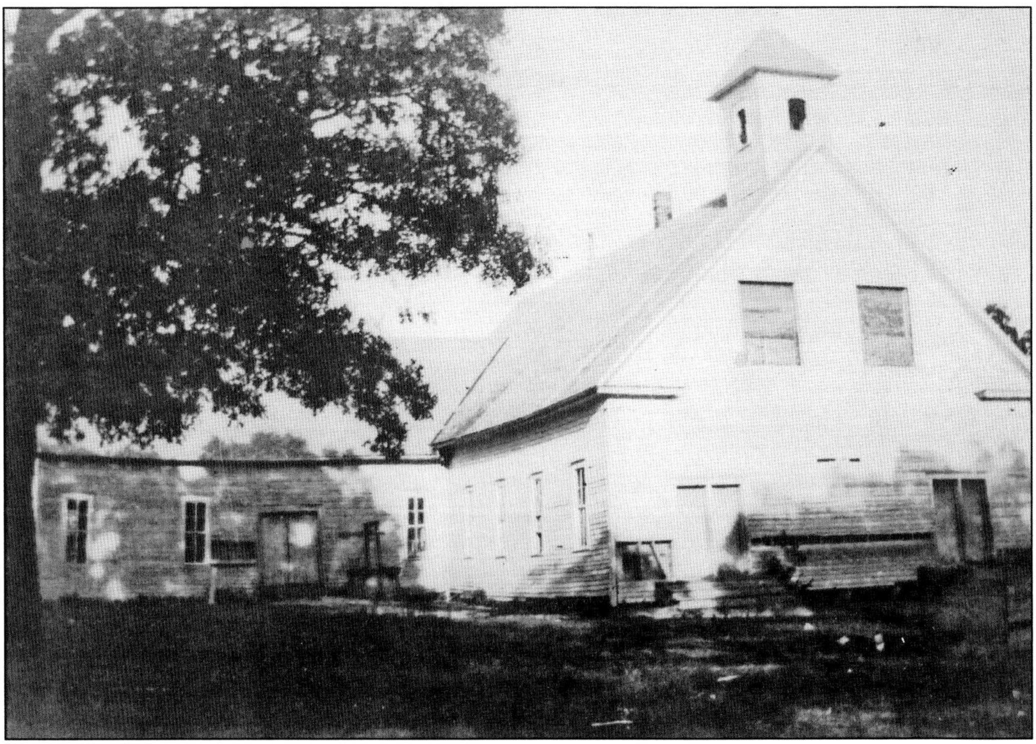

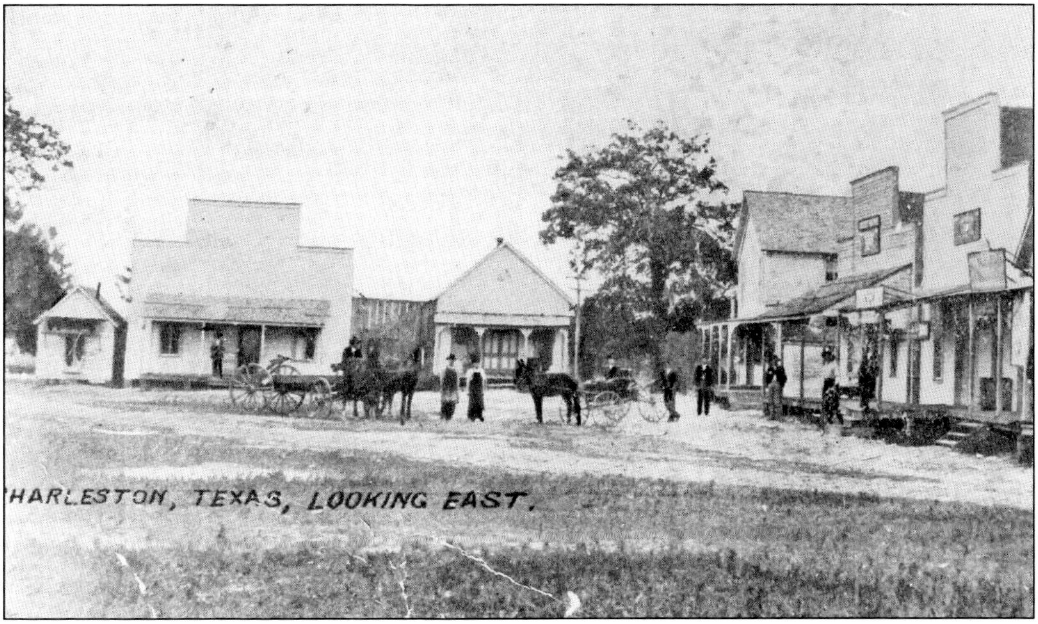

The Charleston square in the early 1900s consisted of stores owned by ? Hargroves, Ed Hendrix, ? Beal (who owned a two-story store), Dutch Akard, ? Latimer, Gazaway Peters, and Grover George. Herman Phillips and Will Worden owned blacksmith shops. Hut Nabors is in the buggy at right. Two fires almost ruined Charleston, one in 1918 that destroyed all businesses on the east side and another in 1924. (Courtesy of Shirley Smith and Katie Malone.)

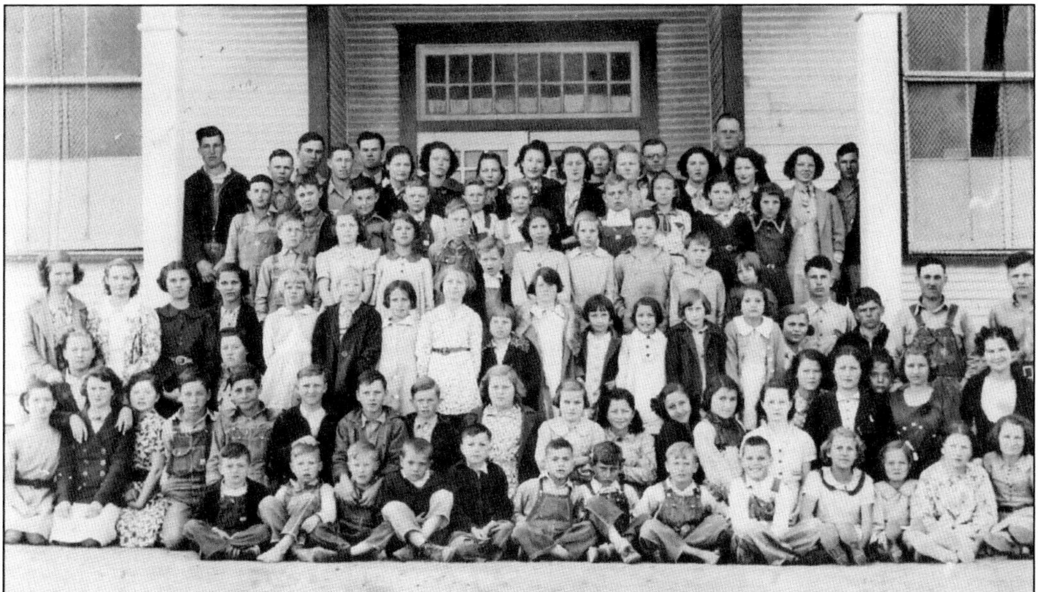

This Charleston School picture shows the children its last year, 1937. The names of the children can be found in the Delta County Library, and the school was located where the county barn is now. The surnames of families are McGuyer, Layer, Oats, Simpson, George, Templeton, Daniels, Beckham, Bettes, Nabors, Stubblefield, Council, Mills, Visor, Chessher, Gardner, Hammett, Slakey, Porter, Helm, Oliver, Click, and Bates. (Courtesy of Shirley Smith and Katie Malone.)

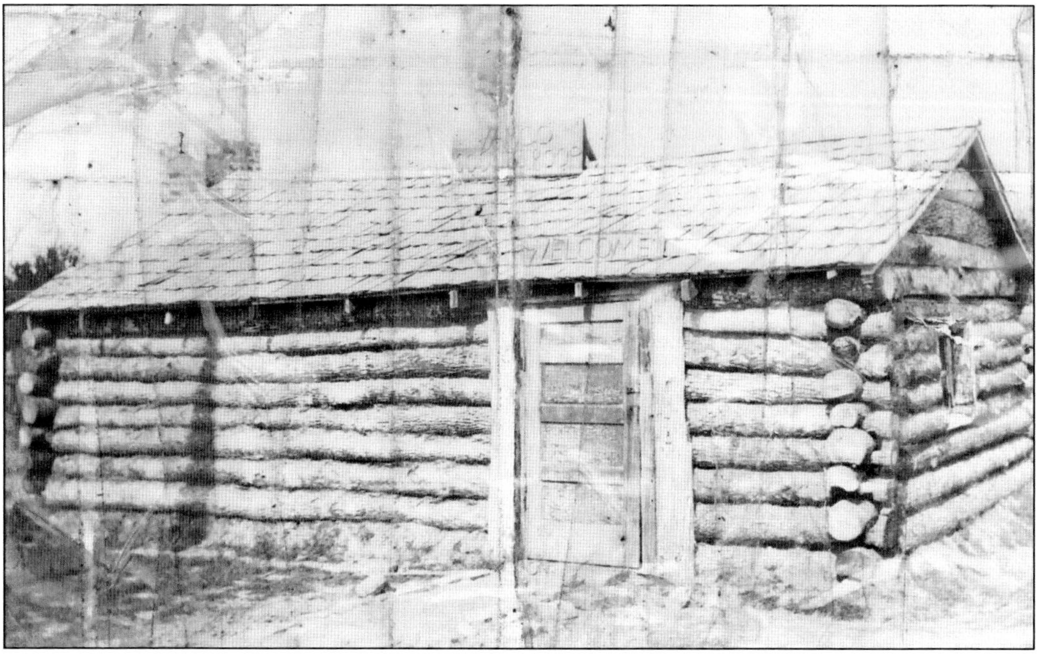

The communities of Vasco, Long Ridge, Cleveland, and Charleston met in this cabin to create the East Delta School in July 1939. The names of the families that were represented included Porter, Martin, Walker, Griffin, Hood, Russell, Harden, Franks, Walker, Beaver, Young, Crumbley, King, and Price. (Courtesy of Mavo Jo Mills Clark and Pauletta Slakey McConathey.)

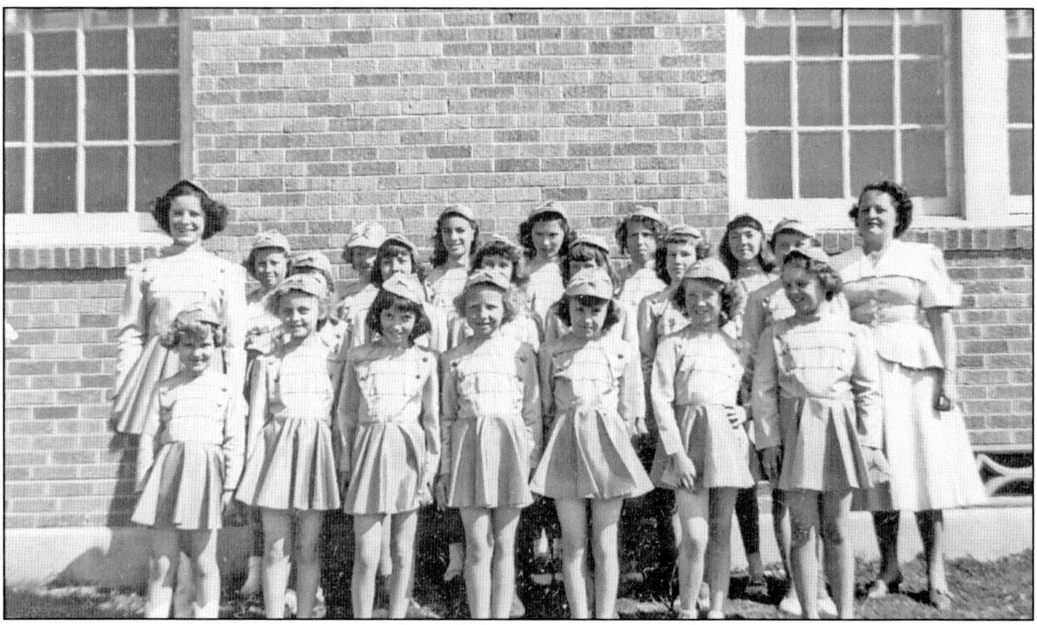

Rural school children had varied opportunities to perform for community functions. The East Delta Rhythm Band was sponsored by Imogene Polk. Among the students are Jean Ann South, Avon Basham, Barbara Johnson, Peggy Layer, Clara Sue Worden, Shelia Hinton, Catherine Stewart, Mary Deweese, Wanda Lawler, Doris Goforth, Carlie McKinney, Sherry Wicks, Joan Daniels, Carolyn Stephens, and Zeneth Cooper. (Courtesy of Shirley Smith and Katie Malone.)

In 1957, these East Delta School students traveled to Beaver's Bend. From left to right are Linda Boyd, Shirley Nabors, June Click, Barbara Johnson, Judy Hornsby, Janice Viser, and Tommie Templeton. (Courtesy of Shirley Smith and Katie Malone)

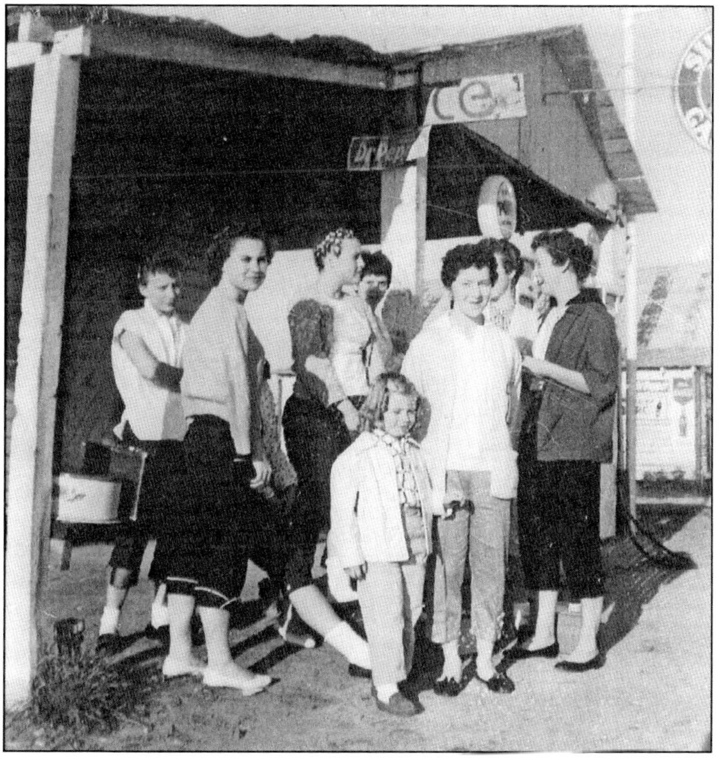

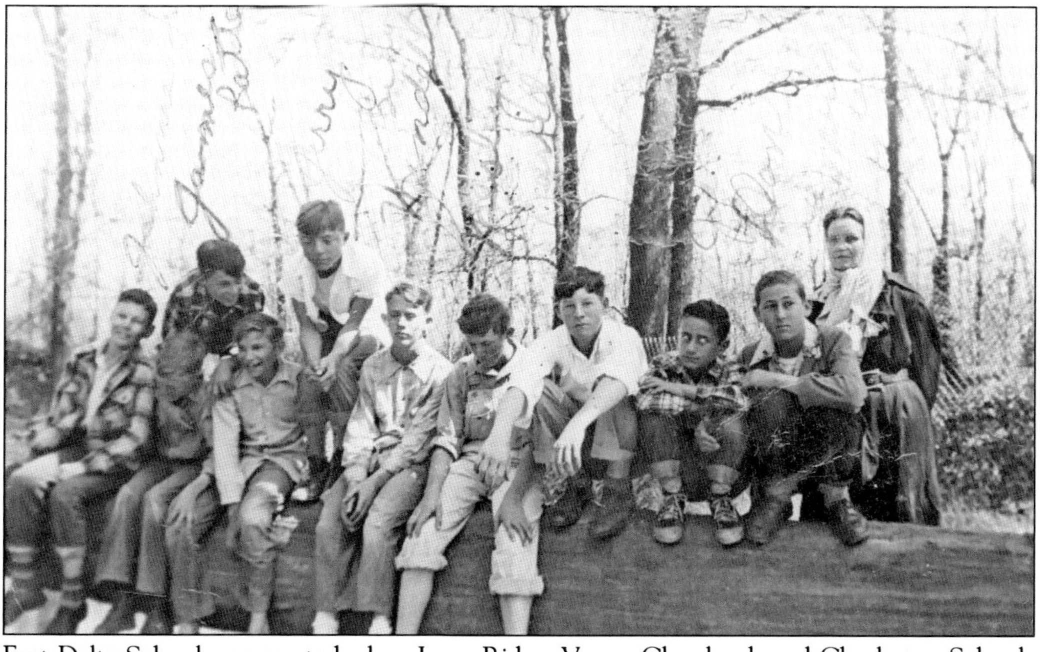

East Delta School was created when Long Ridge, Vasco, Cleveland, and Charleston Schools consolidated in 1939. Teacher Stella Breckeen (right) took, from left to right, Johnny Lawler, James Patterson, Jerry Holcomb, Bennett James, Luther Lawson, unidentified, Wesley Cooper, David Moses, Joe Viser, and Don Woodard on a field trip in May 1954. (Courtesy of Shirley Smith and Katie Malone.)

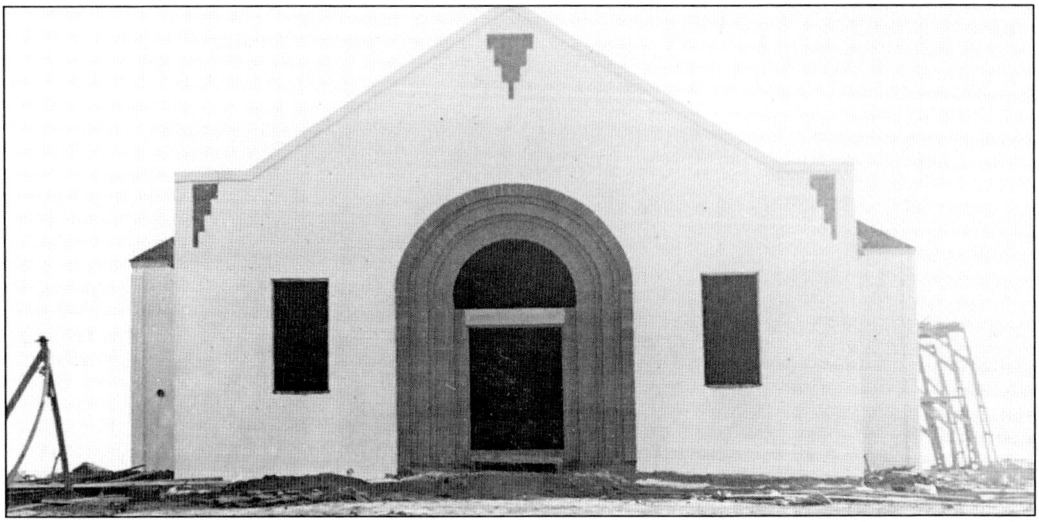

The East Delta Baptist Church was built in 1948 on land donated by Florence and J. C. Terry. The first pulpit committee was made up of E. P. Polk, Travis Young, and T. J. Worden. Carl Jones was the first pastor. T. J. Scott donated 2 acres of land behind the church for a cemetery. The church burned in 2000, and a new church was built. (Courtesy of Shirley Smith and Katie Malone.)

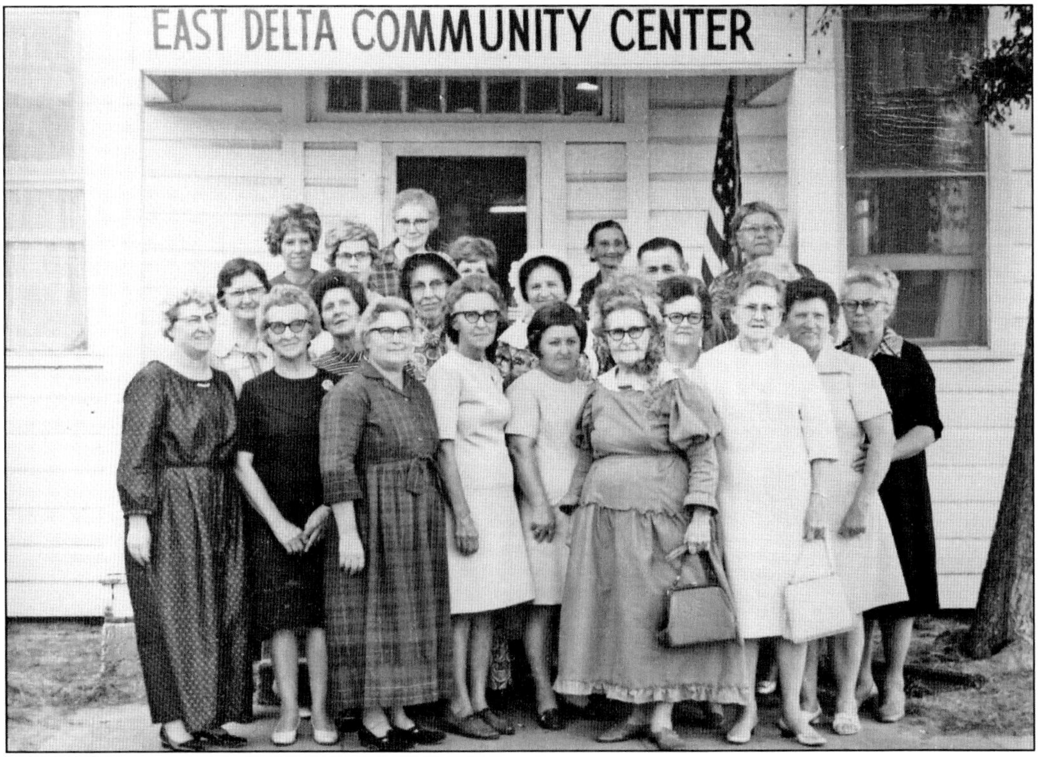

Gathering to celebrate the Delta County centennial in 1970 are, from left to right, (first row) Glenna Scott, Norene Schultz, Venice Worden, Inez Trapp, Lucy Oliver, Nell Peters, Gertha Oats, Ada Oliver, and Maggie Slakey; (second row) Helen Perry, Dolores Jackson, Leo Viser, Olpha Allridge, Oleta Templeton, and Van Worden; (third row) Betty Blagburn, Virginia Bettes, Effie Stubblefield, Grace Moody, and Florene Nabors. (Courtesy of Shirley Smith.)

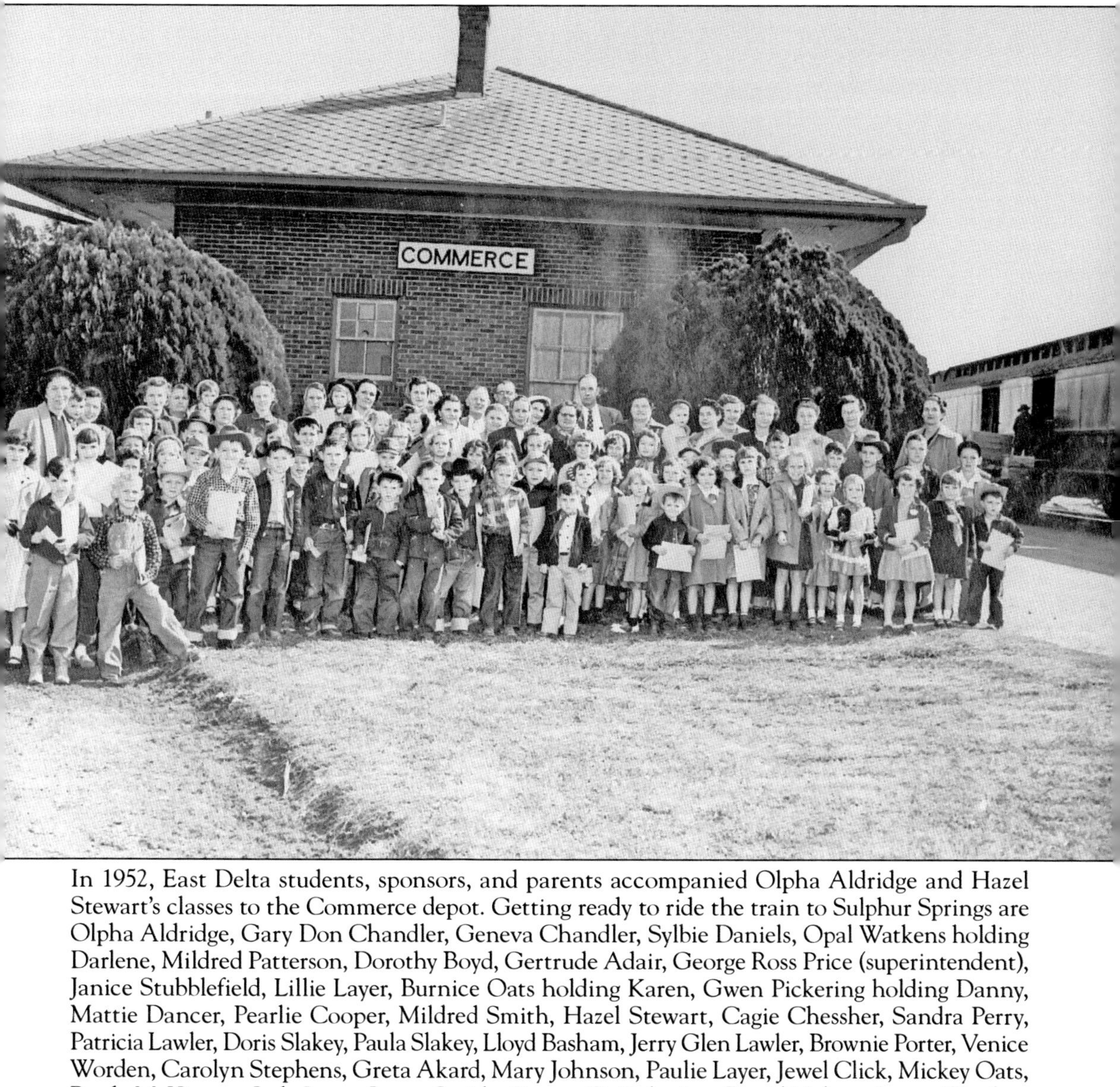

In 1952, East Delta students, sponsors, and parents accompanied Olpha Aldridge and Hazel Stewart's classes to the Commerce depot. Getting ready to ride the train to Sulphur Springs are Olpha Aldridge, Gary Don Chandler, Geneva Chandler, Sylbie Daniels, Opal Watkens holding Darlene, Mildred Patterson, Dorothy Boyd, Gertrude Adair, George Ross Price (superintendent), Janice Stubblefield, Lillie Layer, Burnice Oats holding Karen, Gwen Pickering holding Danny, Mattie Dancer, Pearlie Cooper, Mildred Smith, Hazel Stewart, Cagie Chessher, Sandra Perry, Patricia Lawler, Doris Slakey, Paula Slakey, Lloyd Basham, Jerry Glen Lawler, Brownie Porter, Venice Worden, Carolyn Stephens, Greta Akard, Mary Johnson, Paulie Layer, Jewel Click, Mickey Oats, Brady McKinney, Judy Layer, James Smith, Grover Q. Pickering, David Nabors, Lester Worden, Ted Oats, Charles Elmore, W. C. McKinney, Mickey Oats, Brady McKinney, James Smith, David Slakey, Sally Oats, Bobby George, Lester Worden, Katie Nabors, Carolyn Stephens, Larry Dale Goforth, Bennie Dale Blount, Gary Oats, Sandra Daugherty, Sharron Smart, Donna Kay Watkens, Linda Price, and Ricky Smith. (Courtesy of Shirley Smith and Katie Malone.)

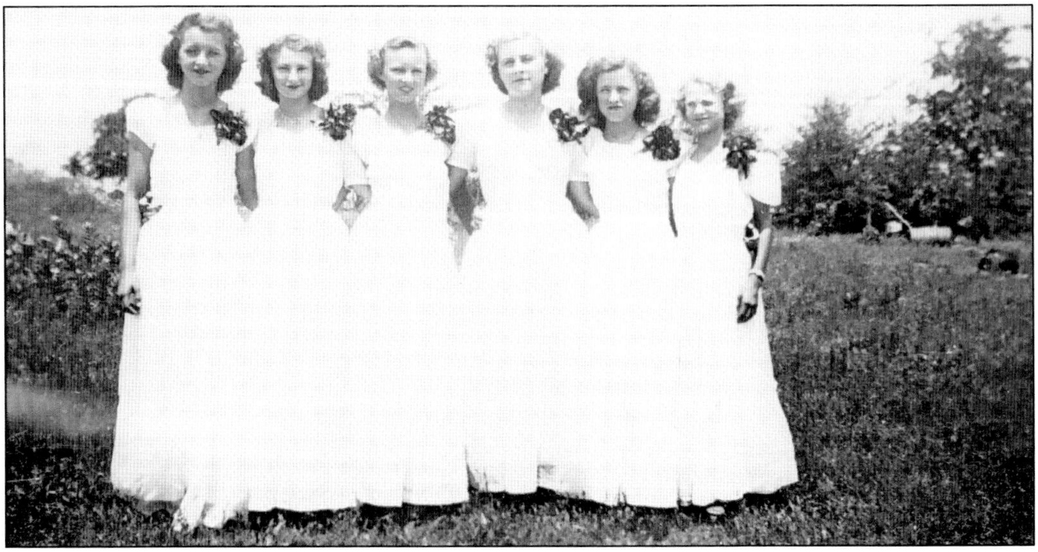

This picture shows the eighth grade graduating class of Kensing School. These young ladies made their own dresses for the occasion. The Kensing School started in 1902 and closed in the early 1950s. Pictured from left to right are Madine Stephens, Evelyn McKinney, Johnnie Simpson, Ema Lold Cooper, Maurice Potts, and Margaret McKinney. (Courtesy of Shirley Smith and Katie Malone.)

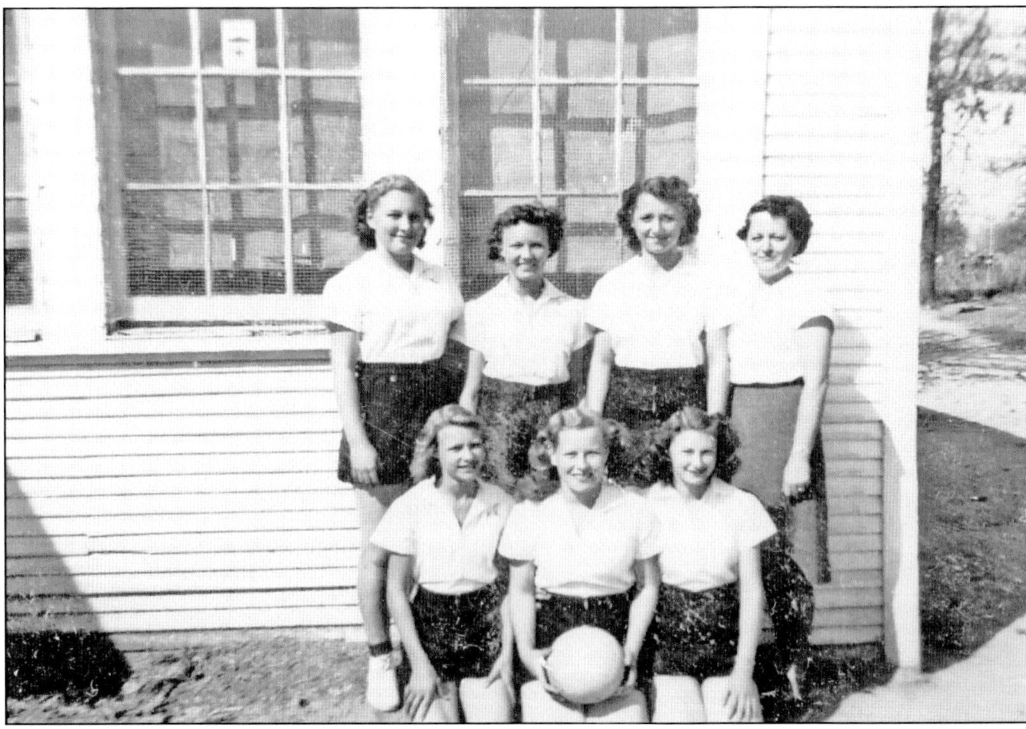

Pictured above is the Kensing School girls' volleyball team and sponsor Imogene Polk. Margaret McKinney is holding the ball, and the others include Eveline McKinney and Madine Stephens. (Courtesy of Shirley Smith and Katie Malone.)

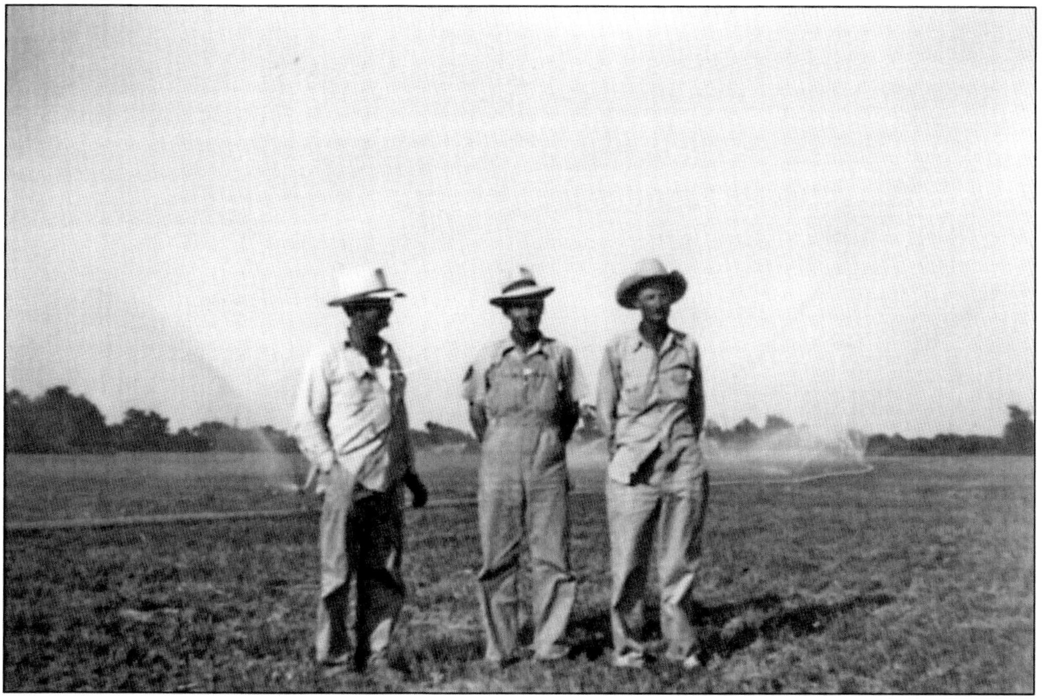

Grover Pickering (left), Stanley Polk (center), and Johnny Thompson are checking the fields at Kensing, which are being irrigated. Grover Pickering was a large landowner in the East End. (Courtesy of Shirley Smith and Katie Malone.)

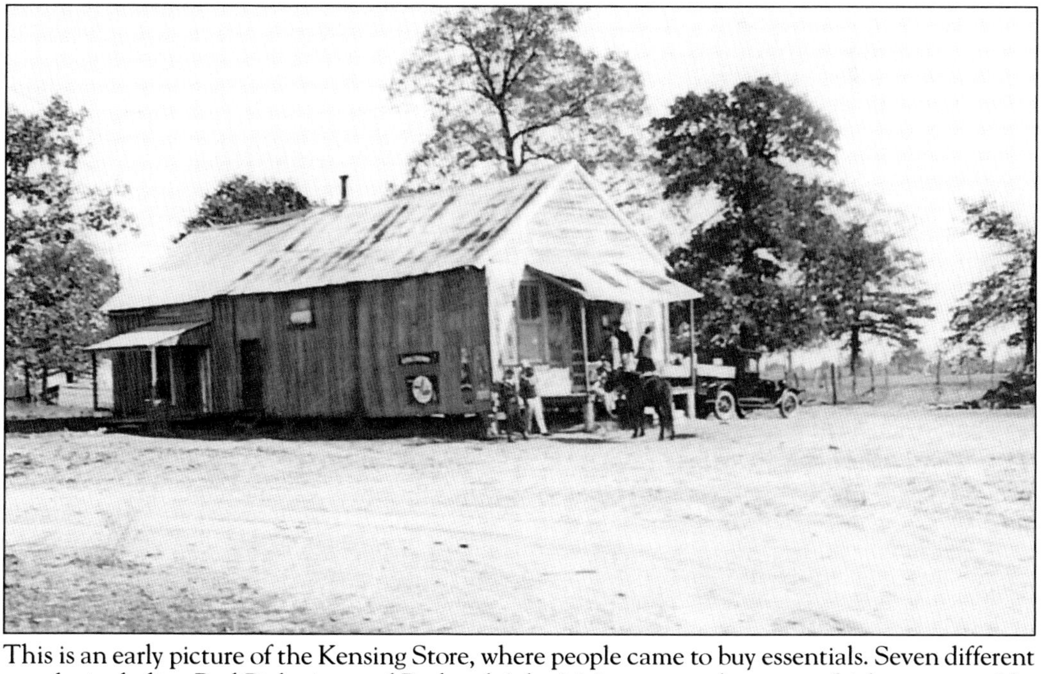

This is an early picture of the Kensing Store, where people came to buy essentials. Seven different people, including Red Pickering and Red and Adra McLarty, ran the store, which was owned by Grover and Teresa Pickering. Thad Moody was the last person to run the store. Shortly before he closed, he was robbed by someone he knew. (Courtesy of Shirley Smith and Katie Malone.)

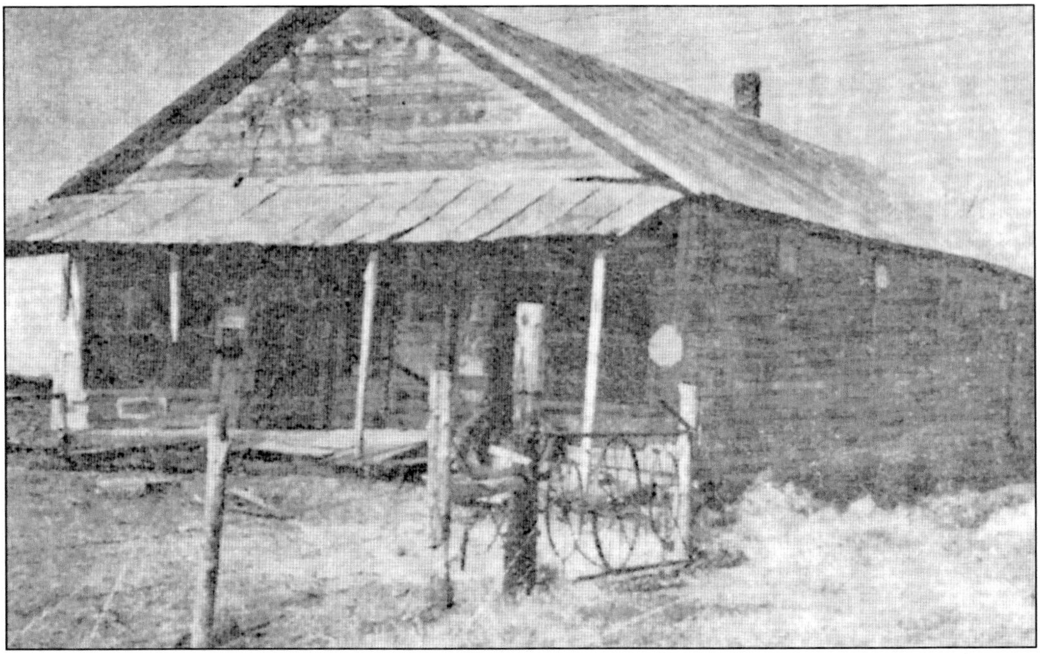

Robert Young bought the Vasco store for his children, Zifton Young and Teresa Young Pickering, as their inheritance in the early 1920s. They operated the store together until Zifton bought out the Pickerings. The store continued in operation until it closed in the 1960s. A gathering place, the store was the scene of many domino games played by area residents in the hot summer afternoons. (Courtesy of Patterson Museum.)

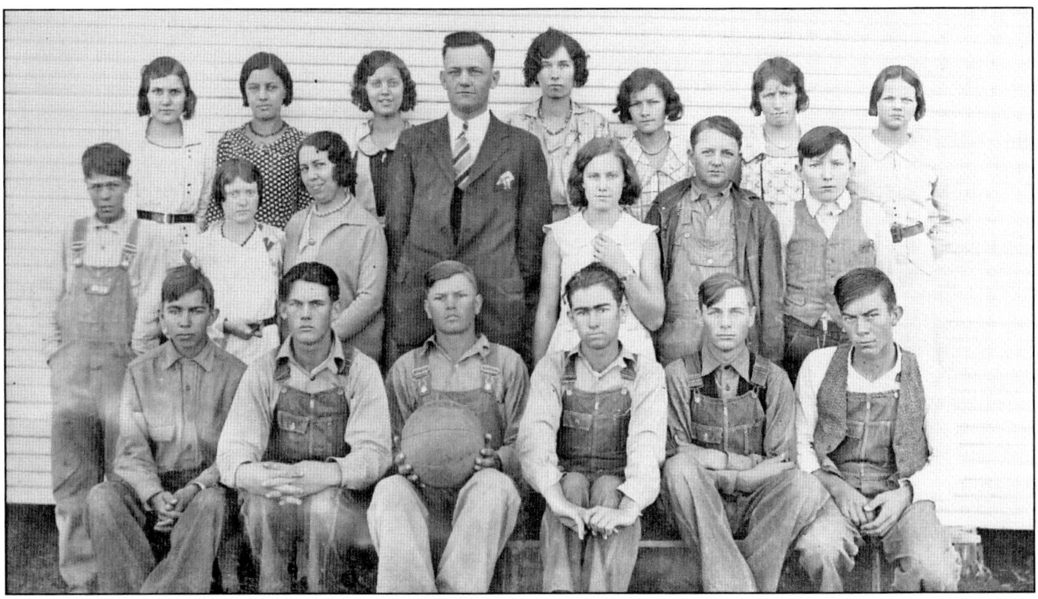

The Vasco School students were, from left to right, (first row) Hulan Westerman, Dennis Daughtery, Woodrow Eppers, Stanley Polk, Clyde Daughtery, and Marshall Driggers; (second row) Hugh Ackard, Della Yarborough, Edna Worden, Alvin Welch (teacher), Edna Williams, Cotton Smith, and Nolan Jenkins; (third row) Louise Mabry, Eddie Lock, Phleta Mitchell, Jessie Mae Ellis, Mildred Hood, Willie Hood, and Rebecca Daughtery. (Courtesy of Stanley Polk.)

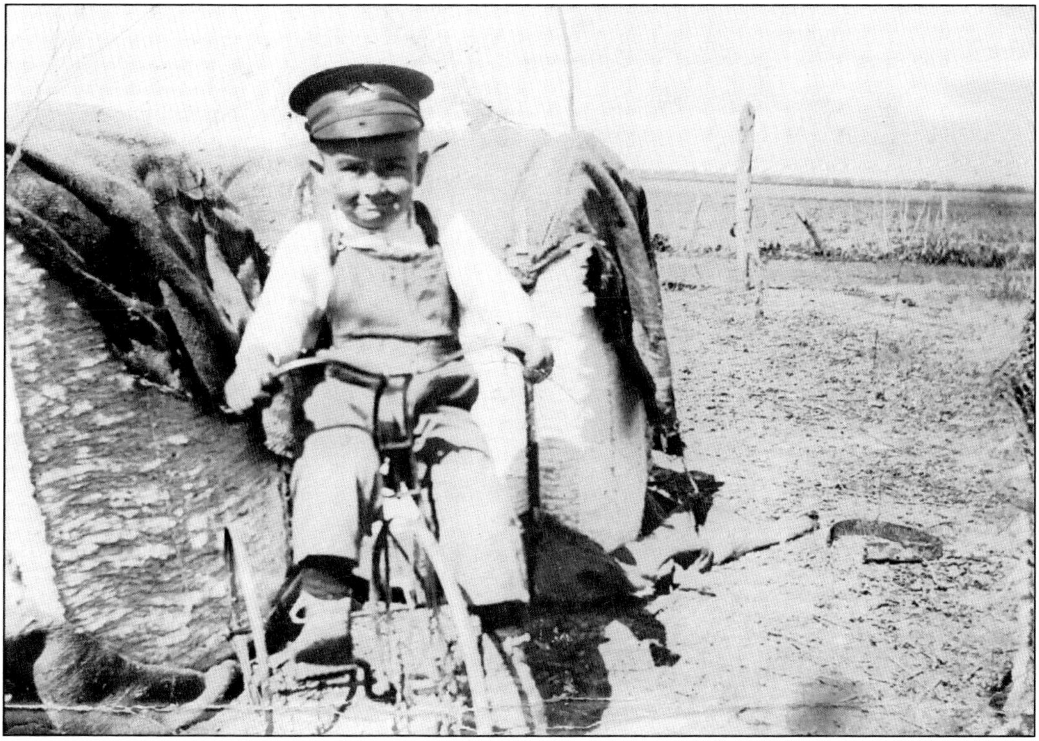

This picture of Stanley Polk, born in 1916, shows him on his tricycle. Stanley rode his tricycle around the bales of cotton at the Vasco Gin in Vasco, Texas. (Courtesy of Imogene Polk.)

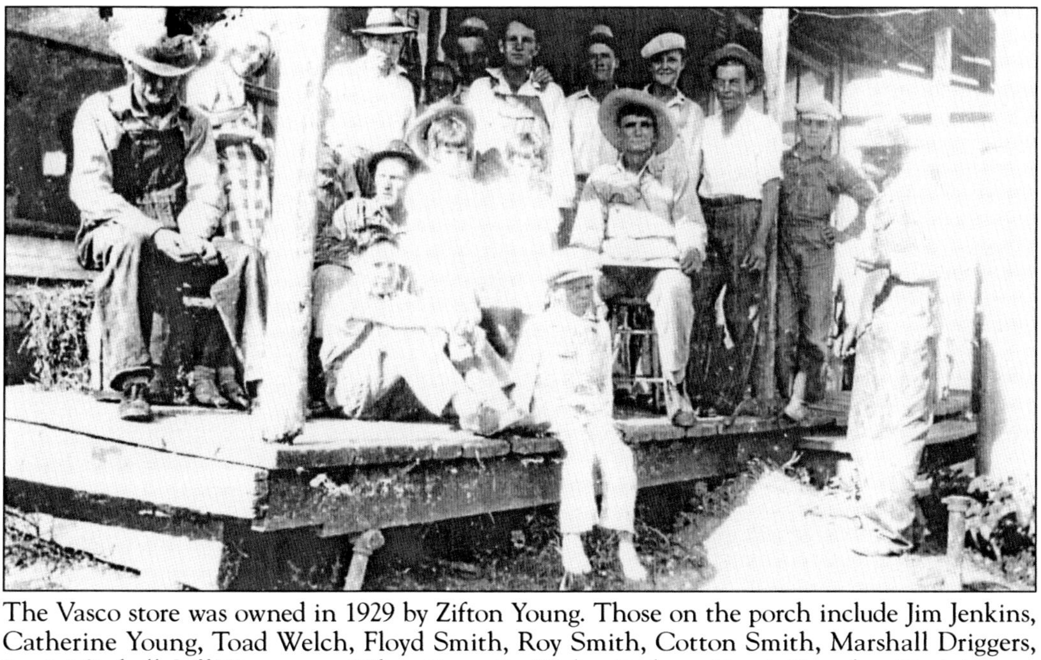

The Vasco store was owned in 1929 by Zifton Young. Those on the porch include Jim Jenkins, Catherine Young, Toad Welch, Floyd Smith, Roy Smith, Cotton Smith, Marshall Driggers, Louis Mitchell, Jeff Westerman, Zifton Young Jr., Walter Barham, Dorris Herndon, Doris Young, Charlie Smith, Grover D. Pickering, and Ershel Driggers. (Courtesy of Shirley Smith and Katie Malone.)

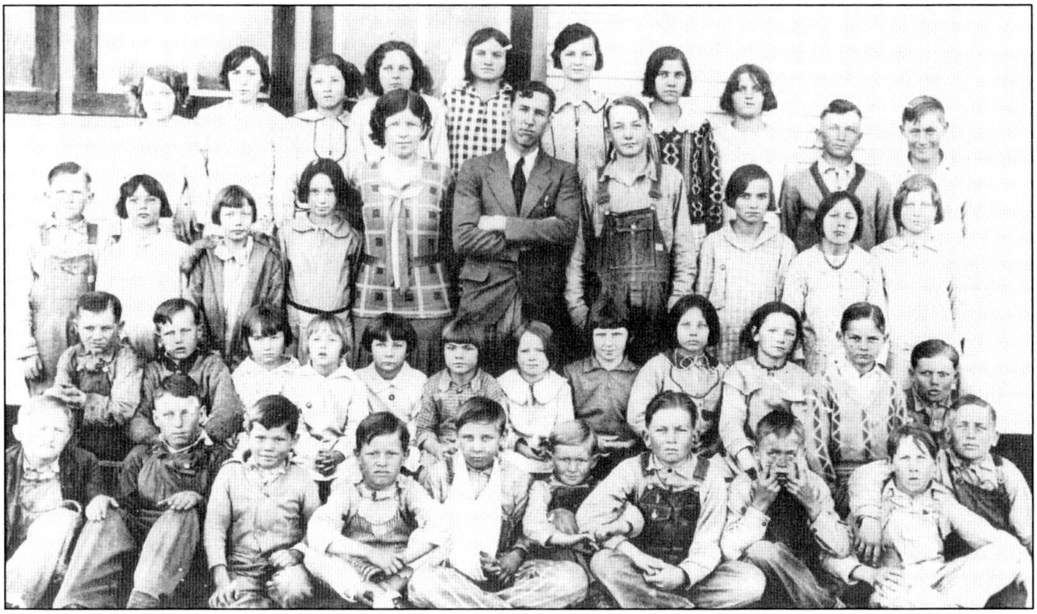

Pictured in 1932 are Long Ridge School students and teachers, from left to right, (first row) Pate Porter, Roy Mills, Jim Woolsey, Eugene Akins, Stanley Rhodes, Clifton Elmore, Houston Elmore, Van Turner, Aubrey Akin, and Seth Lawrence; (second row) Tyree Porter, Thad Lawrence, Mary Francis Porter, Dosha LaRae, Wilda Turner, Millie Porter, Johnny Daniels, Wilma Wright, Odie Boyd, Sybille Daniels, Quinton Woolsey, and Clyde Porter; (third row) Carlton Elmore, Dixie Jo Lile, Christine Lawrence, Fay Daniels, Nettie Wickersham (teacher), R. J. Bryant (teacher), W. T. Lawrence, Murlie Porter, Addison Boyd, and Lucille Mills; (fourth row) Ina Chambers, Nettie Elmore, Faye Cadell, Freddie Lile, Lela Porter, Nettie Wright, Leola Rhodes, Dorthy Lile, Earl Elmore, and Hugh Hammett. Below is a picture of the Union Grove School, which was established before the one in Charleston. The school closed before 1918. (Both, courtesy of Shirley Smith and Katie Malone.)

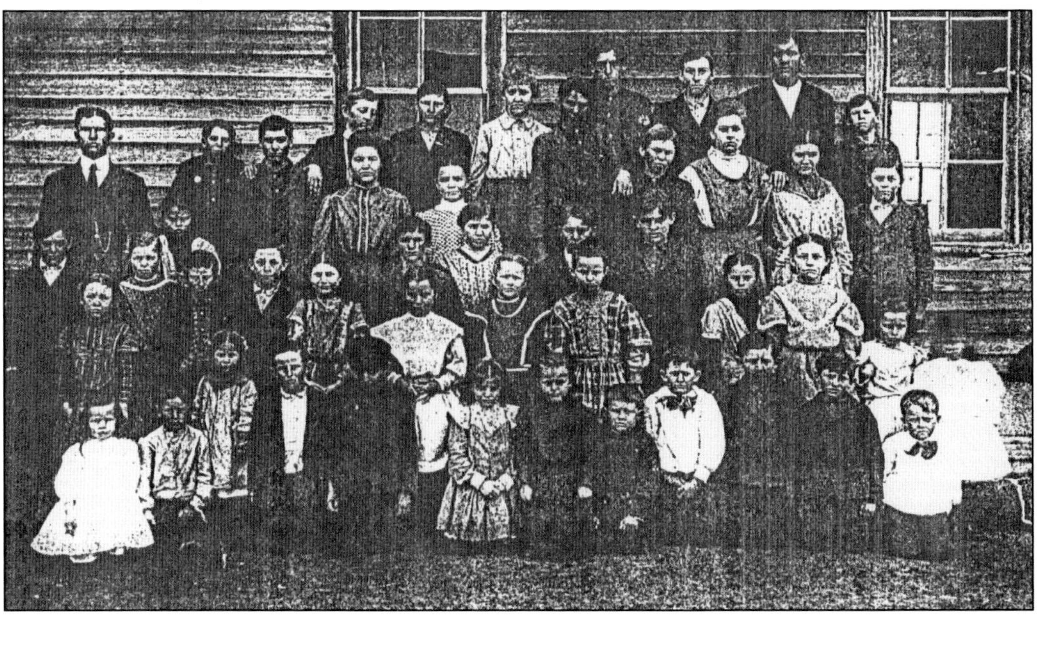

Five

Cooper

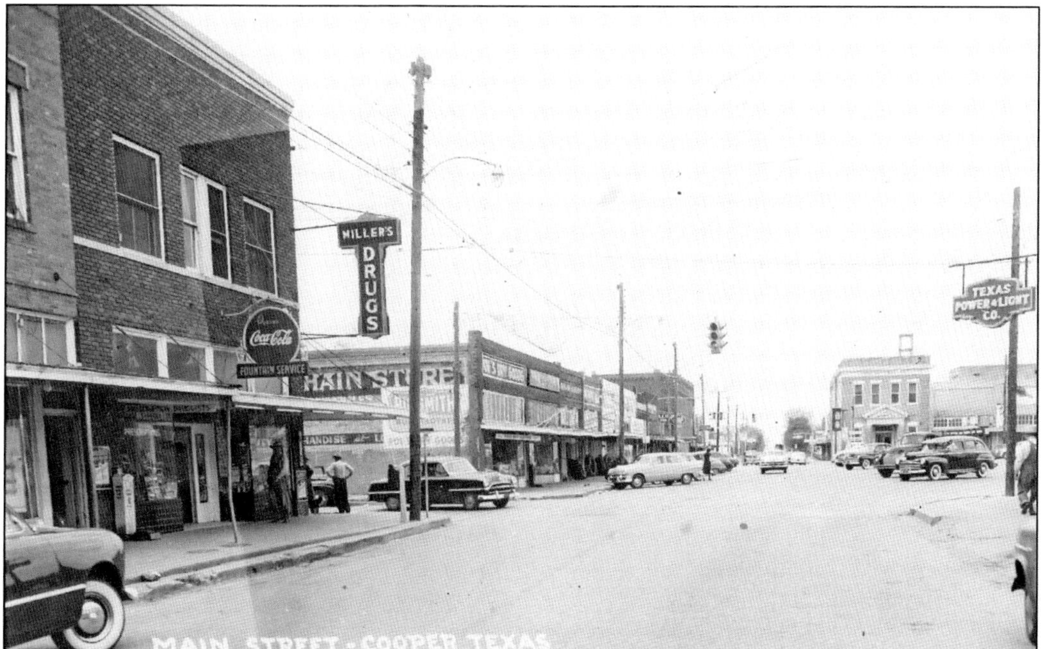

Featured in this photograph is the south side of the square in Cooper. The picture was taken from East Dallas Avenue in 1954. (Courtesy of Marion Miller.)

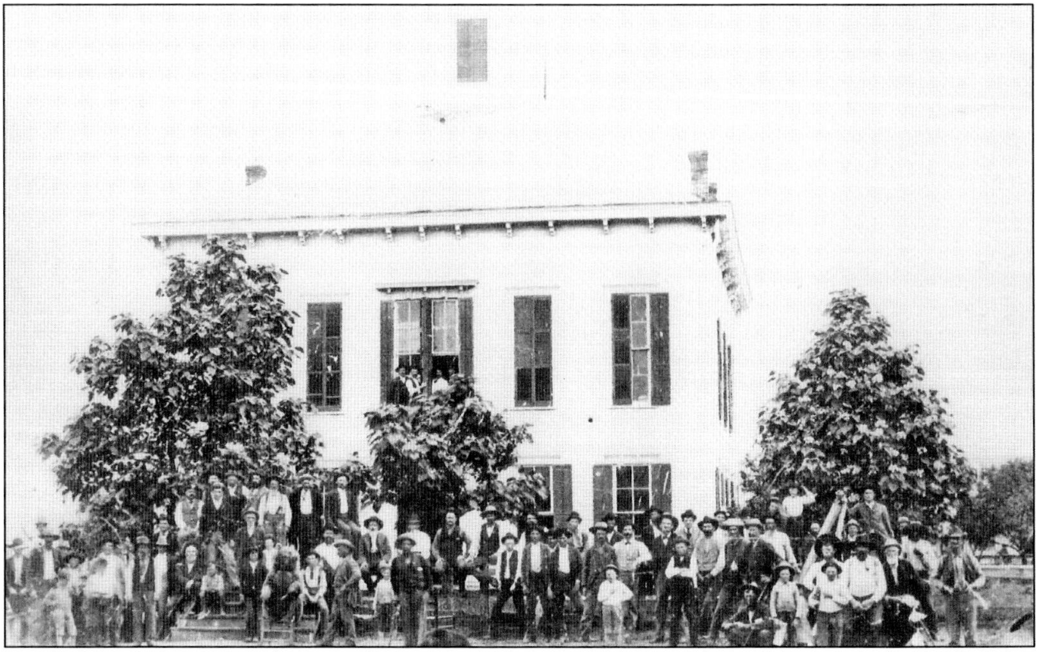

Delta County has had four courthouses. The first was a box house located across from the IOOF building for 10 years. The second courthouse, built in 1881, was a two-story frame structure in the center of the square. In the 1890s, this structure burned, and it was replaced with the third courthouse, which was also located in the middle of the square. (Courtesy of Daphne Story.)

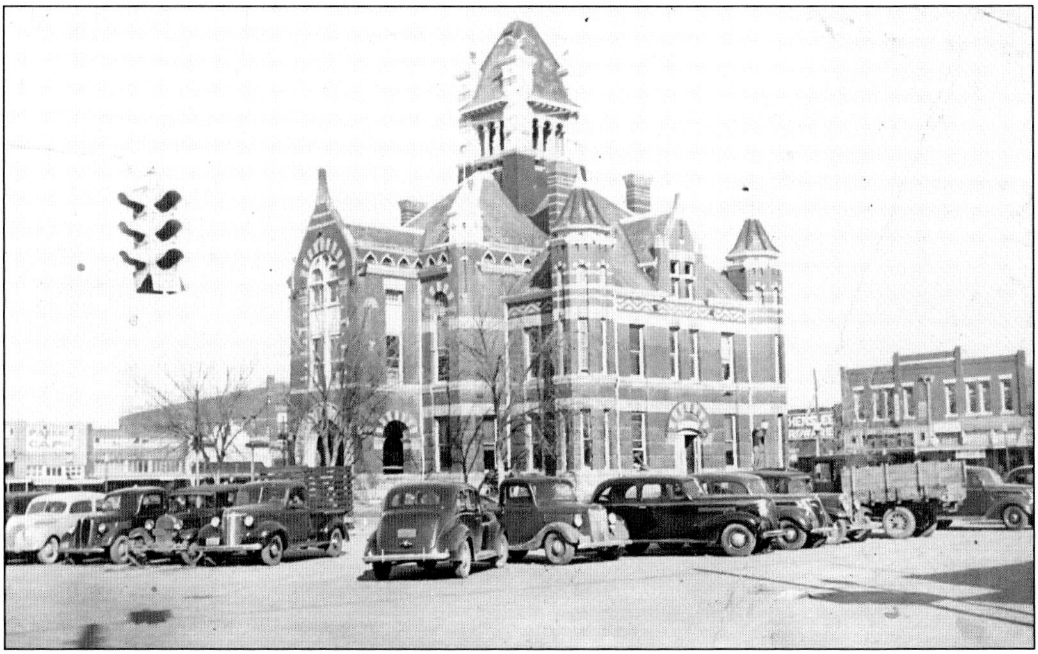

This picture shows the third Delta County Courthouse, which was located in the center of the square. Constructed in 1895, this redbrick Gothic building was an imposing structure and the center of county business, as well as housing civil and criminal courts, community and district records, and county offices. The courthouse was torn down in 1939. (Courtesy of Marion Miller.)

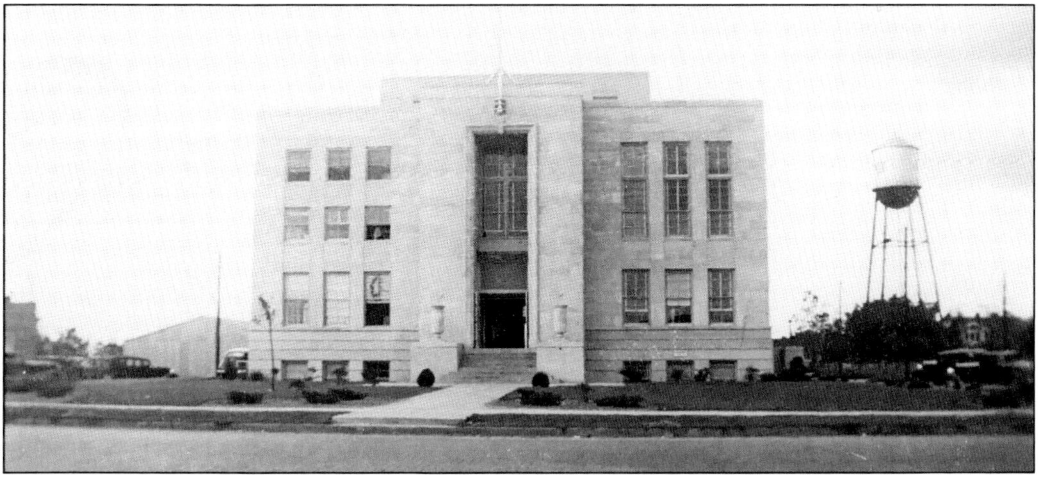

Built in 1940, the fourth Delta County Courthouse is pictured in 1941. According to the instructions of the state, the county seat must be within a day's ride for all residents of the county. The city of Cooper was created in the middle of Yates prairies as the county seat. (Courtesy of Marion Miller.)

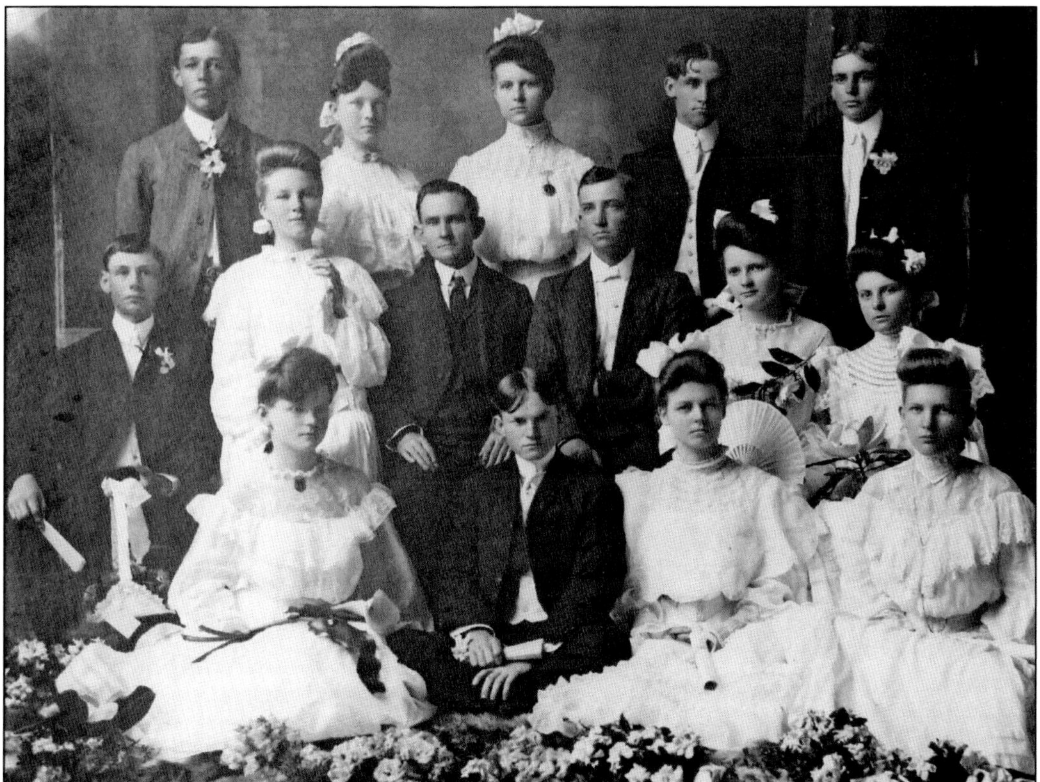

This Cooper High School picture features the class of 1904 with their teachers. From left to right are (first row) Klyde McKinney, Marshall Jones, Celine Webb, and Hattie Havens; (second row) Hale Dickson, unidentified, Professor Hunter, assistant teacher Price, Hallie McKinney, and Carrie McKinney; (third row) Will Pierce, unidentified, Bonnie Blackwell, Clarence Rattan, and John Garrard. (Courtesy of Patterson Museum.)

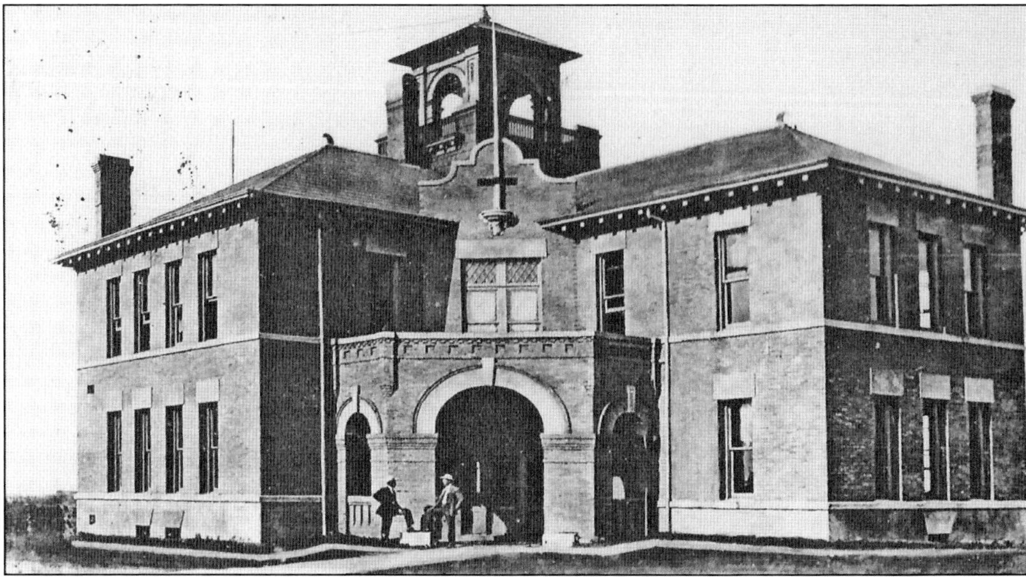

In 1906, W. E. Sharp deeded 4 acres of land for educational purposes on Southwest Fourth Street in Cooper. Bonds were sold, and this building was constructed for $12,700. This building was used until 1926, when it was demolished to build a redbrick high school on the same site. (Courtesy of Nan Olson Beeler.)

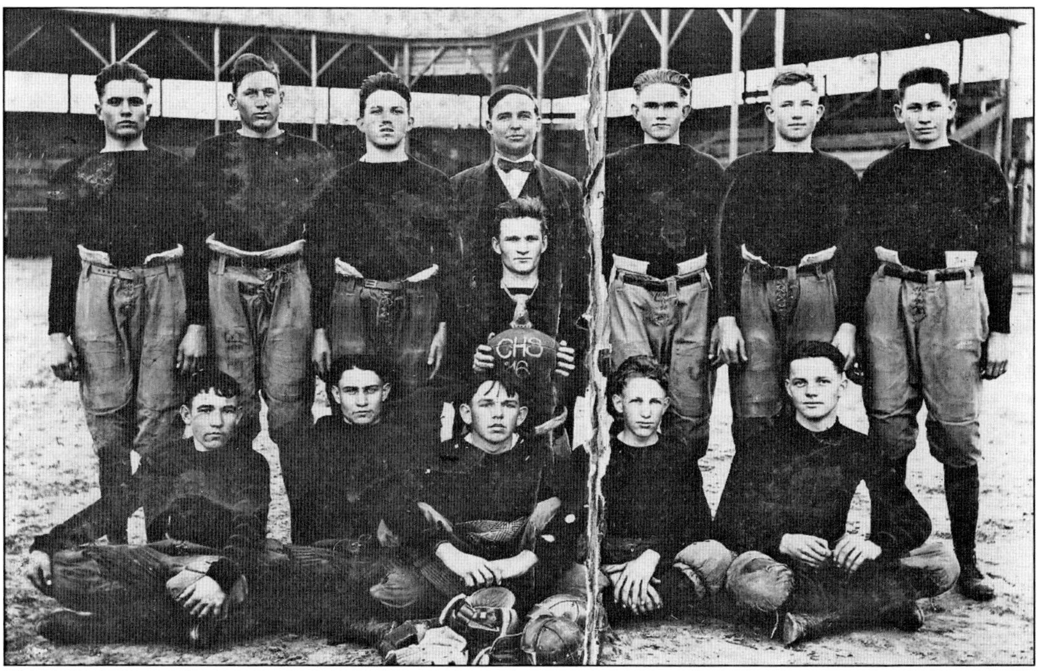

Shown above is the 1916 Cooper High School football team and their coach. From left to right are (first row) Herman Sparks, Bryan Sparks, Thomas Carrell, Lane Tynes, Gibson Ellis; (second row) Dave Hendricks; (third row) Odis "Wart" Adair, Earl Kerbow, Conway Jordan, Coach O. R. Bridges, Sammy Jeter, Haywood Lain, and Hallie Yoakum. Cooper beat Sulphur Springs (12-0), Commerce (6-0), Celeste (7-0), Burleson (18-0), and Rounders (12-6) and tied Paris (6-6). (Courtesy of the Quentin Miller family.)

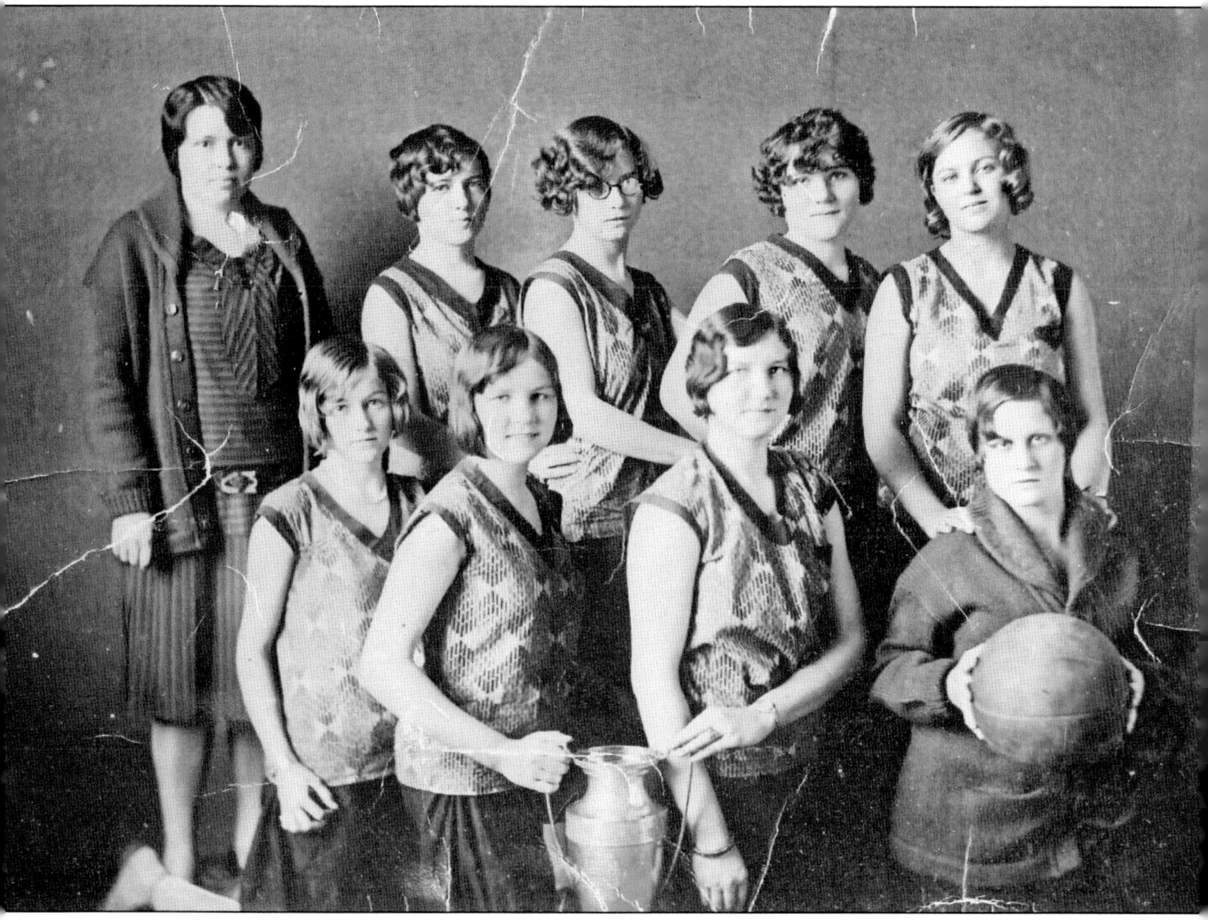

Girls' basketball has always had a special place at Cooper High School. This 1931 group consisted of, from left to right, (first row) Faye McGuire, Nannie Mae Carrington, Leona Carrington, and Ina Hargrove; (second row) Marie Anderson (coach), Juel Oats, Lillian McKinney, Evelyn Taylor, and Thelma Jordan. (Courtesy of Patterson Museum.)

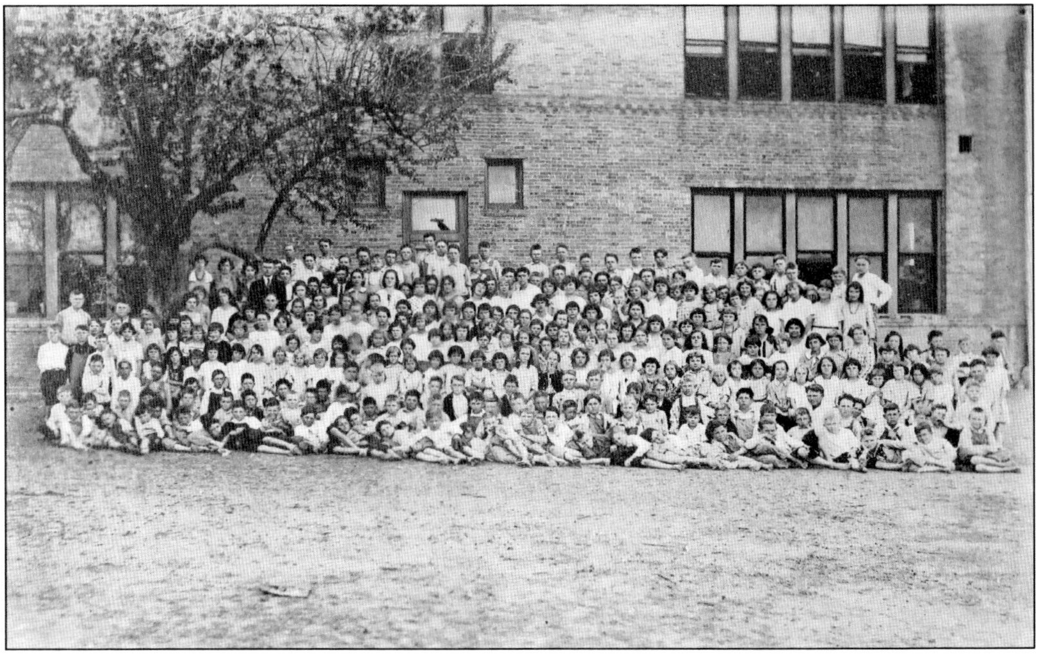

The above picture was taken about 1920 and shows the students in attendance at the East Ward School. It was a two-story brick building on Southeast Eighth Street and East Dallas Avenue. It was used until 1952, when a new elementary school was built on the site of the redbrick high school. Below is a photograph of the building in 1937. (Above, courtesy of Patterson Museum; below, courtesy of Laura Jo Taylor.)

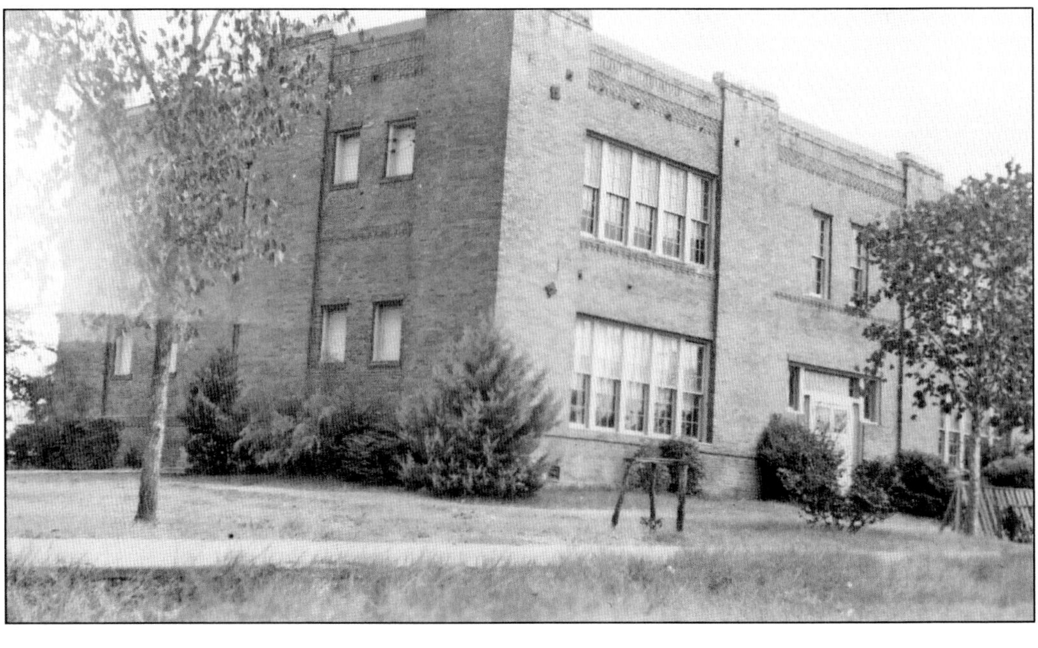

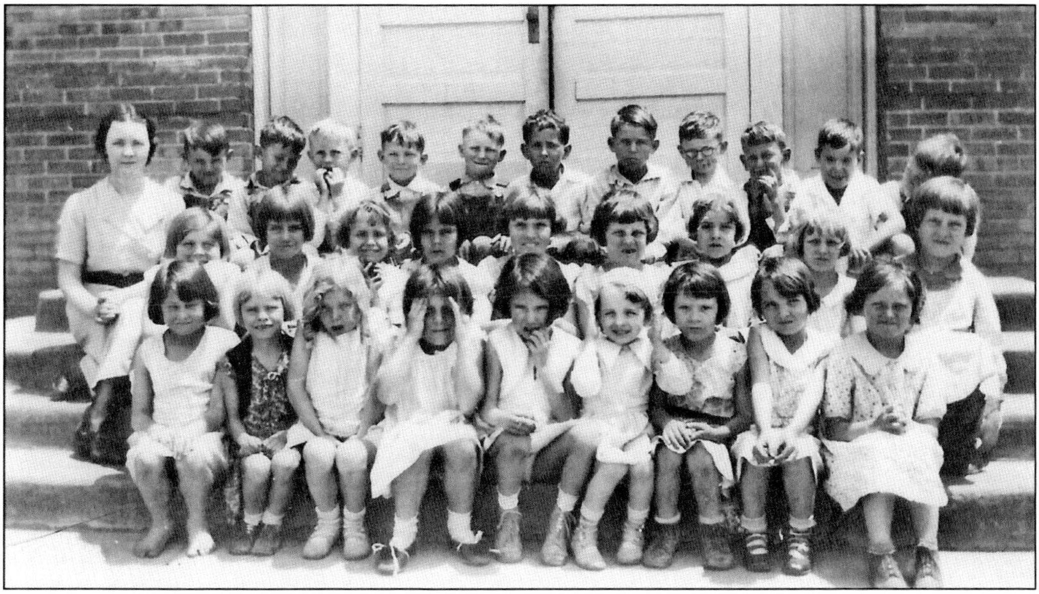

The Little Orphan Annie School was located south of the redbrick high school. This 1930 picture shows students from the following families: Alexander, McDonald, Millard, Harper, Hooten, Sandlin, Taylor, France, Janes, Burnett, Wakefield, Rainey, Boyd, Sharp, Gibbs, Vaughn, Morgan, Robinson, Rhodes, Anglin, Chesner, Haddock, and Burnett. Blanche Carrington is the teacher. (Courtesy of Laura Jo Taylor.)

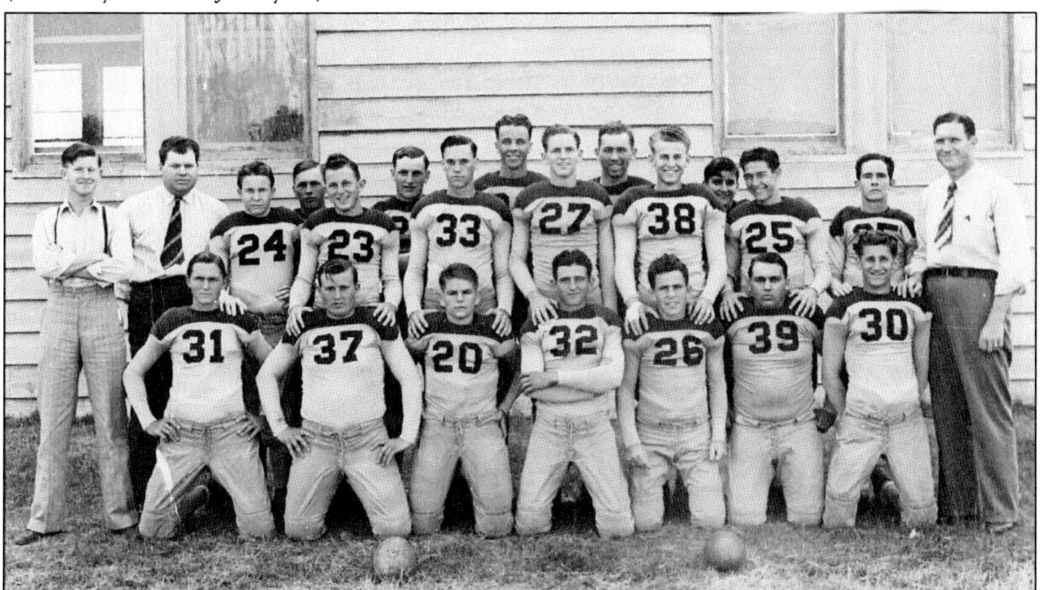

The 1937 district champion Cooper High School Bulldogs opened the season against Paris. They dedicated the first lighted field. The team consisted of Eugene Carrington, Hollis Williams, Don McCombs, Johnny Henson, Ed Robnett, Harry Morgan, Neal Shepard, Shirley Sissel, Joe Kitchens, Robert Stovall, Doyle Smallwood, O. McDonald, Bill Lamb, Byron Anderson, Harold Brock, Sandy Swearigen, Dodie Wood, and coach Woodrow Keahey. (Courtesy of Joe Kitchens and Marion Miller.)

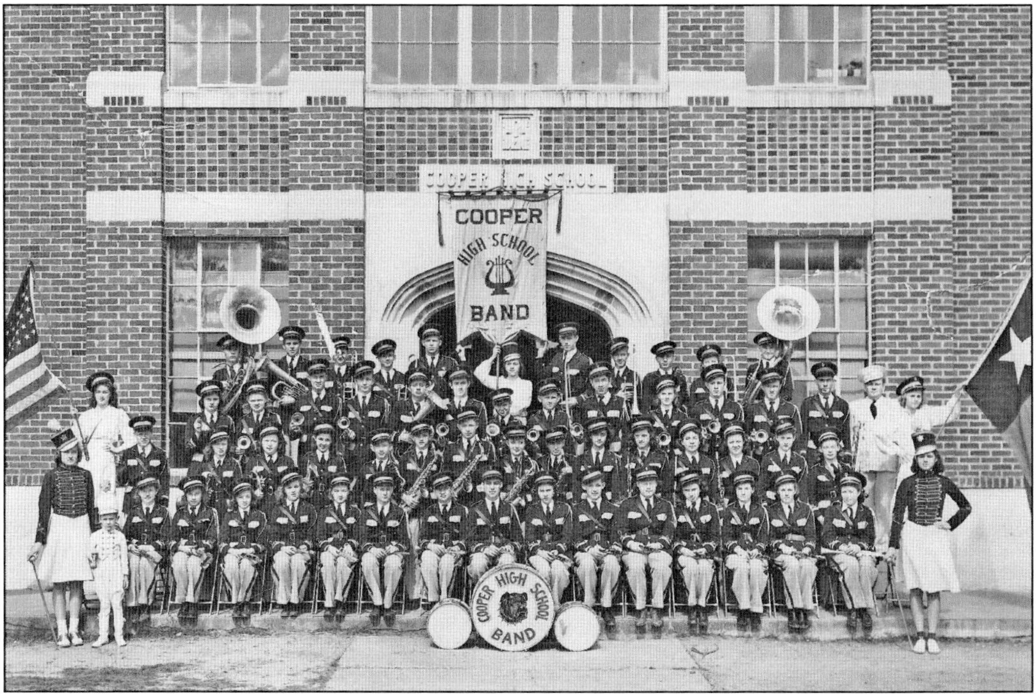

Cooper High School has long placed a value on the musical education of its students. Early records indicate that the band was started in the 1930s. This 1941–1942 Cooper High School Band picture denotes the popularity of the band under the direction of Luther Brown. (Courtesy of Delta County Library.)

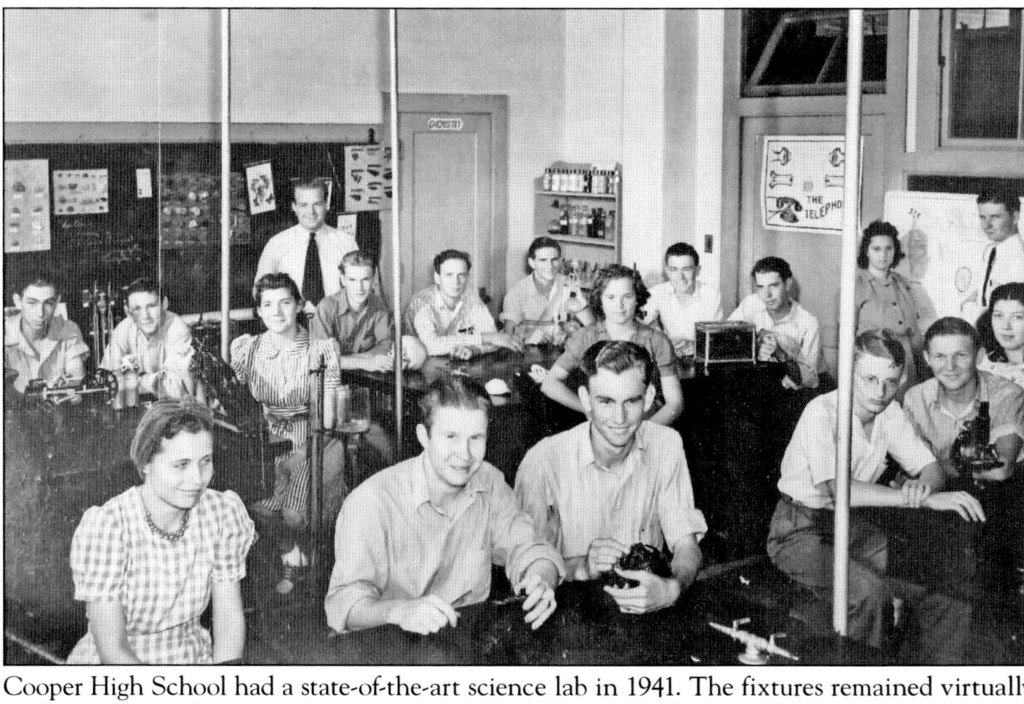

Cooper High School had a state-of-the-art science lab in 1941. The fixtures remained virtually unchanged until the high school closed in 1999. (Courtesy of Patterson Museum.)

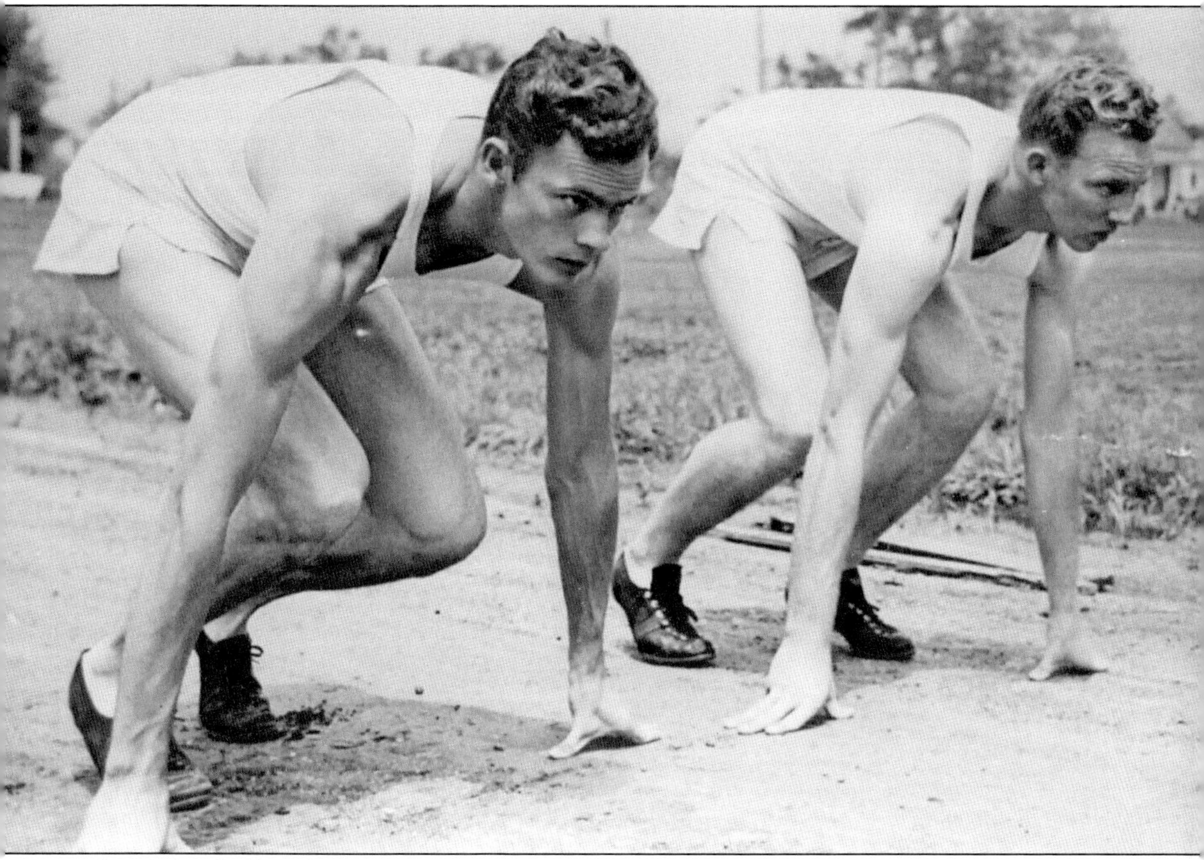

Julius Acker (left) and Don Morgan were members of Cooper High School's seven-man track team in 1949. Both were track stars in the area and on the state level. Both qualified in their senior year for the state track meet in 1949 in the 100- and 220-yard dash. At the state meet, Acker placed third and Morgan placed fifth in the 100-yard dash. Acker was second and Morgan placed fourth in the 220-yard dash. (Courtesy of Julius Acker and Marion Miller.)

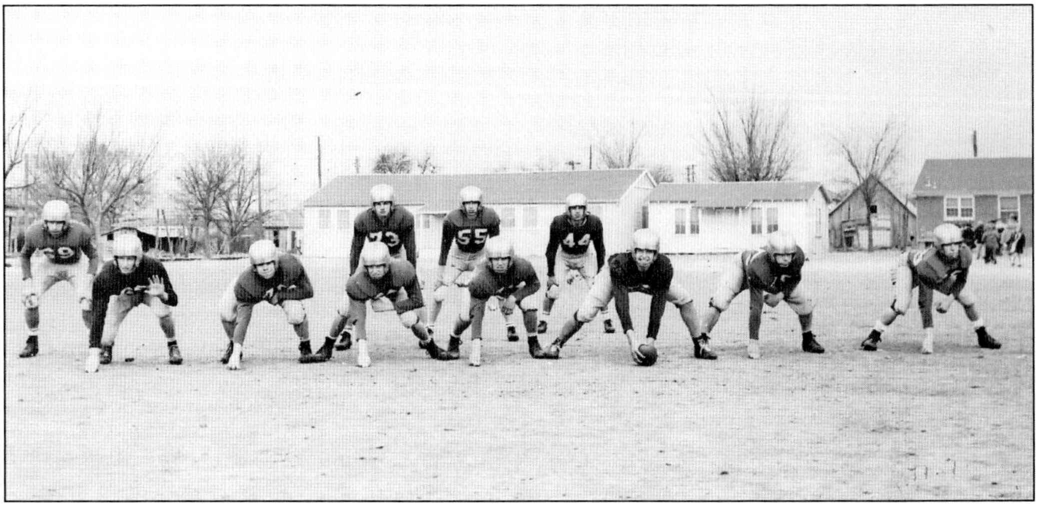

The 1950 Bulldogs were the district champions. Players were, from left to right, (first row) Jack McVay, John Ed Adair, Kendall Wright, James Hooten, Bobby Watkins, Billy Kinard Pratt, and Rip Templeton; (second row) Marion Brown, J. O. Shaw, Billy Huie, and Jimmy Ramon. The Bulldogs beat Wolfe City, Honey Grove, Leonard, Ladonia, and Celeste. Jack Wright was the coach. (Courtesy of Rip Templeton.)

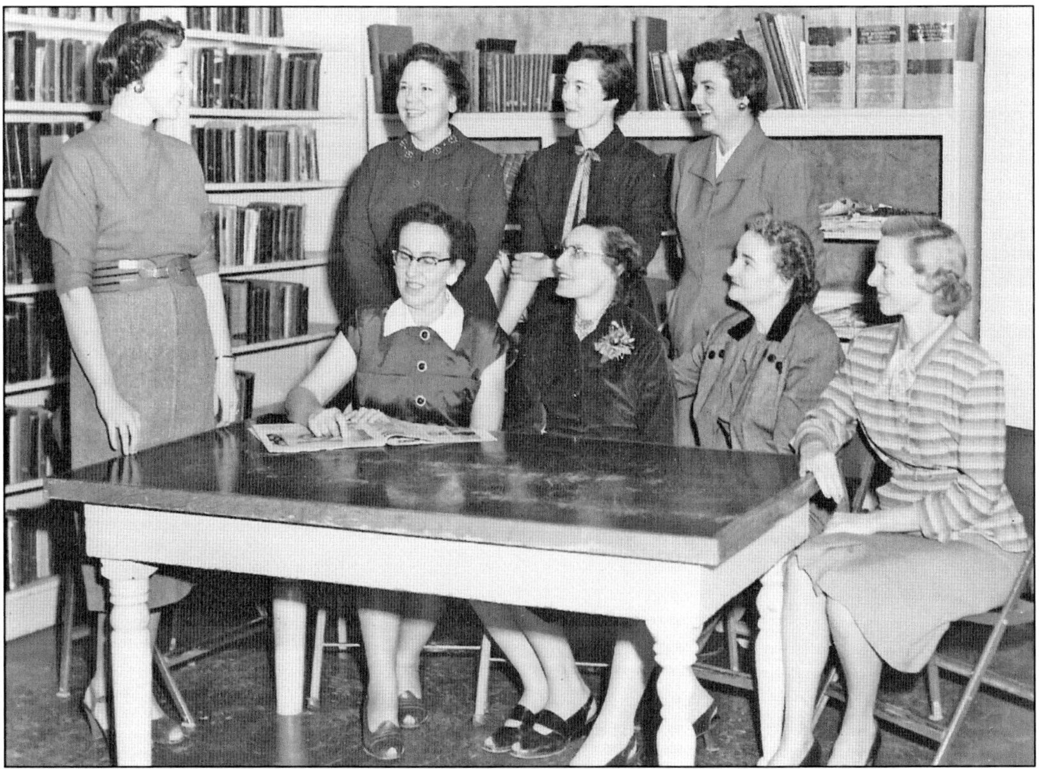

In the 1950s, the PTA was very active. This picture shows the officers for 1955. From left to right are (seated) Mrs. Alton Wright, Mrs. Truman Whitlock, Mrs. Goebel Templeton, and Mrs. G. H. Jaynes; (standing) Mrs. Harry Ward, Mrs. Verlee Morgan, Mrs. Richard Stringfellow, and Mrs. Lundy Hooten. (Courtesy of Judy Falls.)

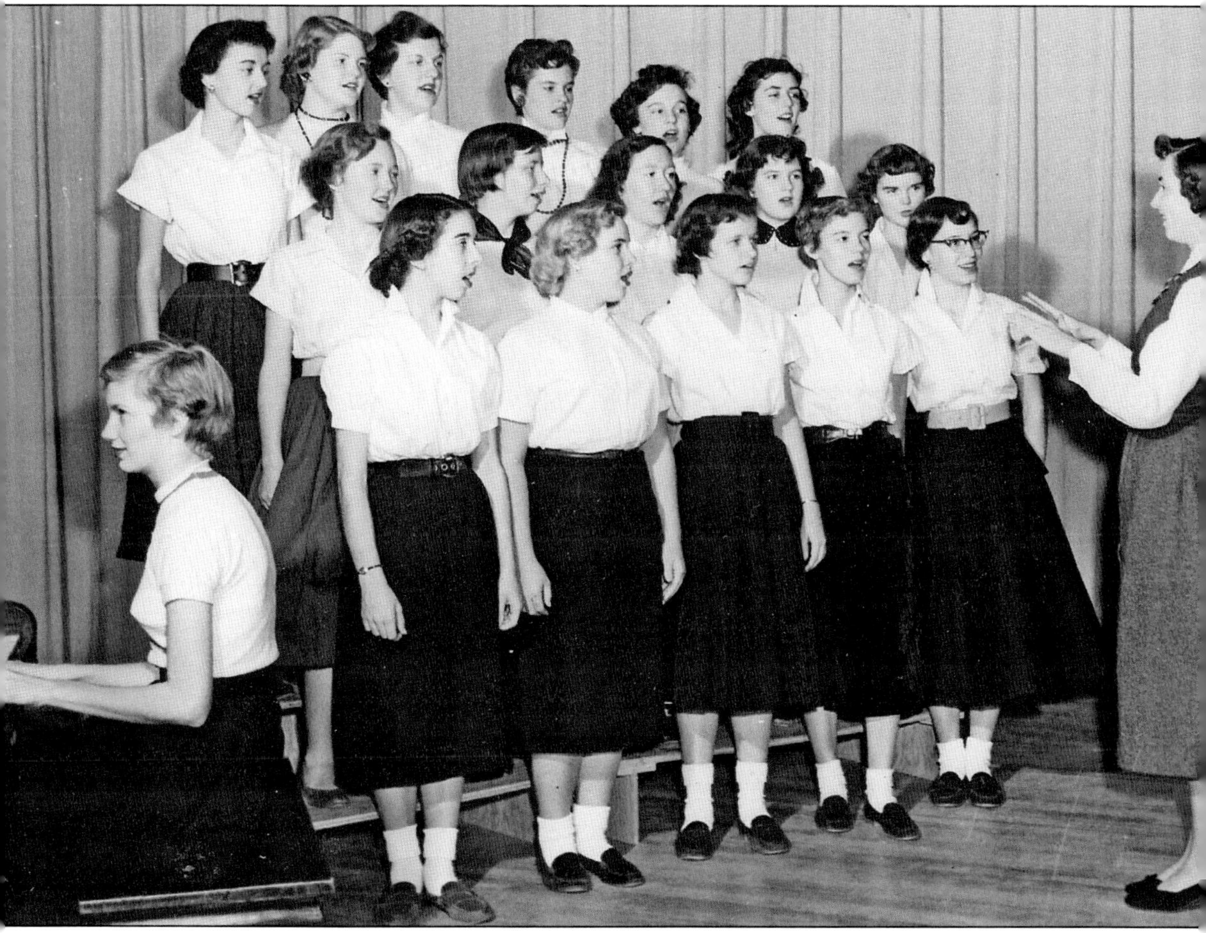

The Girls Ensemble of 1955 for Cooper High School included, from left to right, Marilyn Whitlock (pianist), Sarah Good, Nina Wicks, Bobbie Thomas, Marna Johnson, Carole Bolger, and Mrs. Richard Pruitt as director; (second row) Betty Young, Nada Holmes, Avon Bradford, Carolyn Morgan, and Bobbie Toon; (third row) Ellen Janes, Carolyn Wallace, Barbara Wright, Brenda Cain, Wanda Rouse, and Peggy Garner. (Courtesy of Judy Falls.)

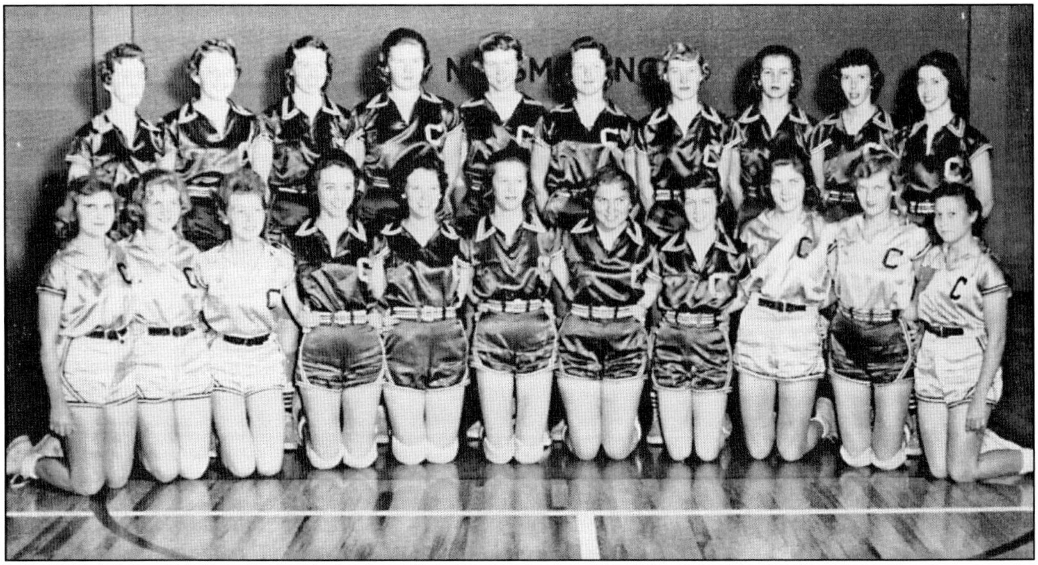

The 1957–1958 girls' state champion basketball team was, from left to right, (first row) Carolyn Nance, Bennie Gibbs, Sherria Choate, Joyce Lovelady, Martha McMillan, Carolyn Boles, Mary Owen, Fredda Newman, Doris Stanley, Martha Whitlock, and Anne Simpson; (second row) Norma Cauley, Bab Janes, Jane Gregory, Brenda Holmes, Sharline Garrison, Glynana Steward, Betty Miller, Linda Harris, Laquieta Day, and Linda McGaha. (Courtesy of Cooper Growl.)

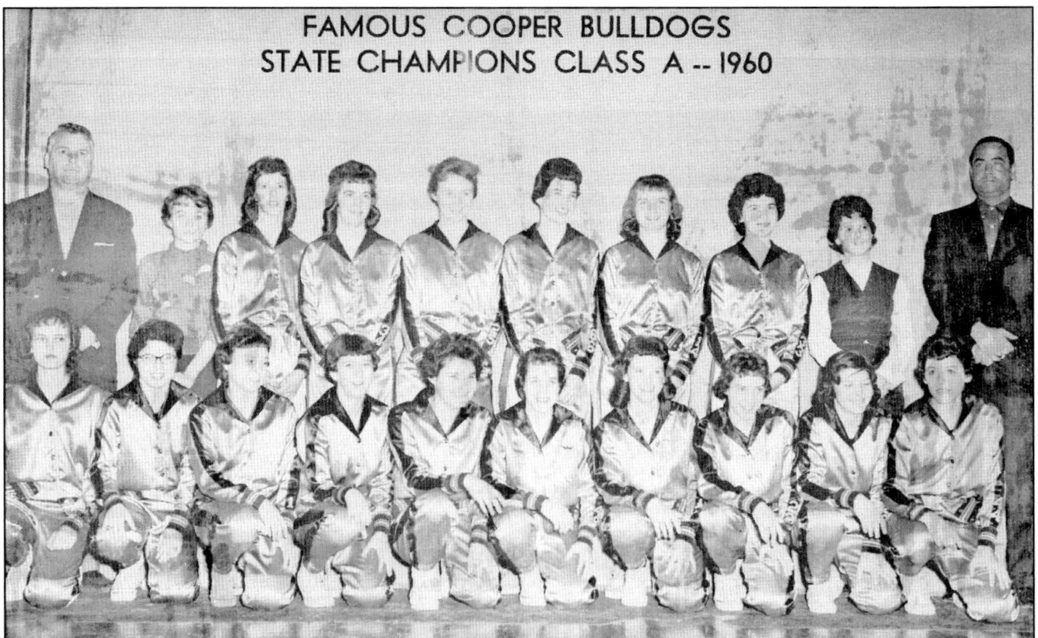

The famous 1960 Cooper Bulldogs Class A state champion basketball team was, from left to right, (first row) Carolyn McKee, Betty Lane, Anne Simpson, Nancy Willson, Sue Stanley, Mickey Newman, Martha McMillan, Fredda Newman, Peggy Wood, and Kay Toney; (second row) Joe Daniel (coach), Ann Ray (manager), Laquieta Day, Carolyn Boles, Sharline Garrison, Dixie Mendenhall, Glynana Steward, Sandra Perry, Judy Little (manager), and Davis Floyd (coach). (Courtesy of Cooper Growl.)

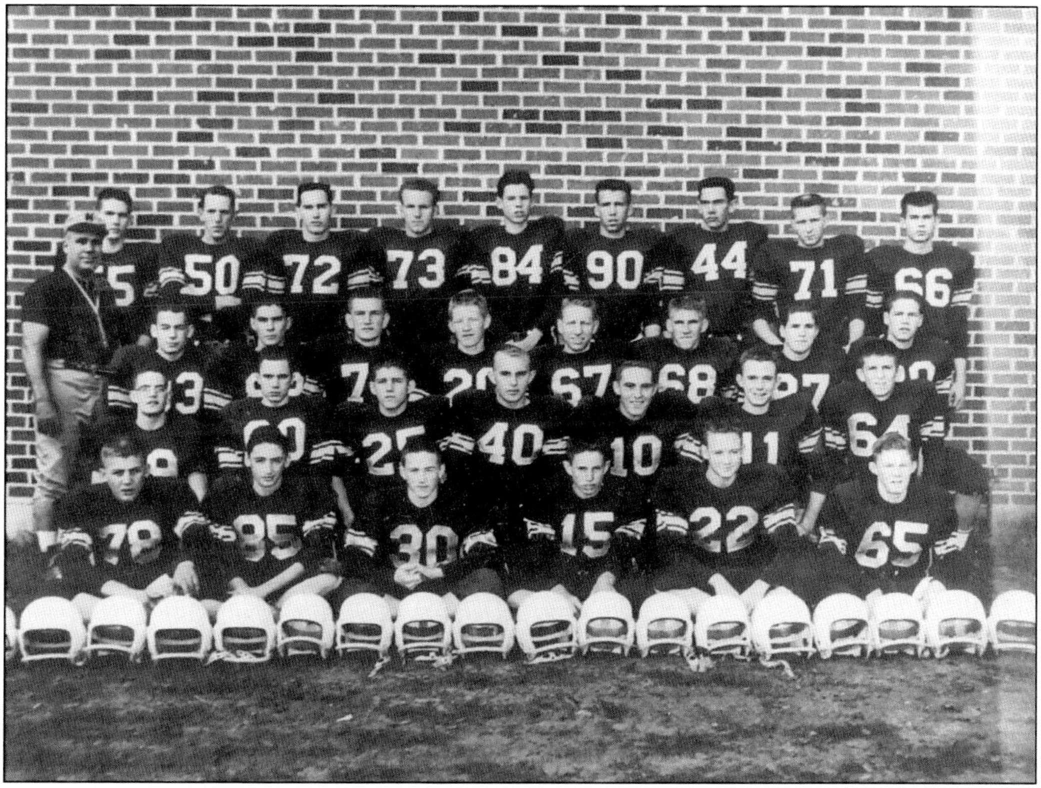

Above, the Cooper High School Bulldogs of 1957 were the District 14A cochampions with Plano High School. The team was coached by Hollis F. Williams, T. O. McClung, and Davis Floyd. Below, the 1958 Cooper High School Bulldog team poses for its official picture. The team was coached by, from left to right in the third row, Davis Floyd, Tom King, and Joe Scott. (Both, courtesy of Marion Miller.)

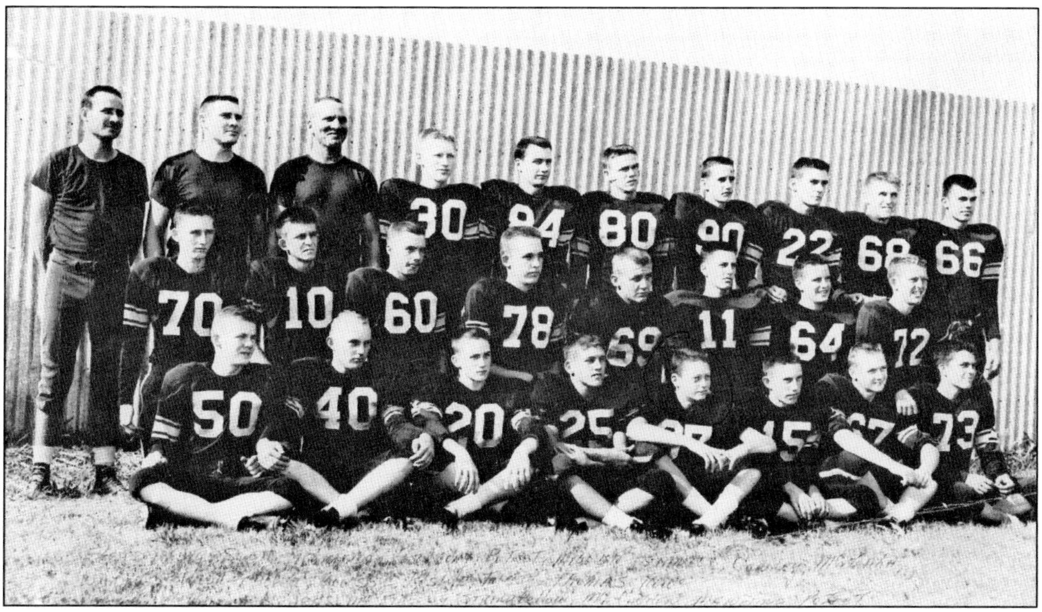

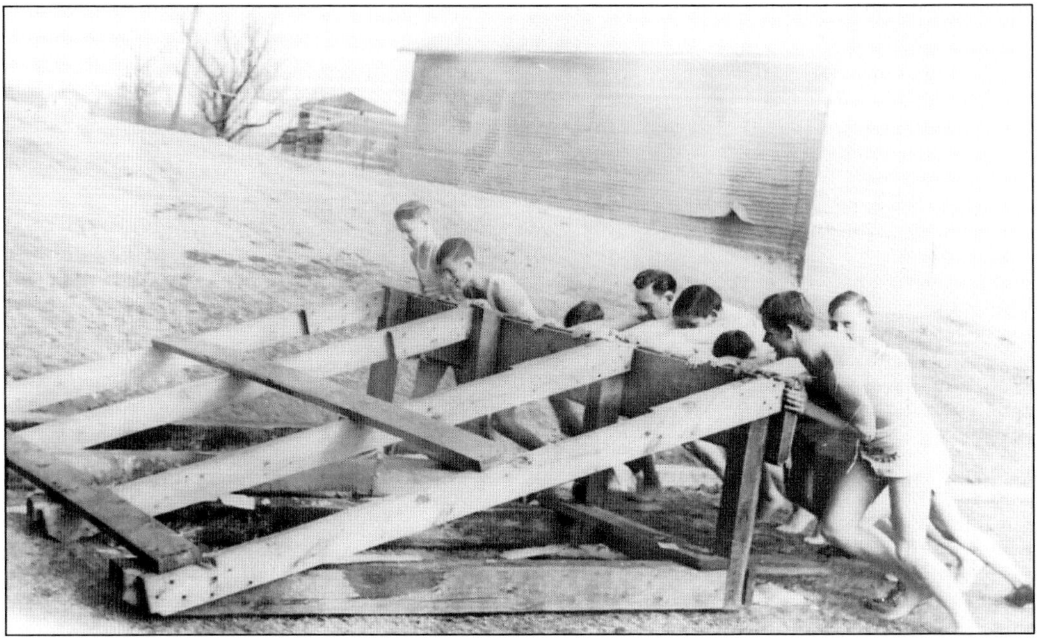

Learning how to block and developing strength are parts of football training and conditioning. Seen here are some Cooper High School Bulldogs developing their skills. This picture was taken about 1940. To the players of the 21st century, this blocking sled seems awfully crude and primitive. (Courtesy of Marion Miller.)

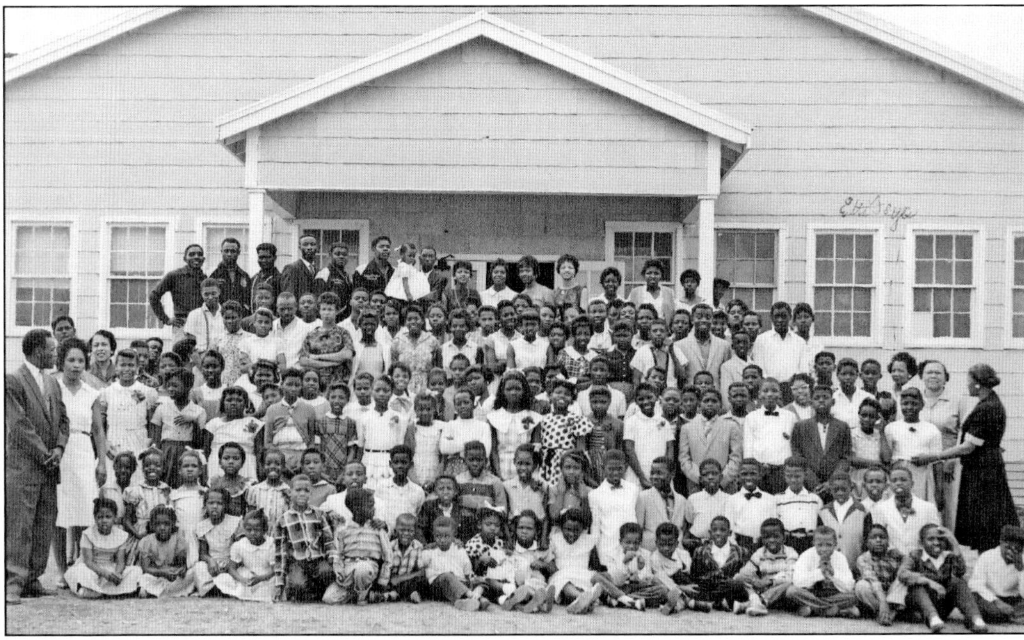

This was the second Booker T. Washington School. In 1961, the principal was Tom Pleasant (standing in the middle at left), and his wife was Wailene Pleasant, a teacher. Among the students in the center of the top row are Eddie Owen, Edna Shanklin, Willie Wilburn, Nadine Turner, Maureen Parks, and Bobby Hubbard. Etta Roseman, Lovie McGuire, and Fannie Mays are the teachers on the far right. (Courtesy of Carlton Thomas.)

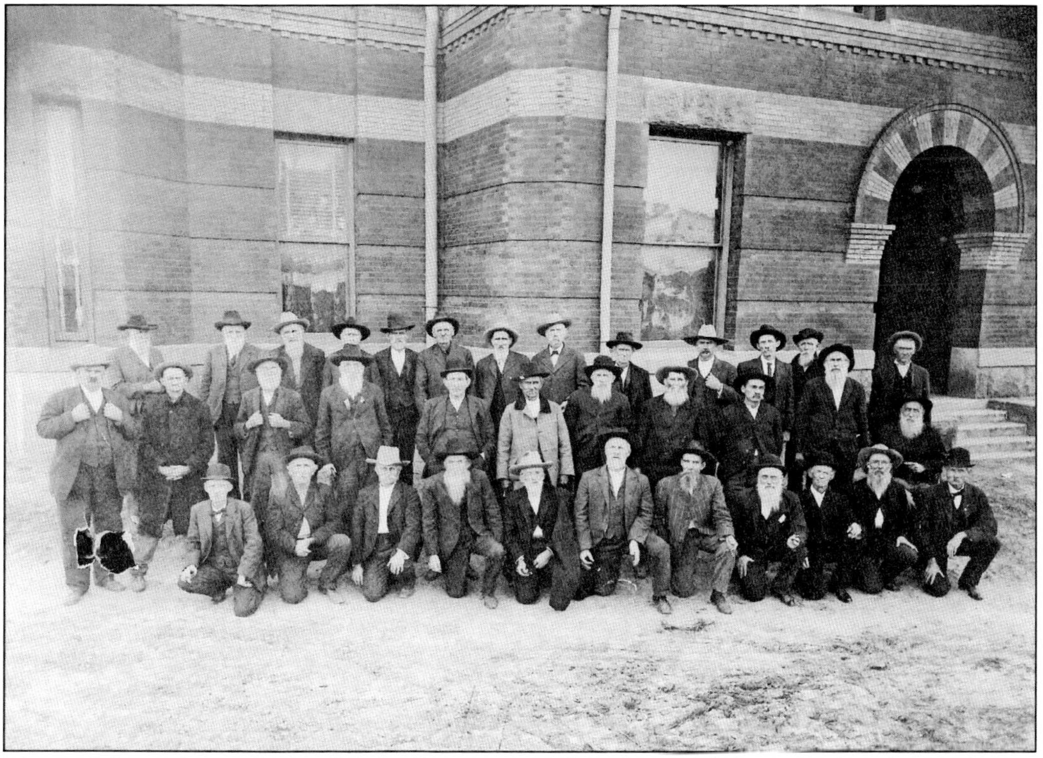

Many of the early residents of Delta County served in the Confederacy. After the Civil War, groups of veterans gathered to reminisce. This picture was taken in front of the courthouse in Cooper. On October 22, 1908, Congressman Morris Shepherd addressed 51 of the Delta County Confederate veterans at the Thornton Hotel in Cooper. (Courtesy of Kathy Thomas.)

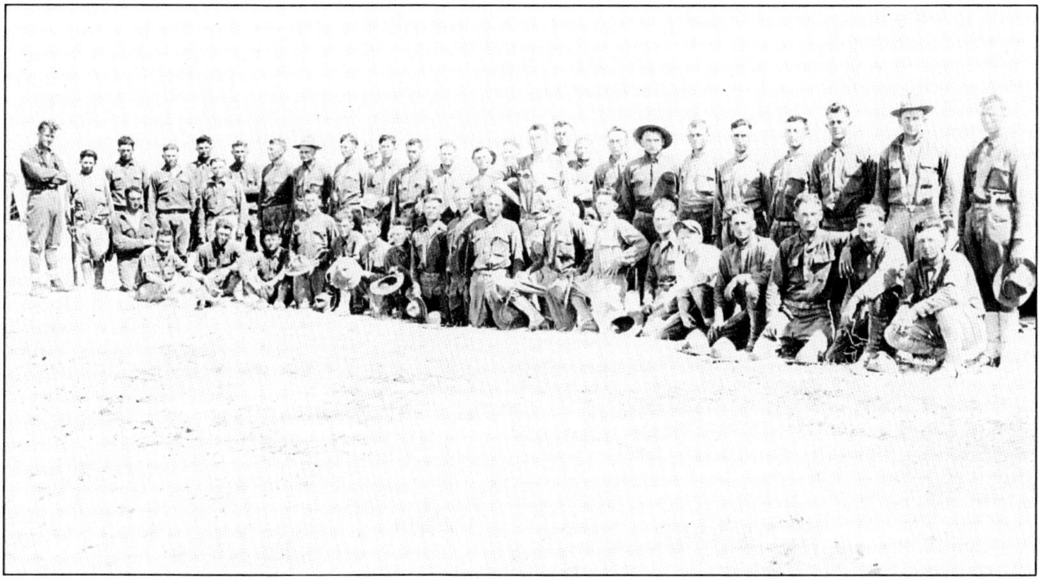

Many of the young men of Delta County served in World War I. The photograph documents their service to their country. The names of the soldiers as well as the date are unknown. (Courtesy of Pattie Brack Pettigrew.)

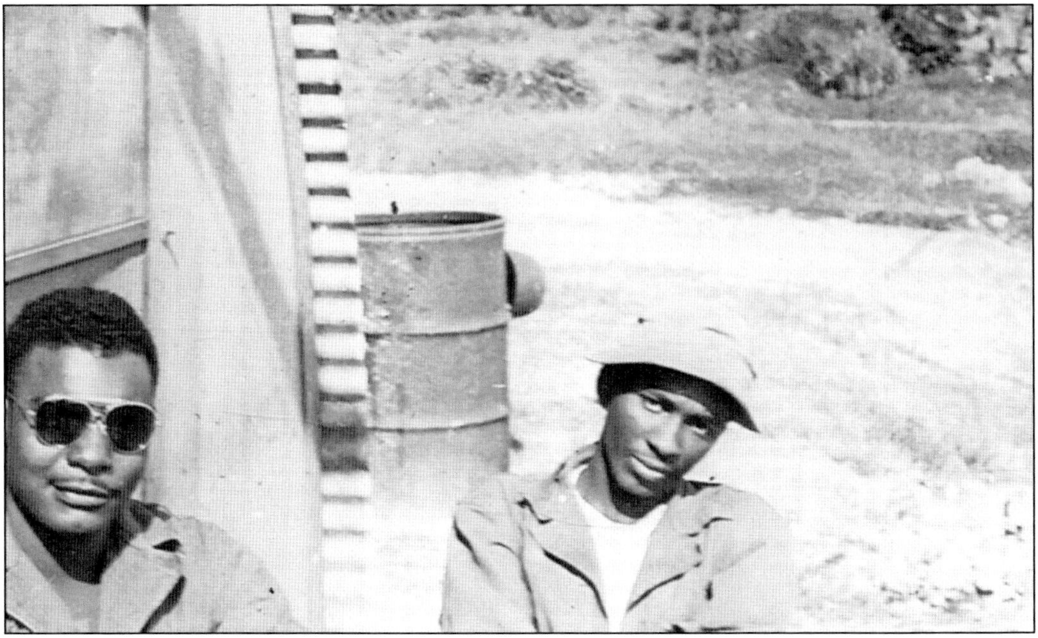

Many men from Delta County have served in the armed services. Odell Alston, left, served in the U.S. Army and was awarded the Bronze Star. (Courtesy of Willie Bear Wilkins.)

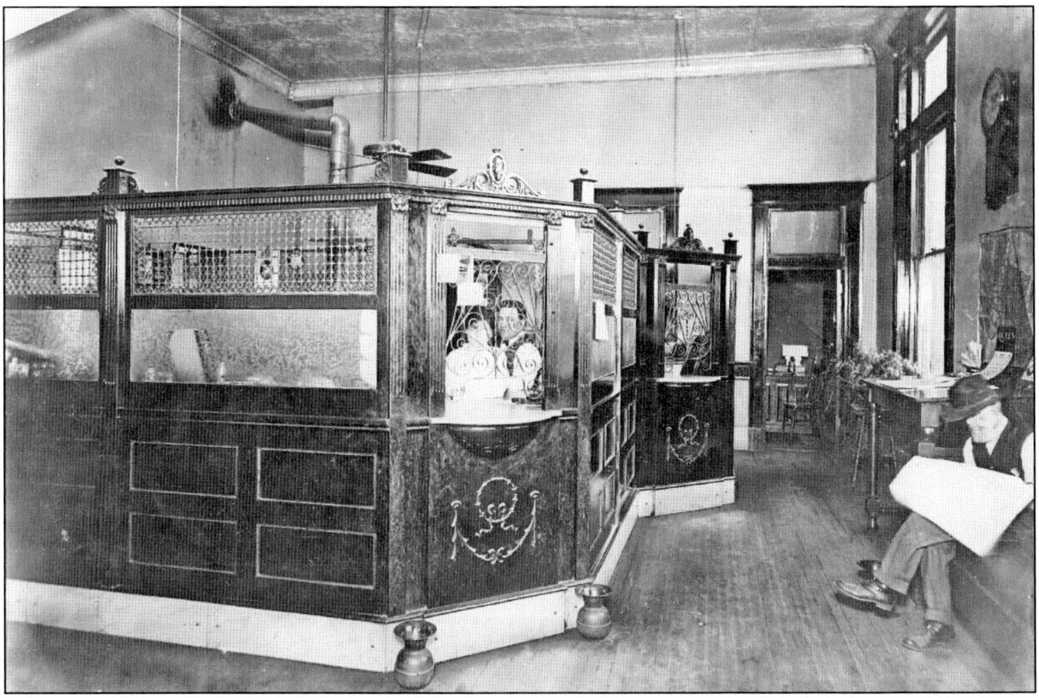

The Delta National Bank organized in 1900 with S. C. Ratliff, J. A. Blackwell, C. E. Anderson, J. L. Darwin, and T. J. Record as original directors. James A. Smith was the first cashier. The bank successfully operated through two world wars and the Great Depression, and it remained a viable force until it merged with the First National Bank in 2007. (Courtesy of Mildred Morgan and Marion Miller.)

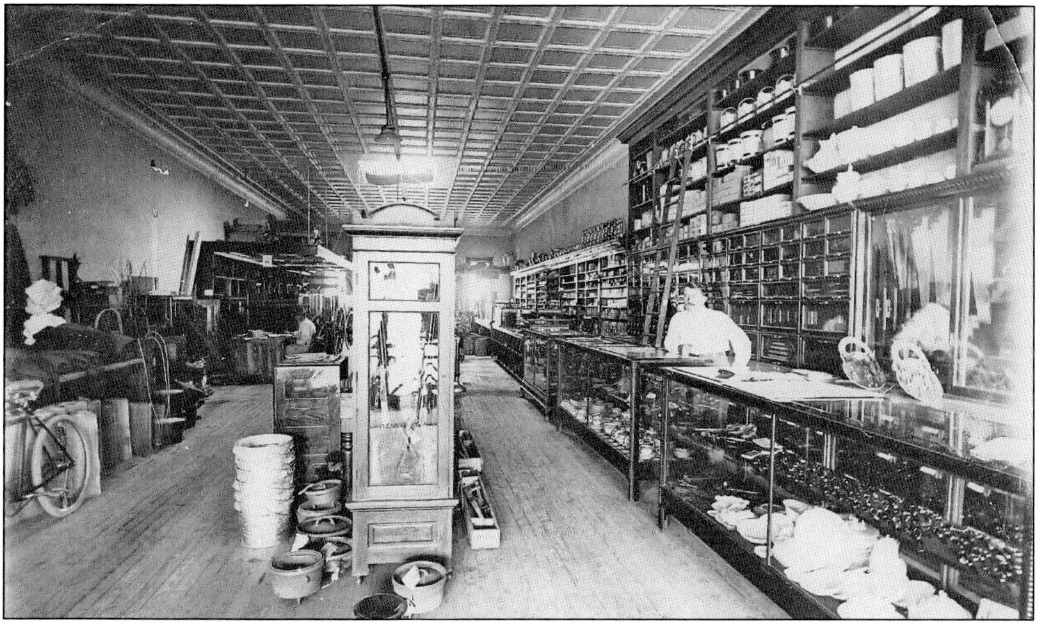

John Franklin Henslee opened a hardware store under a tent and later constructed a building where it remains in operation today, 120 years later. He sold farm implements, guns, kegs, whiskey, caskets, nails, black powder, dynamite, and other sundry items. He died in 1938, and the store passed to his grandson, Quentin Miller. The store is now owned by Judy, Jan, and Frank Miller. (Courtesy of the Miller family.)

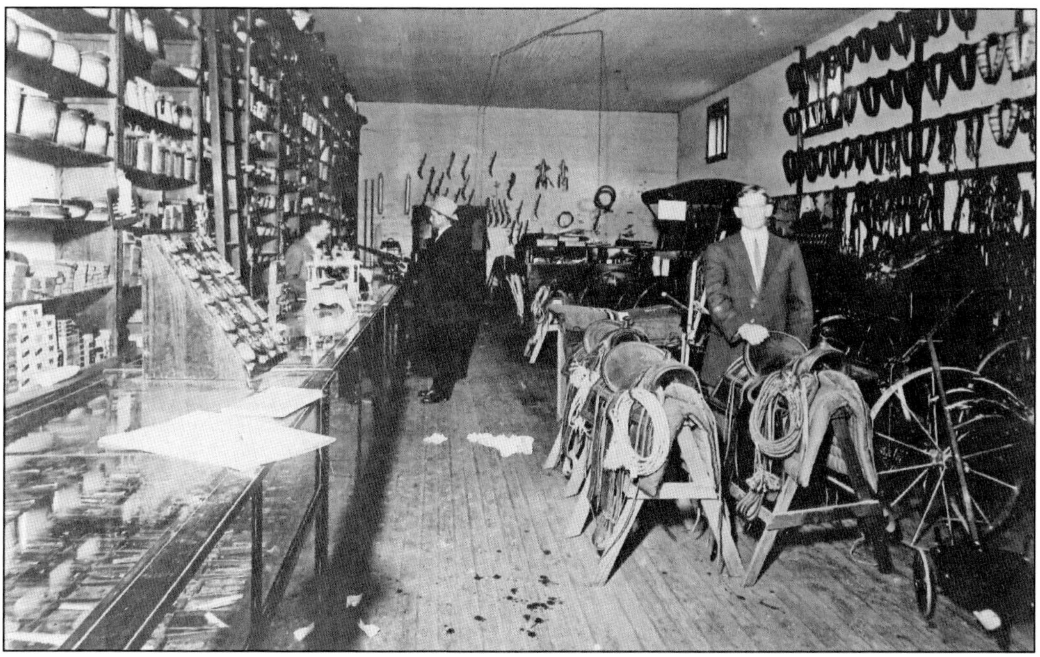

Stovall Hardware, located on the corner of West Dallas Avenue and Southwest First Street, was originally owned by Robert Norman Stovall. He operated this store until he died in 1944. After his death, his son Robert ran the hardware and implement business until he closed it in 1964. This picture features Robert Stovall and Charlie Sissell in 1912. (Courtesy of Patterson Museum.)

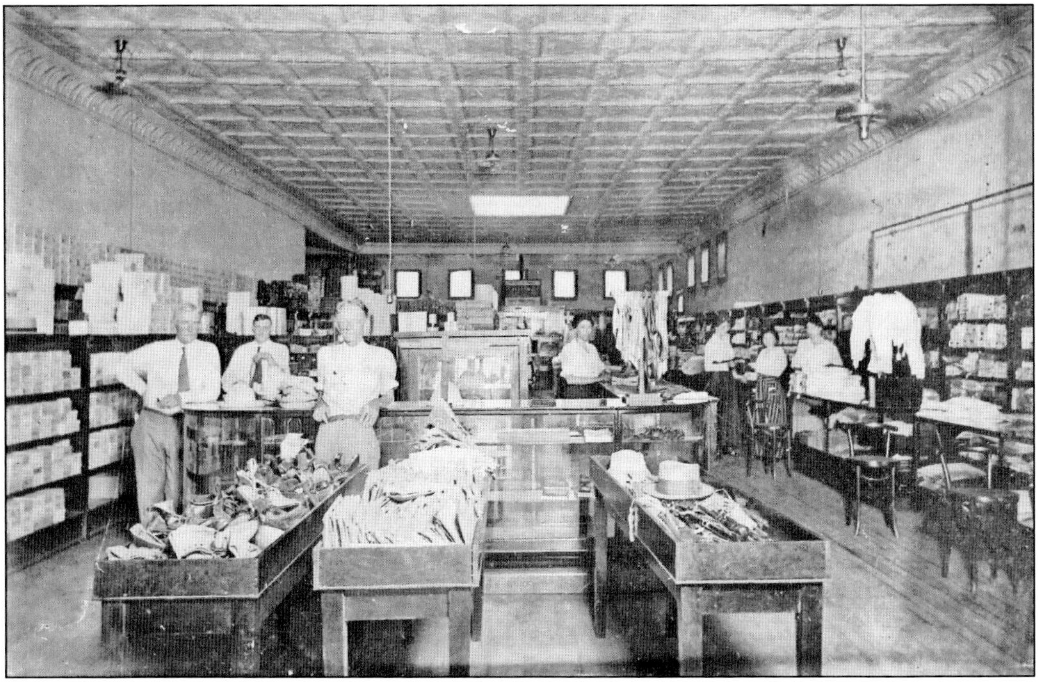

The Crawford-Norris-Stevens Dry Good store in Cooper was typical of these types of stores. This 1910 picture features Georgia Townsend, Guy McAlexander, Charlie Stevens, Ethel Wheat, Irene Sabestien, and Maggie Todd. It was located on the square. (Courtesy of Patterson Museum.)

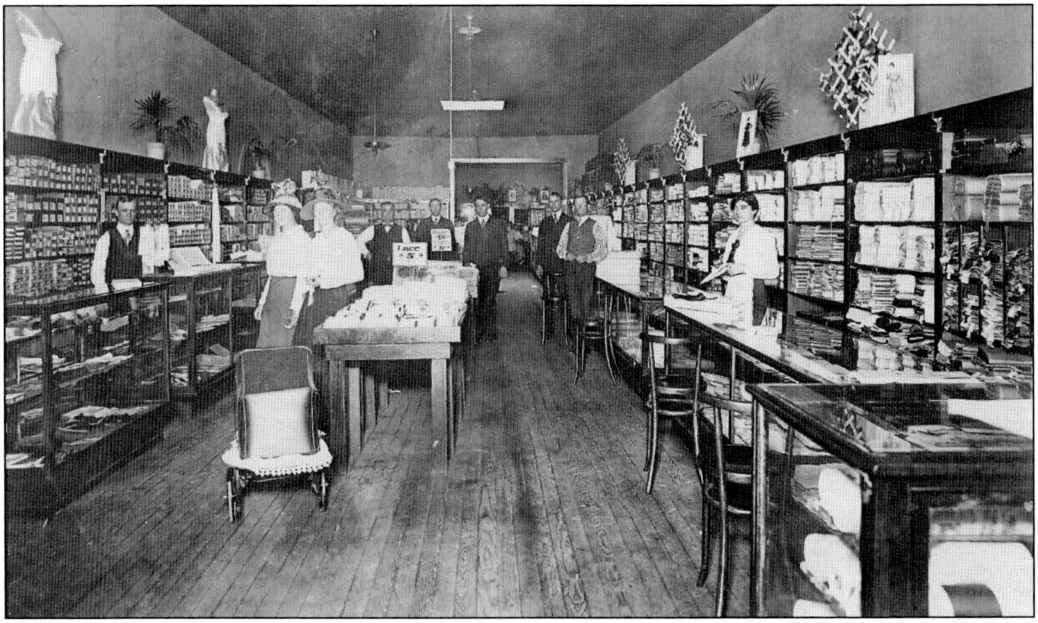

Ed Hendricks opened this dry goods store in Cooper after leaving Charleston about 1910. This store had a men's department and a women's department. A Mrs. Evans made hats in the back part of the store. Ed Hendricks traveled to St. Louis, New Orleans, and New York to buy stock for the store. He later left the dry goods business and opened a grocery store. (Courtesy of Lucille Bledsoe.)

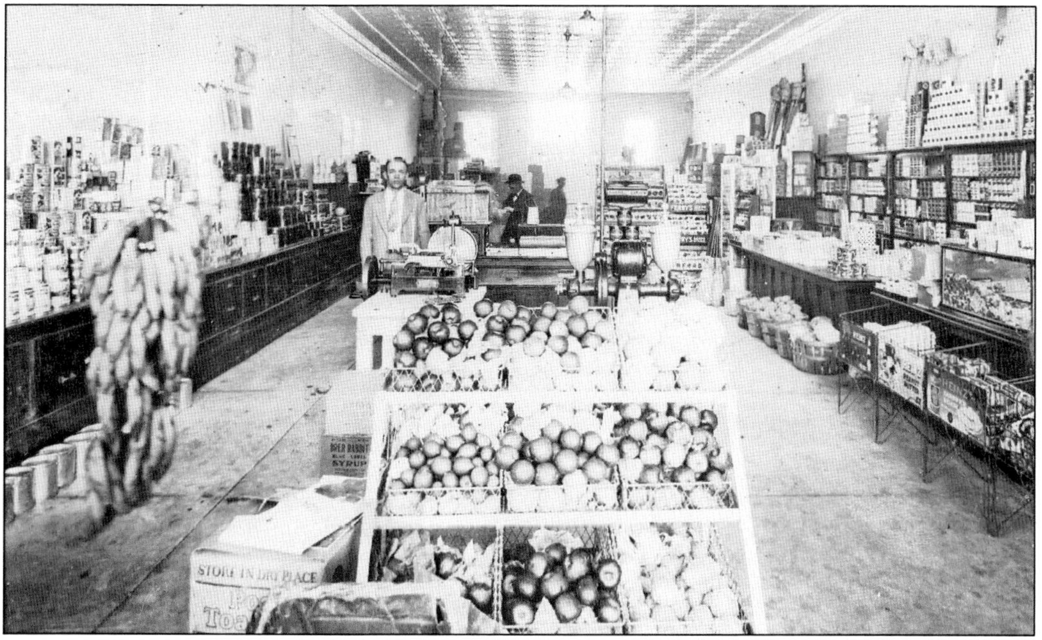

Ed Hendricks Grocery was located on the northwest corner of the square. Hendricks purchased the store about 1916 and moved it to the center of the north side of square. He operated it until he sold the store to Johnny Pollard. Nolan Hendricks is at left, and Ed Hendricks is at right. Note the two coffee grinders and the stalk of bananas. (Courtesy of Lucille Bledsoe.)

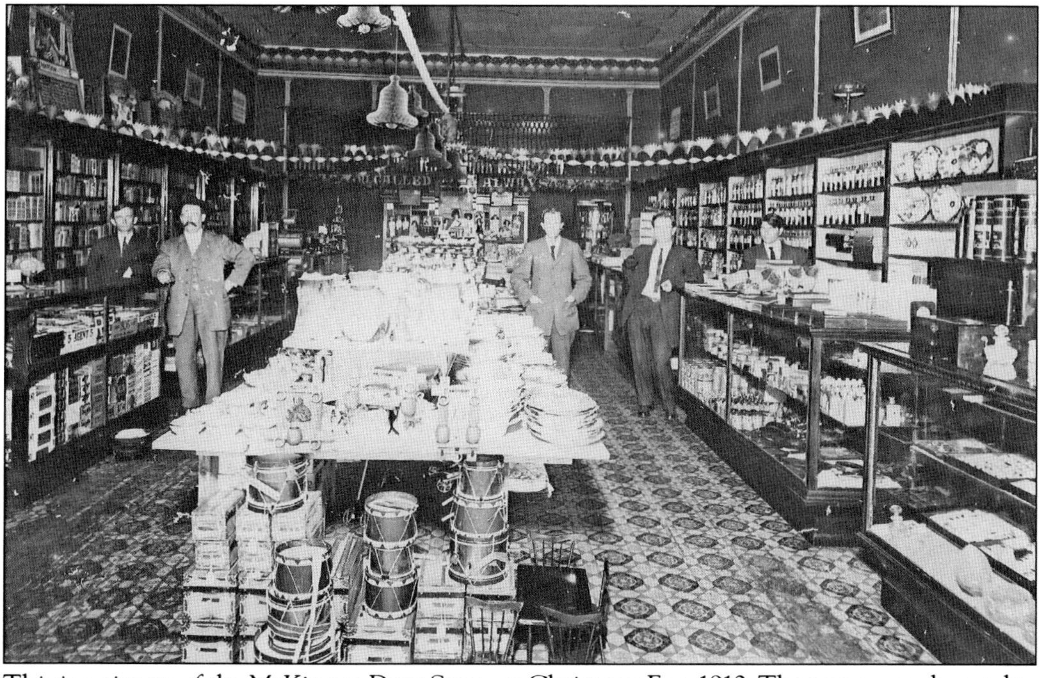

This is a picture of the McKinney Drug Store on Christmas Eve, 1910. The name was changed to Hooten Drug Store when Lundy Hooten bought the store from Howard McKinney and Dr. J. H. McKinney. Hooten Drug Store operated until 1984. (Courtesy of Delta County Public Library and Patterson Museum.)

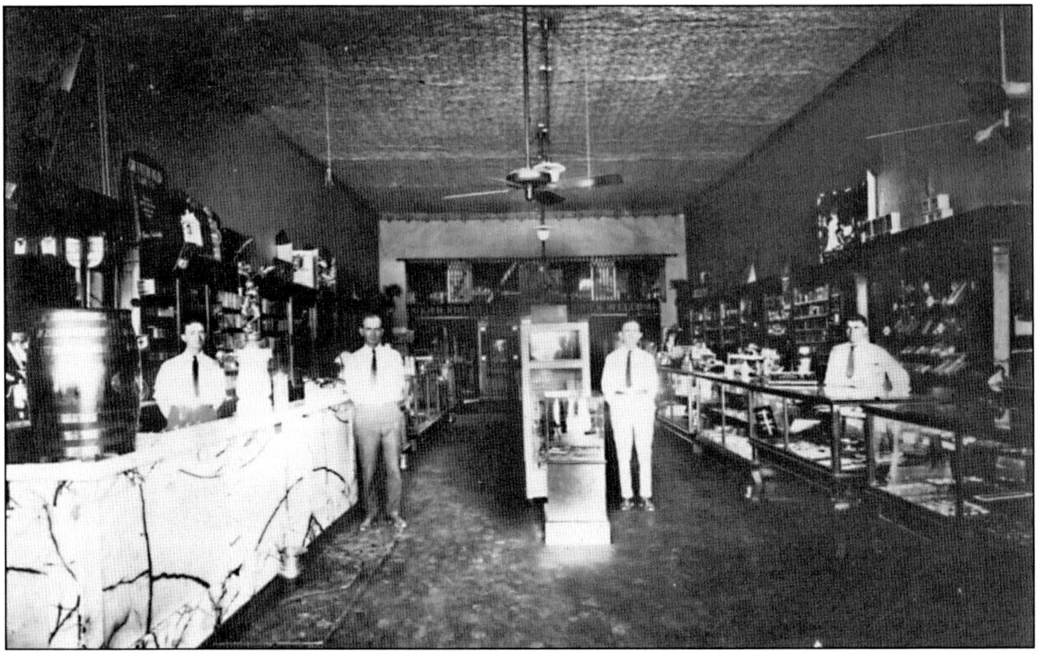

In 1921, the Hooten Drug Store was owned by Lundy and Clovis Hooten. Owen Hooten worked as a clerk, Doney Fisher was the jeweler, and Dr. Fritz Engle was the pharmacist. Dr. Engle is not pictured. (Courtesy of Marion Miller.)

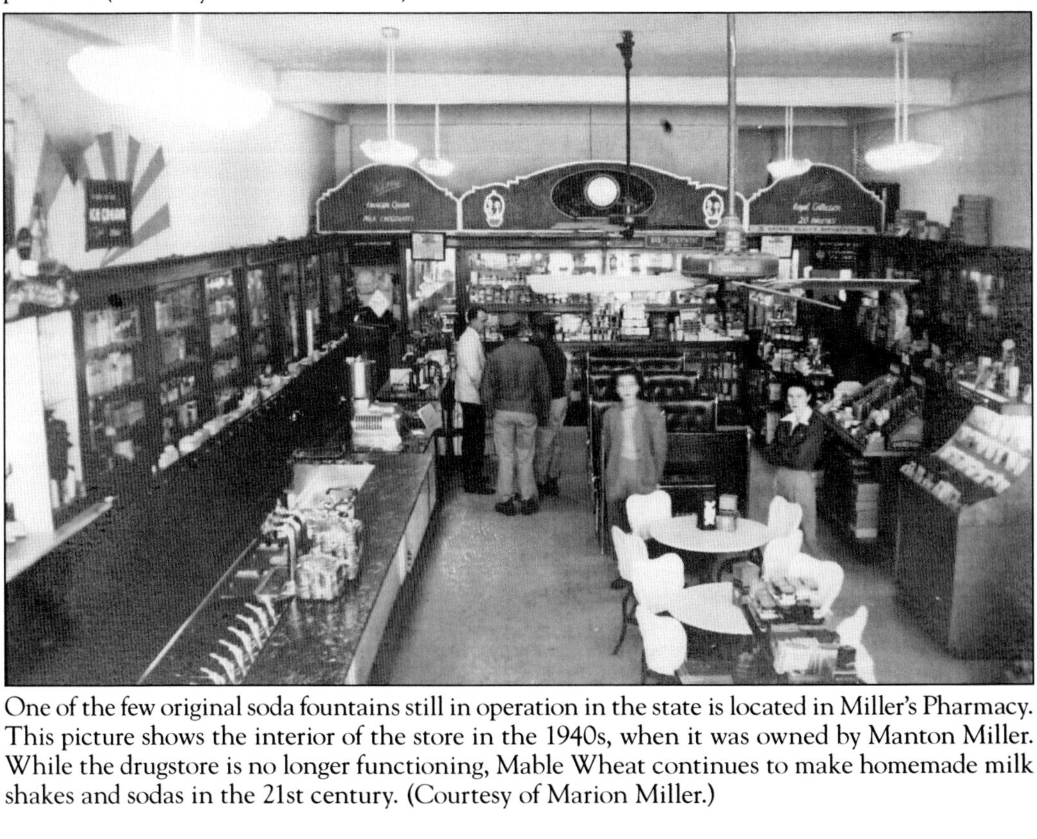

One of the few original soda fountains still in operation in the state is located in Miller's Pharmacy. This picture shows the interior of the store in the 1940s, when it was owned by Manton Miller. While the drugstore is no longer functioning, Mable Wheat continues to make homemade milk shakes and sodas in the 21st century. (Courtesy of Marion Miller.)

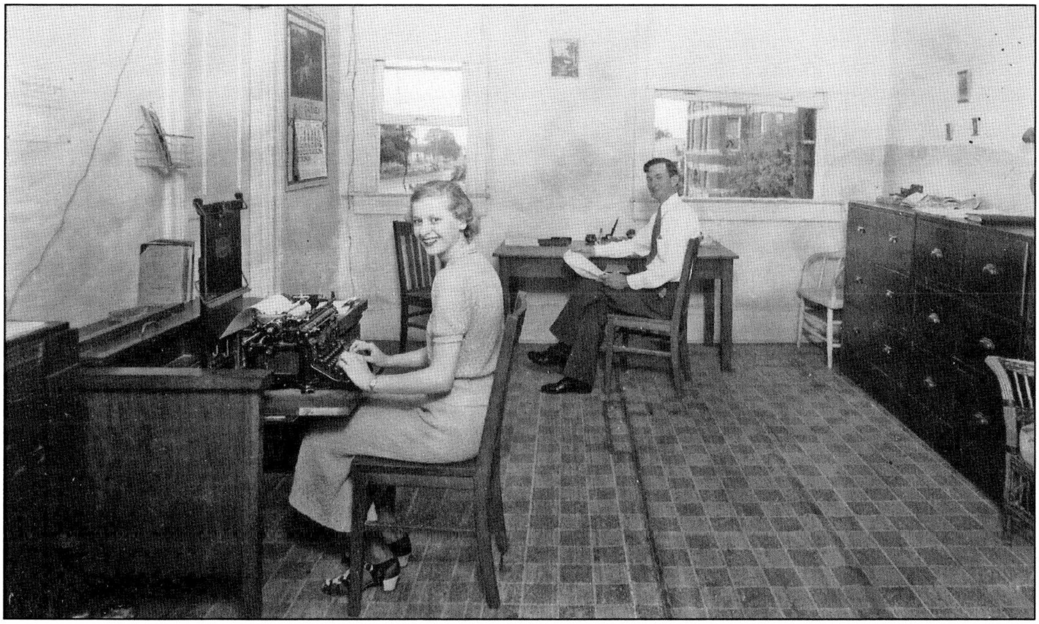

Hubert Smith owned the Smith Furniture Company, which was located on the west side of the square next to the Delta National Bank. Above the furniture company was an insurance company. The picture, made about 1930, shows Helen Anderson (left) and Louis Taylor. (Courtesy of Laura Jo Taylor.)

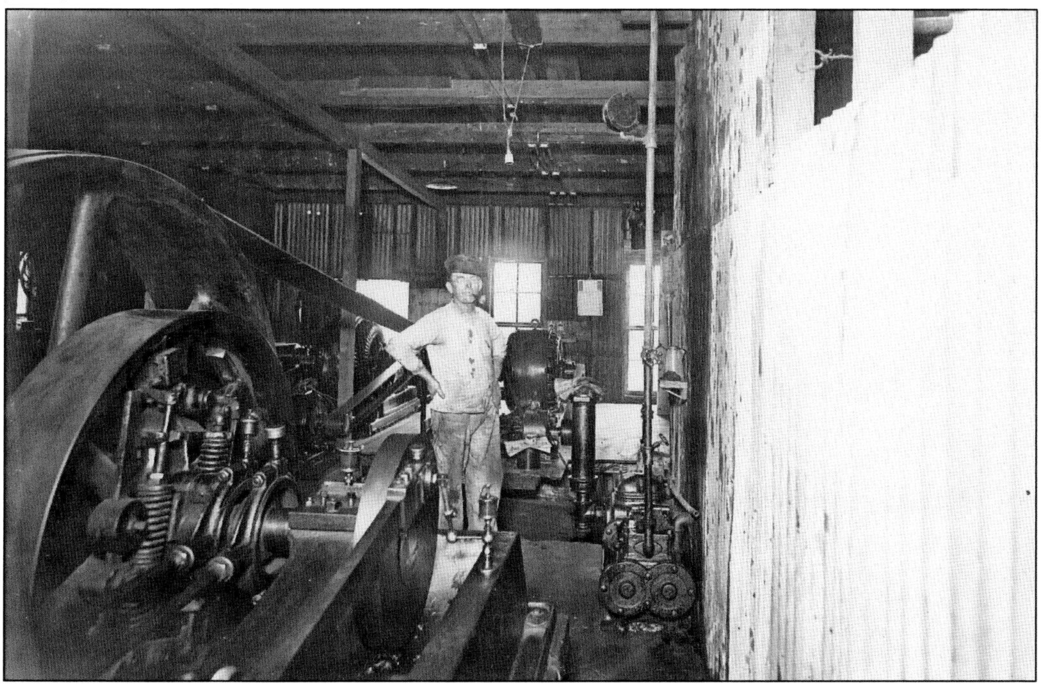

The Cooper Cotton Oil Mill was a popular business. Cottonseeds were pressed for their oil, and the oil was used to make cottonseed cake cattle feed. The building still stands near the railroad tracks southwest of the old cotton yard, now Delta Logistics. (Courtesy of Mildred Morgan and Marion Miller.)

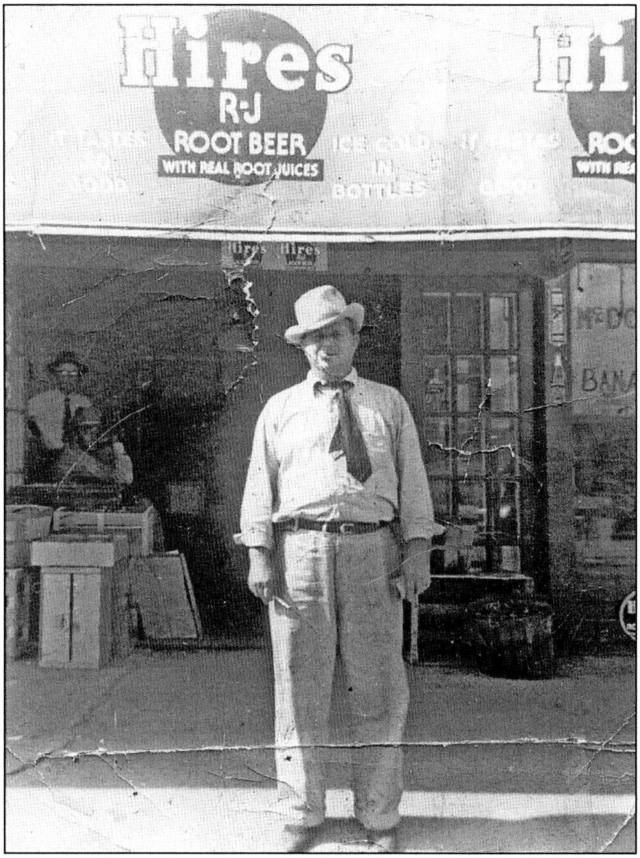

Fruit stands were as prevalent yesterday as today. Brack McDonald first owned and operated a fruit stand on East Dallas Avenue just off the square. (Courtesy of Marion Miller.)

The George Bakery was a popular place for citizens of Cooper. From left to right are Opal George, Carl Bowman, and Cas George. Their slogan was "Baked fresh every day / Will drive the blues away / Our cakes and pies will put you wise / To eat our cookies so nice will make you think you are in paradise." (Courtesy of Shirley Smith and Katie Malone.)

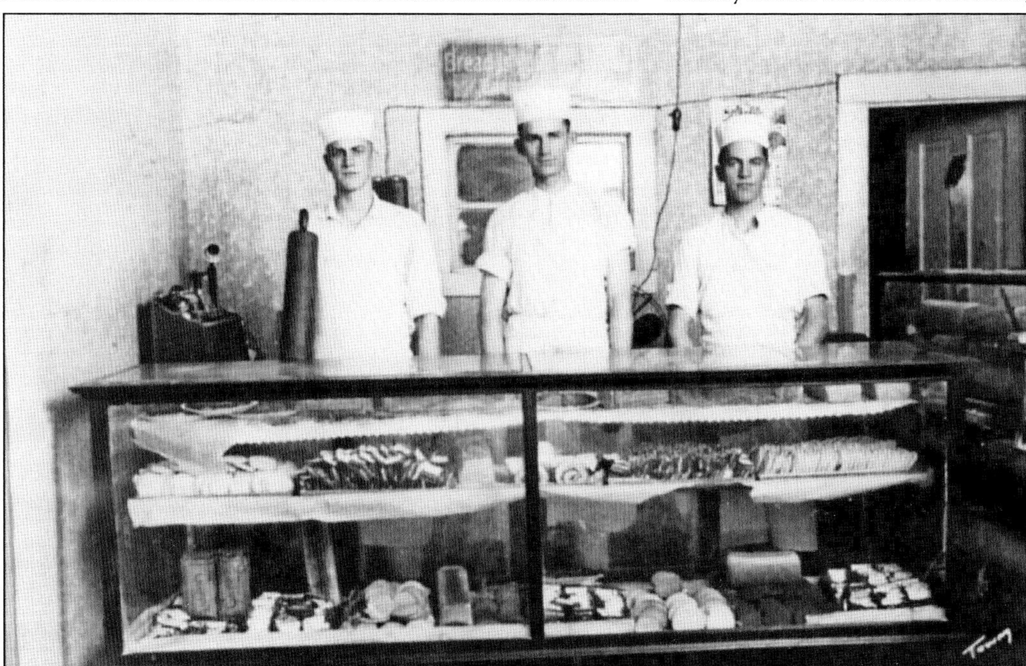

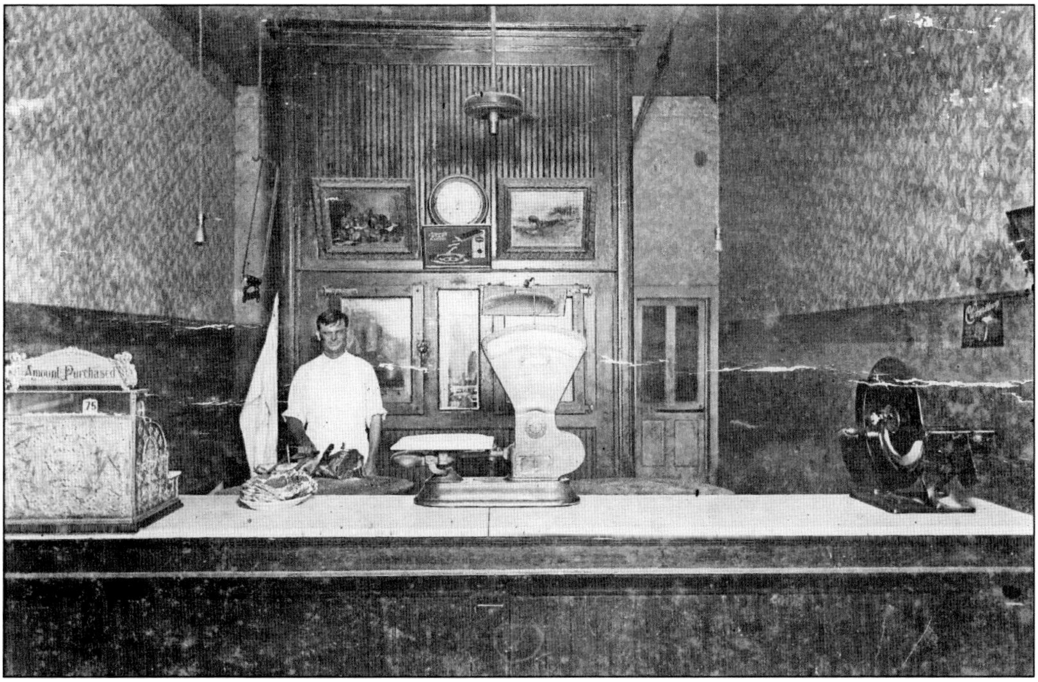

Walter Chandler Sr. had a meat market on Northwest First Street in 1911. He sold the shop when he left Cooper. When he returned to Cooper, Chandler opened a shop on Southeast First Street. (Courtesy of E. J. and Joyce Cates.)

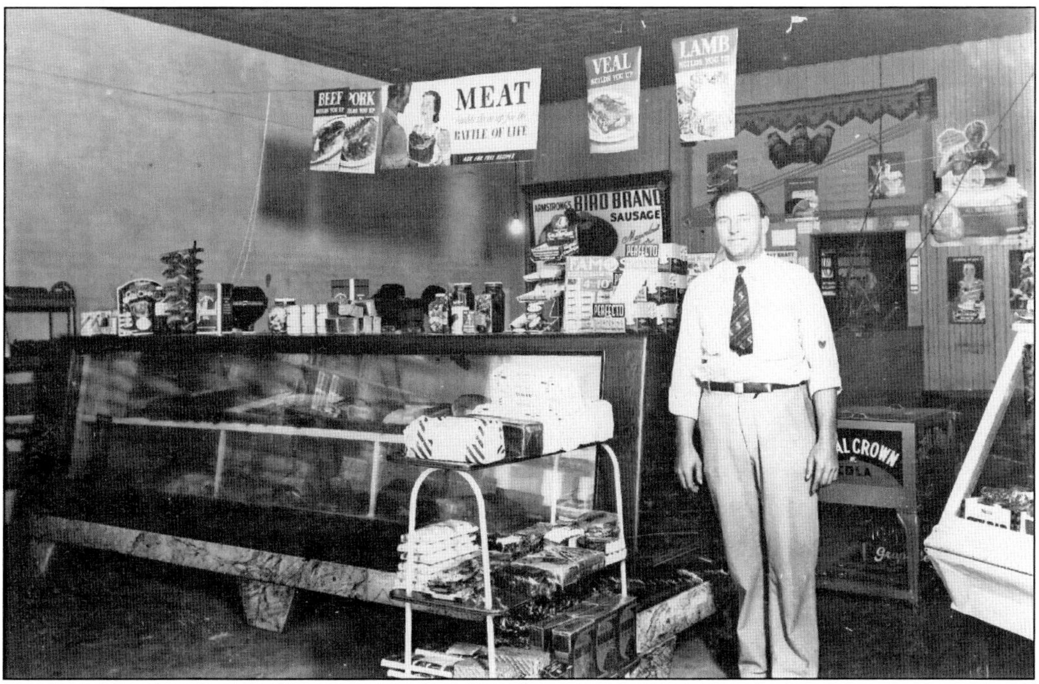

Walter Chandler owned the Chandler's Grocery and Meat Company. The market was located behind the present-day Cumby Telephone on Southeast First Street. Pictured is Enon Cates, who ran the meat market and store. (Courtesy of E. J. and Joyce Cates.)

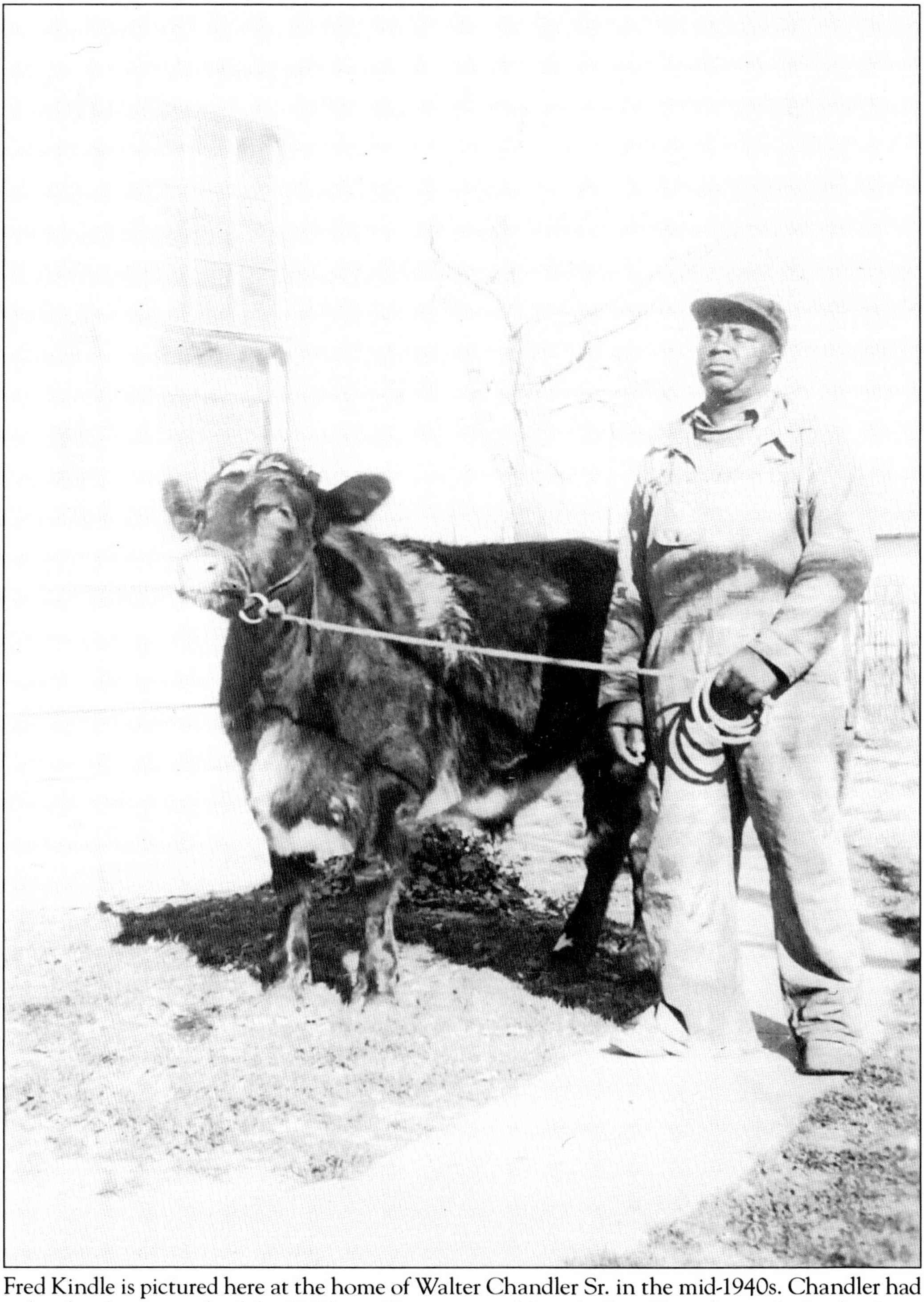

Fred Kindle is pictured here at the home of Walter Chandler Sr. in the mid-1940s. Chandler had a slaughterhouse south of the Oaklawn Cemetery, and he raised and bought cattle for slaughter. Fred was his right-hand man in his cattle and slaughterhouse operation. (Courtesy of E. J. and Joyce Cates.)

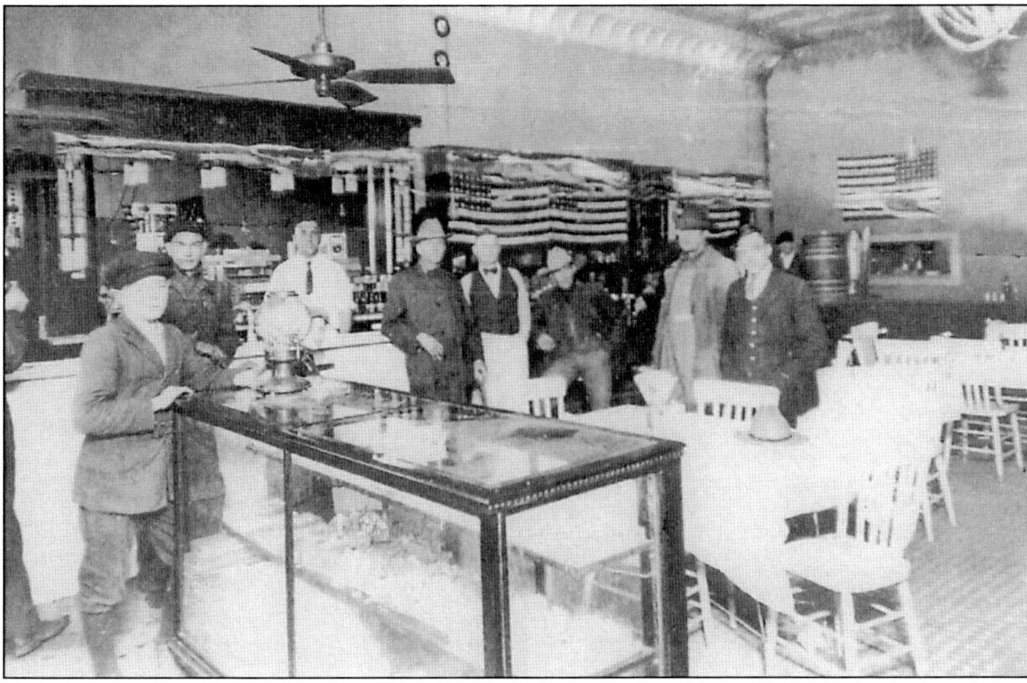

Frank Schell owned and operated the Schell Café from about 1912 to 1922. The family story indicated that Schell closed his café when political activities, which he did not like, began in Cooper. In the 1918 picture above are, from left to right, ? Moss, Ira McDaniel, Bill Starks, Dick Waters, J. J. Ralls, Claud Glaspie, unidentified, and Frank Schell (owner). (Courtesy of Quentin Miller.)

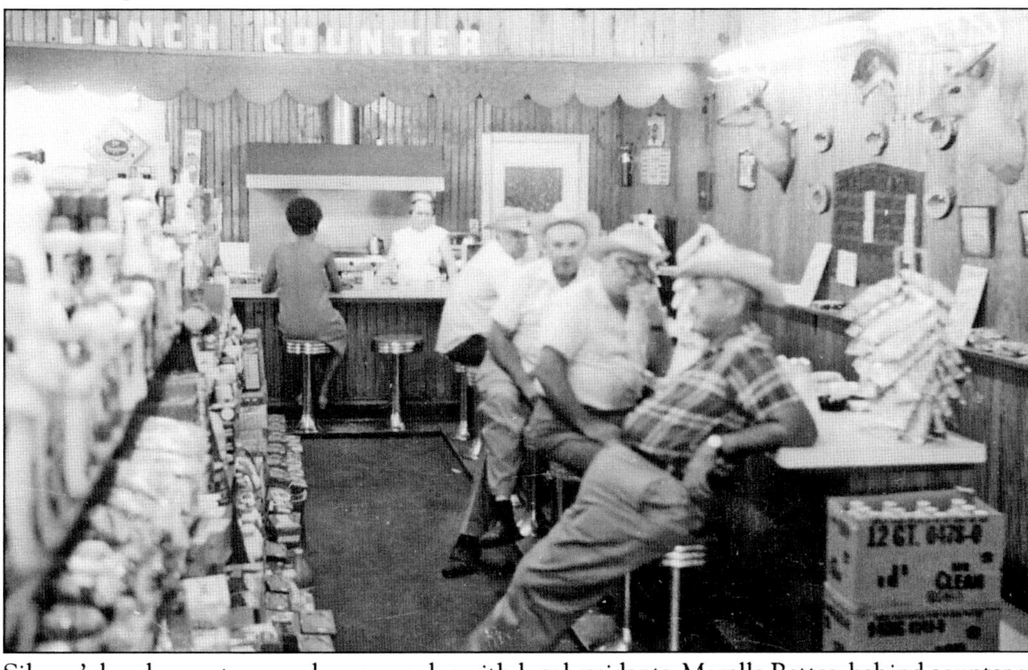

Silman's lunch counter was always popular with local residents. Mozelle Bettes, behind counter at the far back, is pictured with, from left to right, Goebel Templeton, Wolfe Lowery, L. E. Hadaway, and Roger Love. (Courtesy of Billy Jack and John Bartley Silman.)

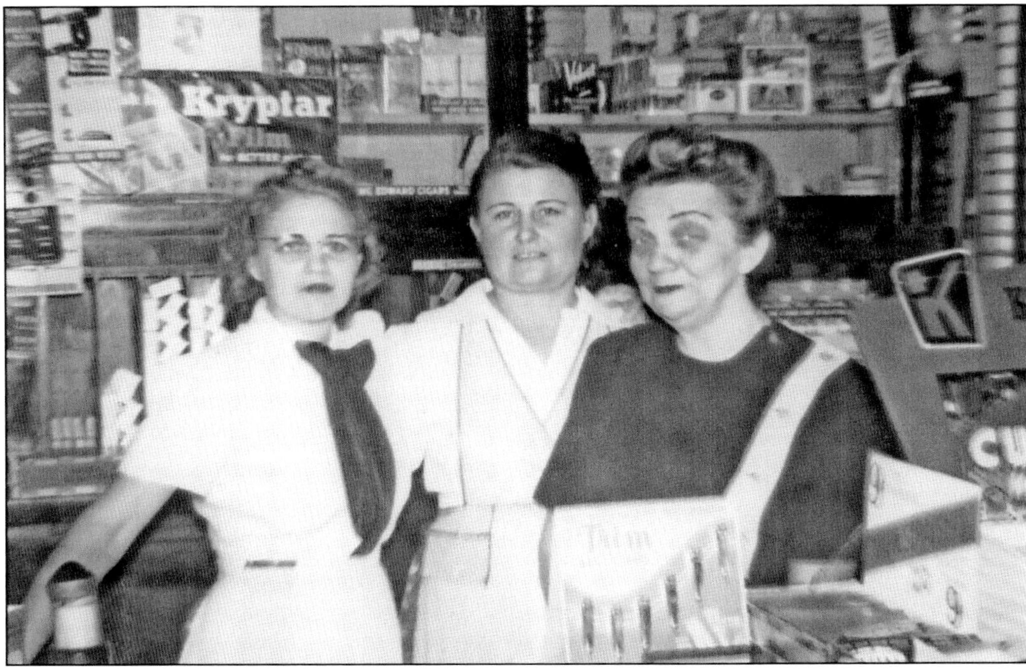

Pete and Maude Parkhill first owned Parkhill Sweet Shop, above, then turned it into Parkhill Café in the mid-1920s. During the Depression, they fed many people who were just passing through and were in need of a meal. Some years later, a nicely dressed man reappeared and handed Maude some money to pay for the meal she had given him. A favorite of residents and schoolchildren, the café sold in the mid-1960s. Maude is the woman on the right, and the other two are unidentified. Below, Pete Parkhill is pictured behind the counter of the café at lunchtime. (Both, courtesy of the Parkhill family.)

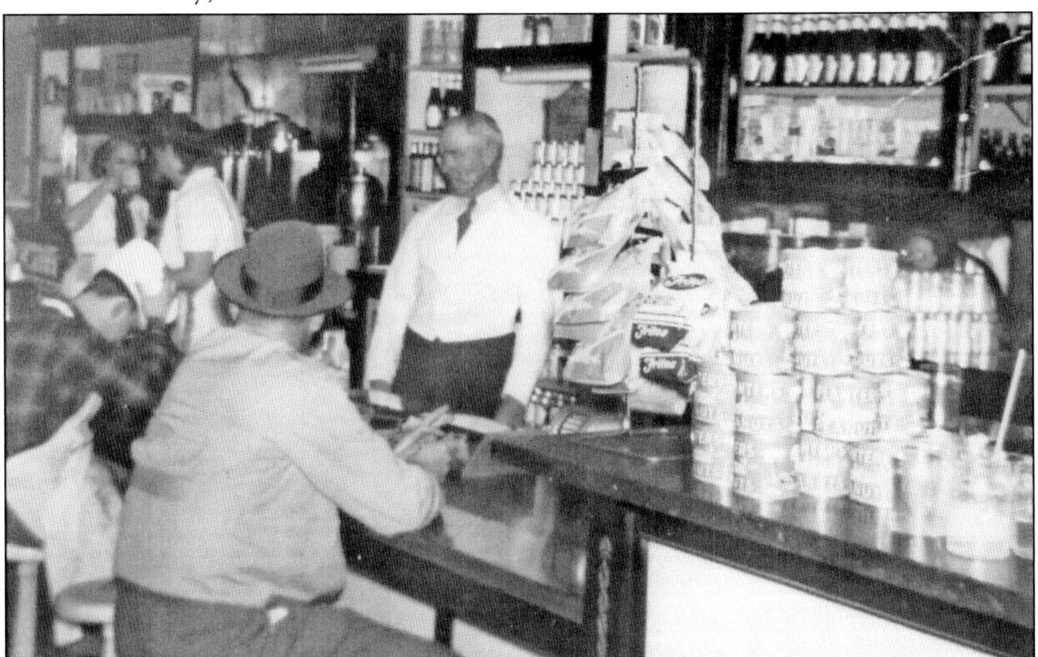

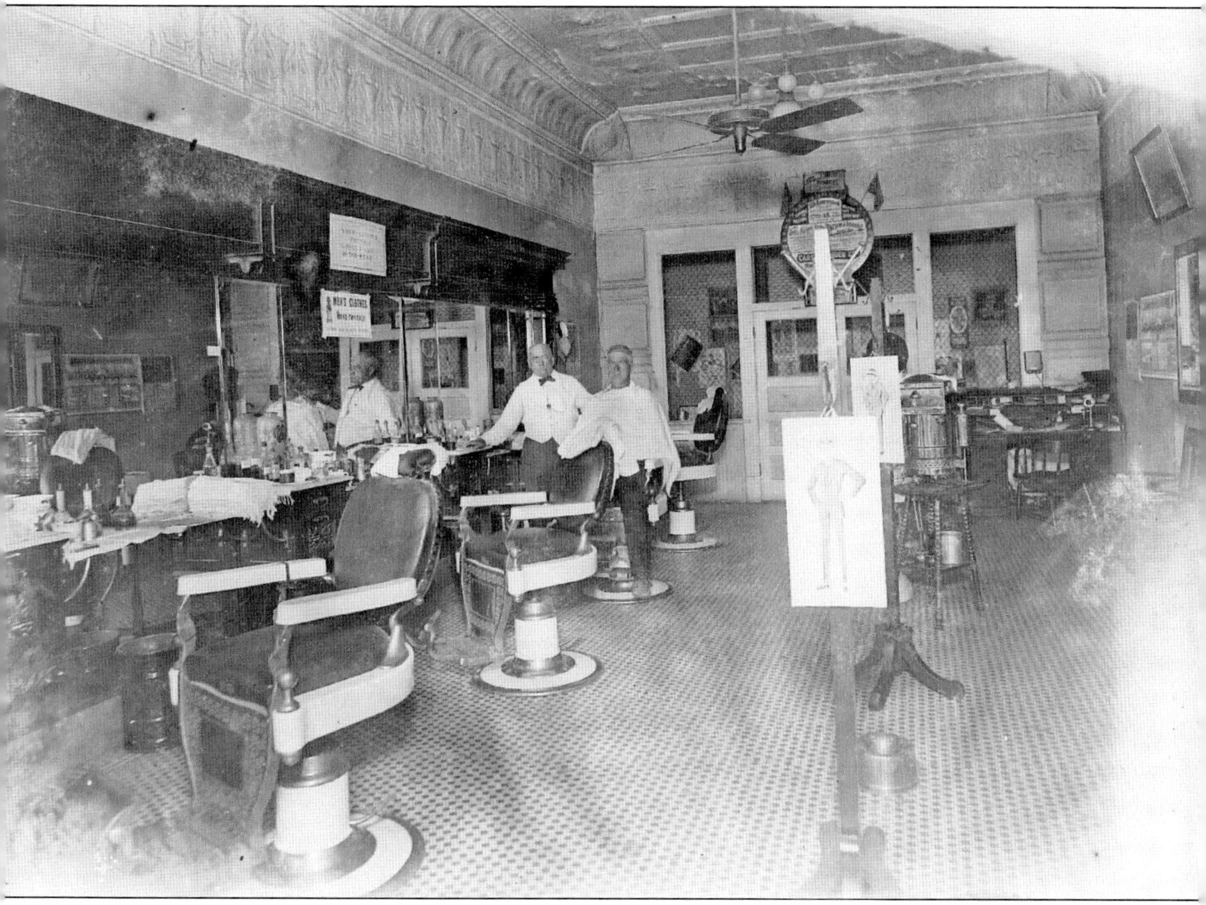

Barbershops were important businesses in Cooper, as in any community. Pictured here is the Parkhill Barber Shop. It was located on the west side of the square, where the Parkhill's Café was later located. (Courtesy of Marion Miller.)

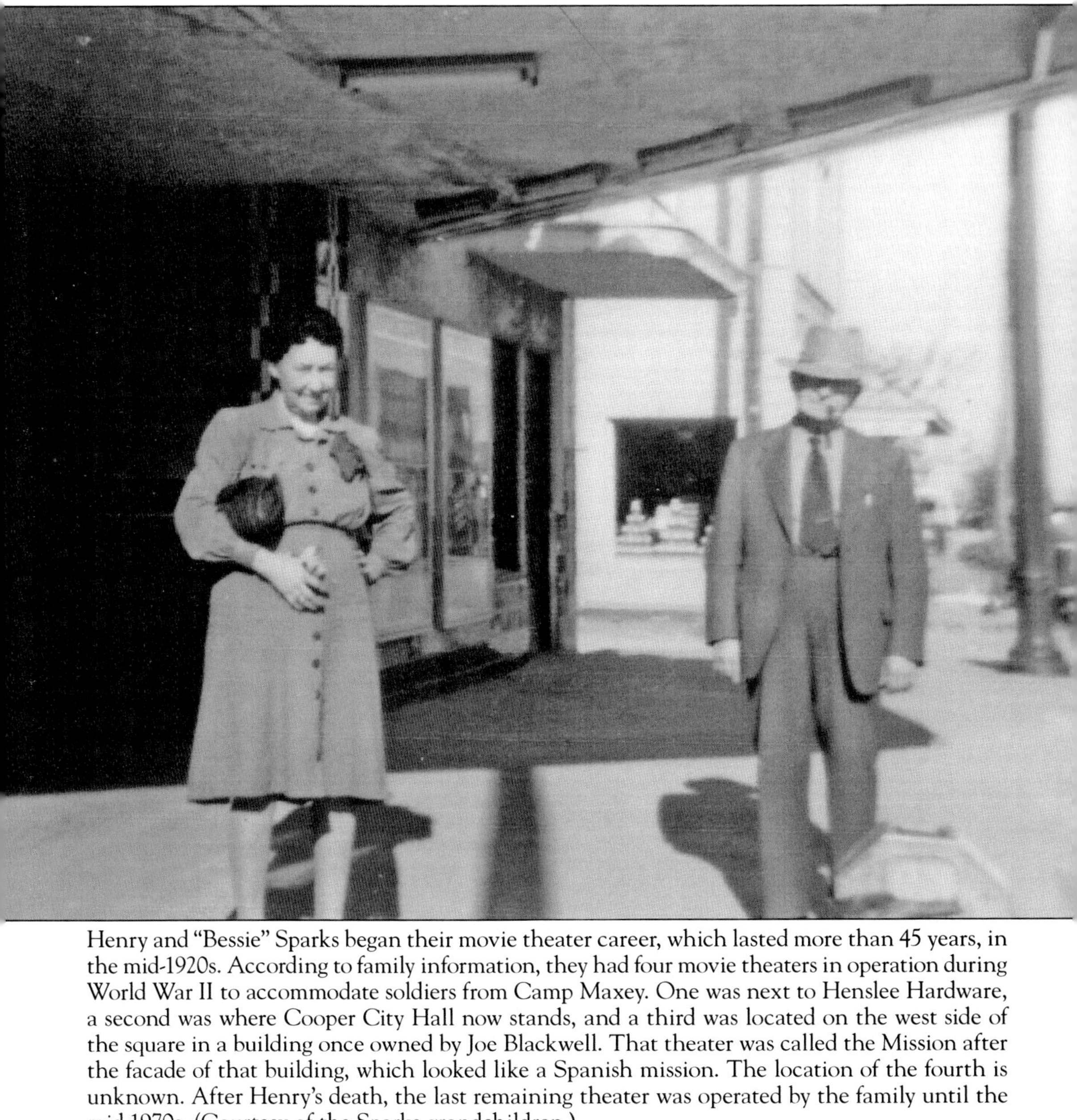

Henry and "Bessie" Sparks began their movie theater career, which lasted more than 45 years, in the mid-1920s. According to family information, they had four movie theaters in operation during World War II to accommodate soldiers from Camp Maxey. One was next to Henslee Hardware, a second was where Cooper City Hall now stands, and a third was located on the west side of the square in a building once owned by Joe Blackwell. That theater was called the Mission after the facade of that building, which looked like a Spanish mission. The location of the fourth is unknown. After Henry's death, the last remaining theater was operated by the family until the mid-1970s. (Courtesy of the Sparks grandchildren.)

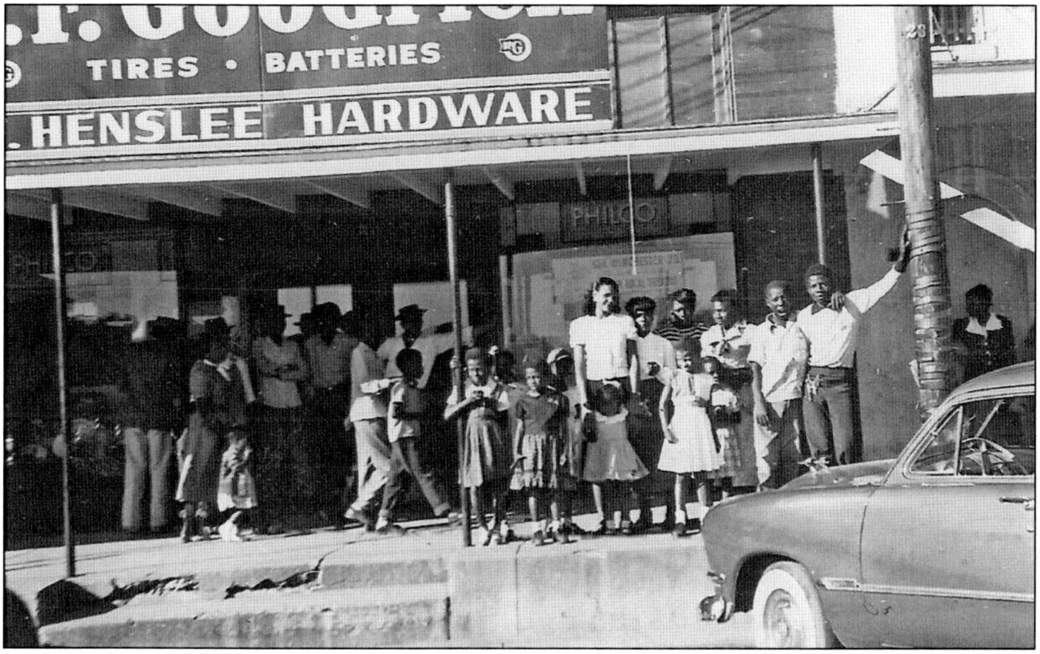

Henry Sparks owned two movie theaters on the north side of the square in Cooper. The children above are lined up for the afternoon movie at the theater located next to Henslee Hardware. This movie theater was in operation until Pollard's Grocery burned in 1957, also destroying the theater. At right is Theolous Wilson, who probably saw every movie that was shown at the Sparks theaters, as he ran the picture projector for many years. (Both, courtesy of Willie Bear Wilkins.)

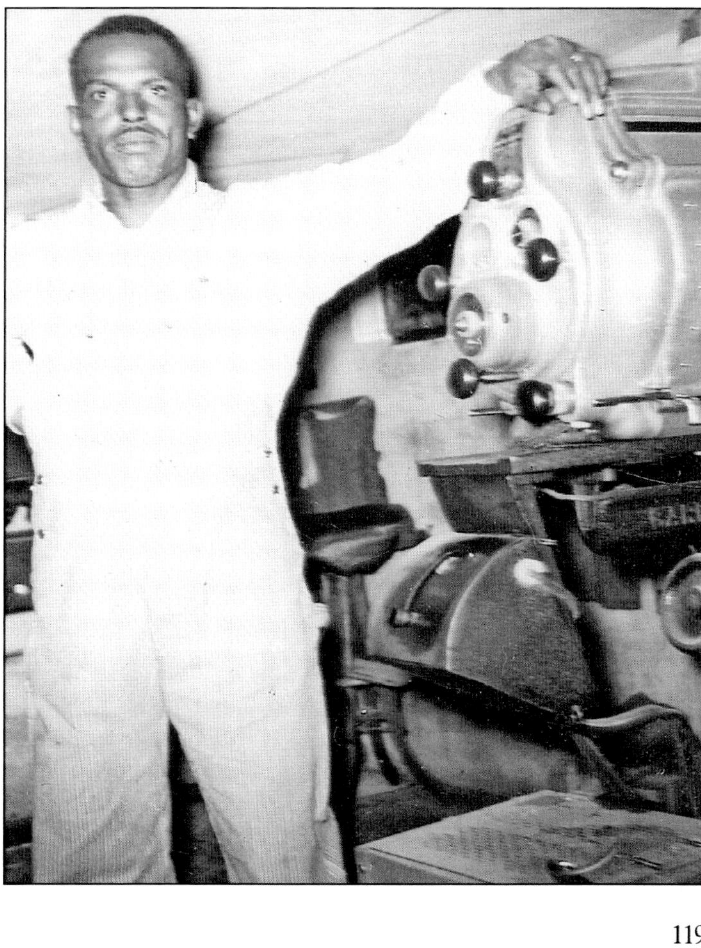

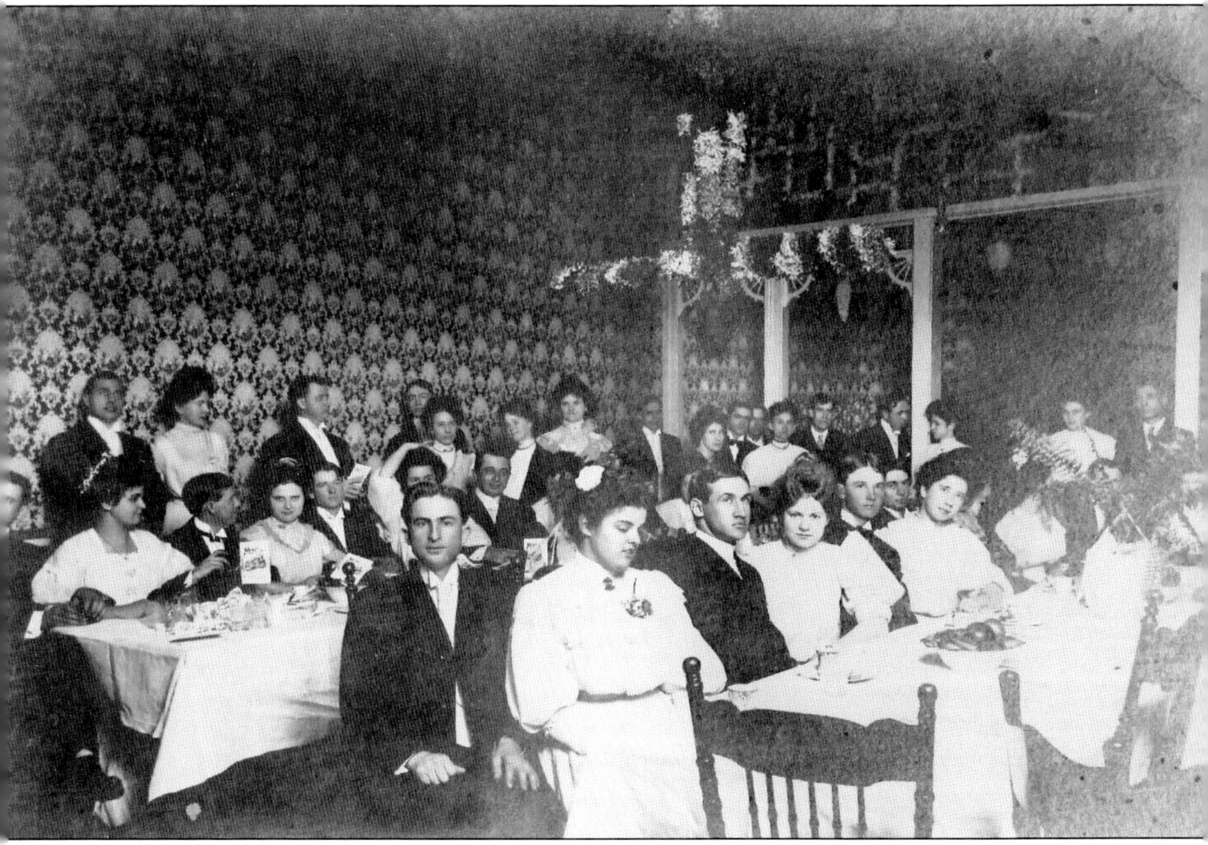

Banquets were popular at the beginning of the 20th century. This 1907 banquet at the Palmore Café shows many of the young adults of the community. From left to right are (first row) Grundy Stevenson, Beulah Henslee, Clarence Rattan, Velma Lester, Floyd Lain, Corinne Culver, Tom Robertson, Mabel Cabeen, and unidentified; (second row) Tom Snell, Minnie Pillman, Oscar Kelton, Hallie McKinney, John Garrard, Jennie Albright, and John Young; (third row) W. D. Hart, Willie Kate Fisher, Carl Tynes, Arthur Kenyon, Laura Wilson, Tom A. Lambeth, May Garrard, unidentified, Bess Daniels, Pete Parkhill, Dr. J. H. McKinney, Frankie Custer, Frank Cannell, Ollie Talley, Mamie Rattan, Dulcie Havens, and Hugh Moore. (Courtesy of Patterson Museum.)

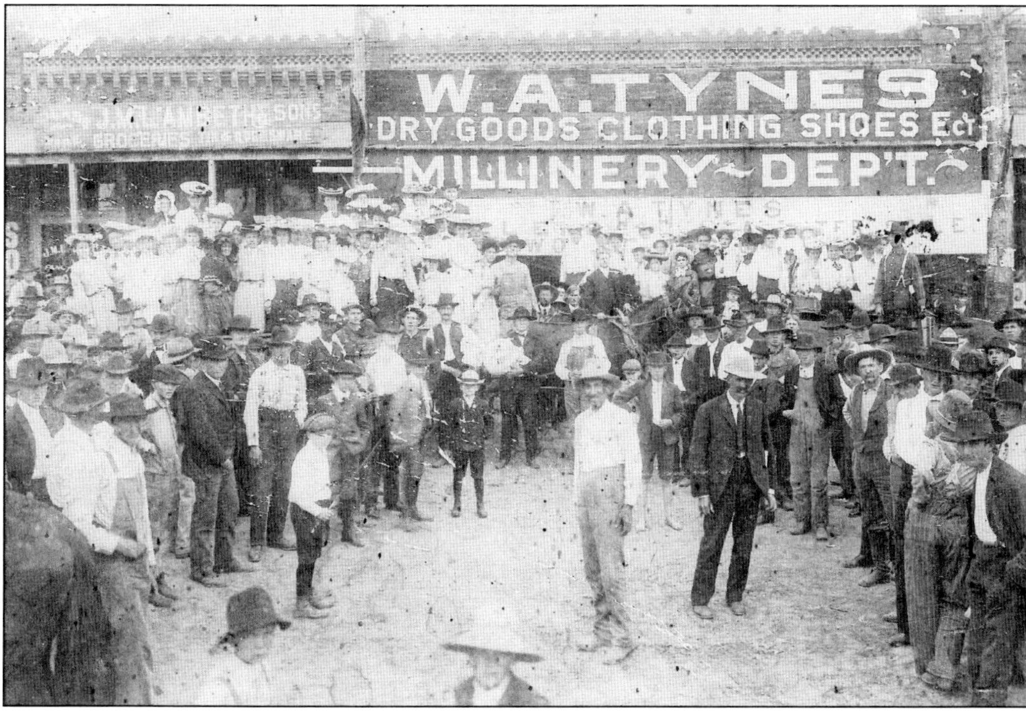

This picture was taken in 1905 in the Cooper Square, where people gathered to learn the outcome of elections, hear political speakers, and attend community meetings. (Courtesy of Delta County Library.)

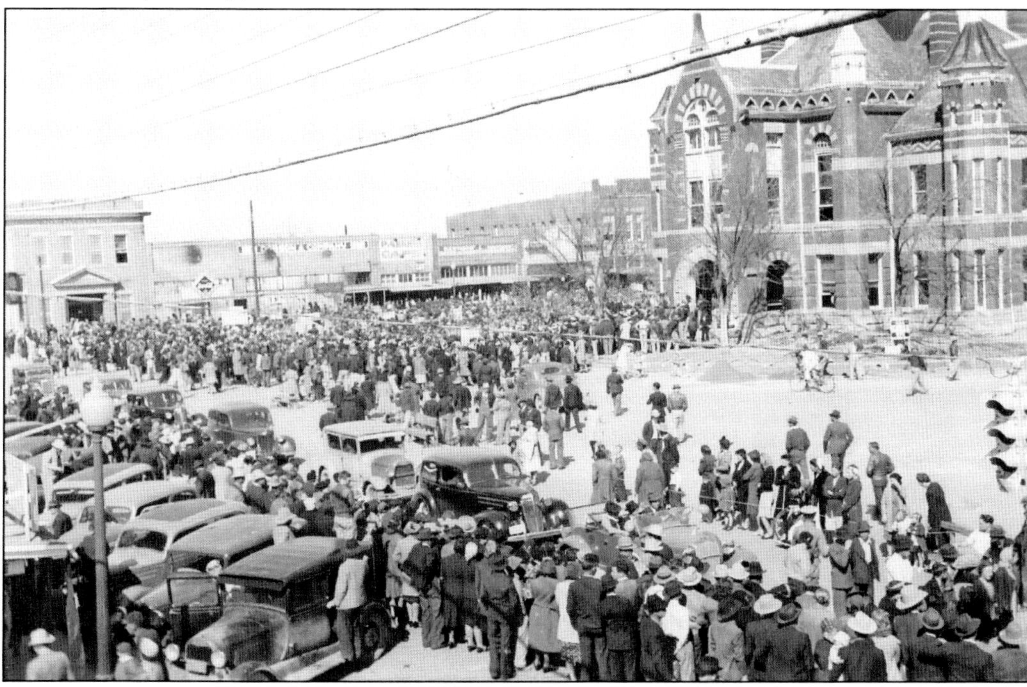

A parade always attracts crowds, and in the 1930s, people came to enjoy the sights. This picture shows the county courthouse and the west side of the square. (Courtesy of Marion Miller.)

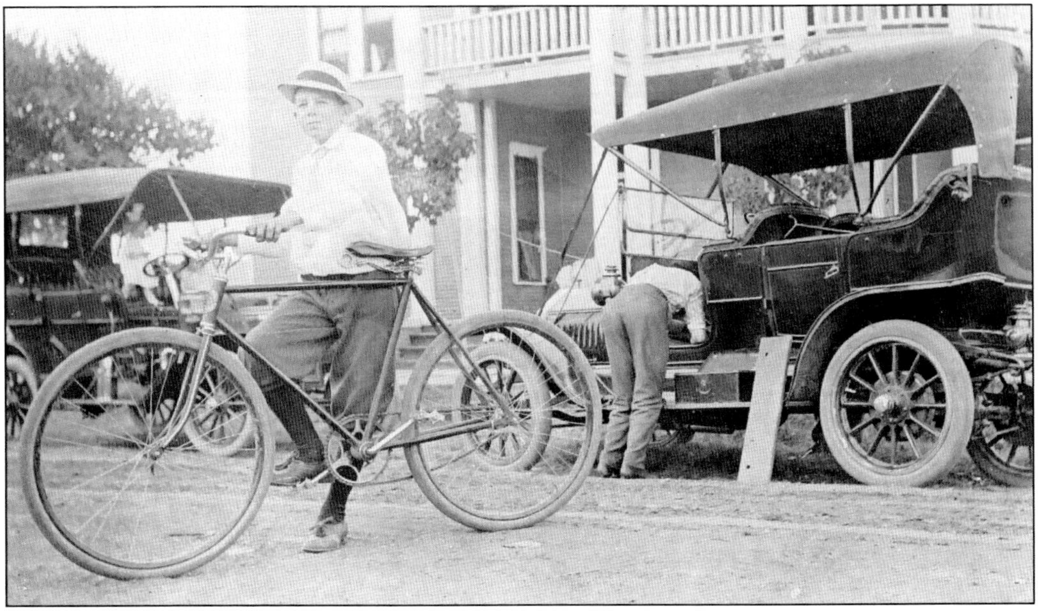

Bicycles were used for transportation and pleasure at the beginning of the 20th century. Greaver Miller is seen with his bicycle, and Wesley Miller is bending over the car on Southwest First Street about 1910. (Courtesy of Marion Miller.)

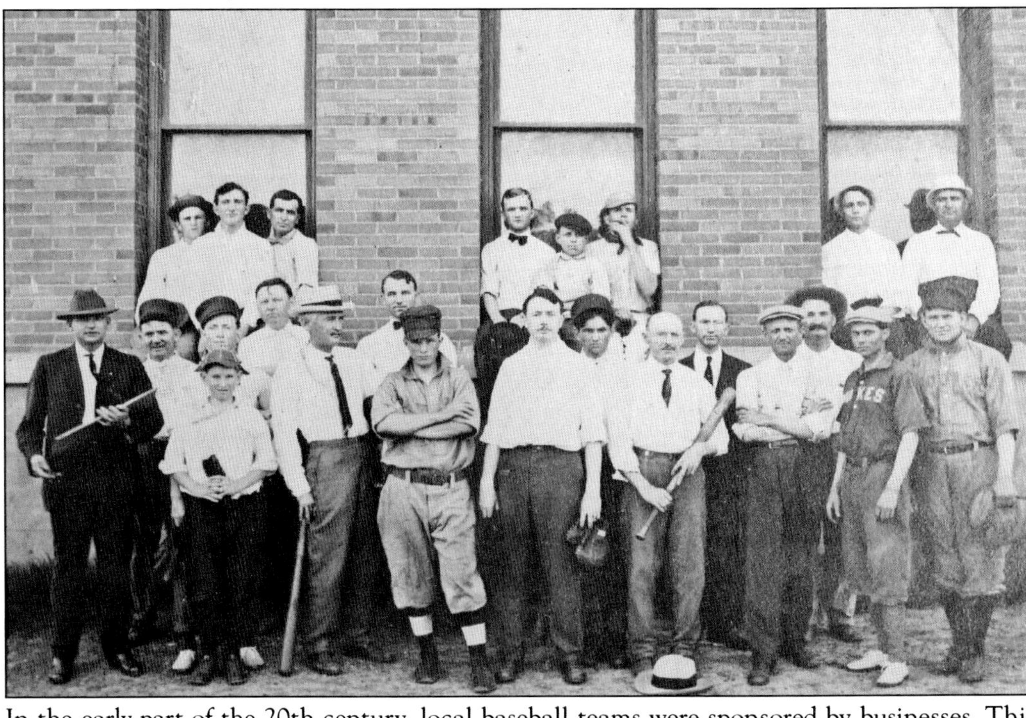

In the early part of the 20th century, local baseball teams were sponsored by businesses. This team was sponsored by Crawford-Norris-Henderson and featured John Garrard, George Lane, Fred Cooper, C. L. Stevenson, Lucen Hatcher (in suit), Arthur Kenyon, Sam Leverette, Seth Townsend, Floyd Tanner, Guy Alexander, Walter Chandler, William Brackeen, Tom Steely, Bob Hendrick, Jess Spencer, Carter Anderson, and Ed Hendrick. (Courtesy of Patterson Museum.)

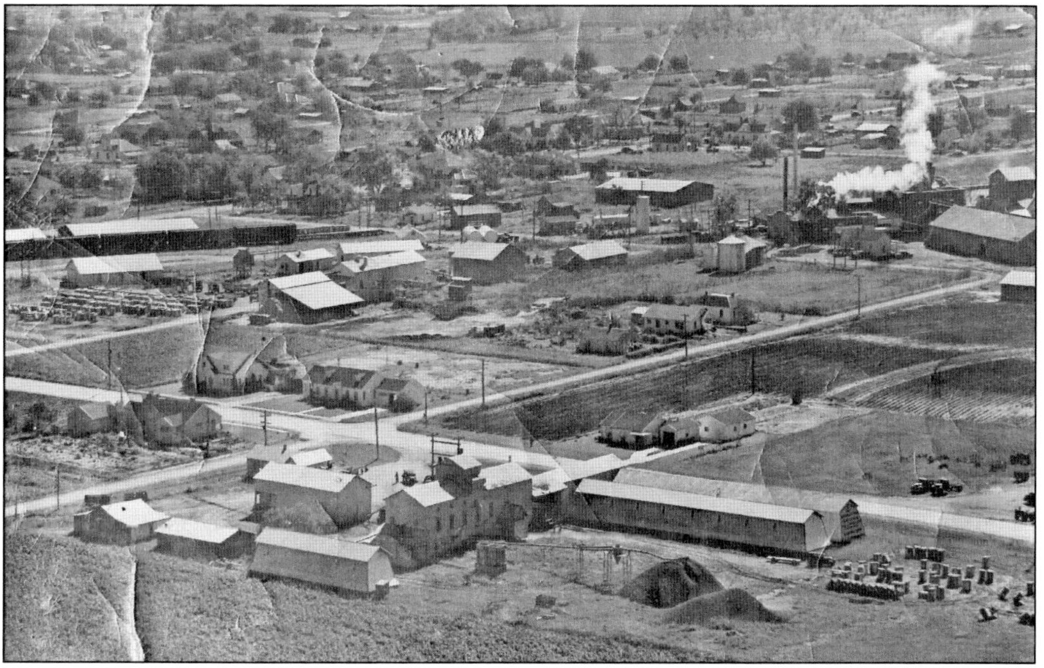

The gin in the forefront of the photograph is Hurley's Gin, and it was located on West Dallas Avenue and Northwest Twelfth Street. The smoke in the upper right is the Cooper Oil Mill. Bales of cotton at the Cooper Warehouse can be seen in the middle left of the picture. (Courtesy of Patterson Museum.)

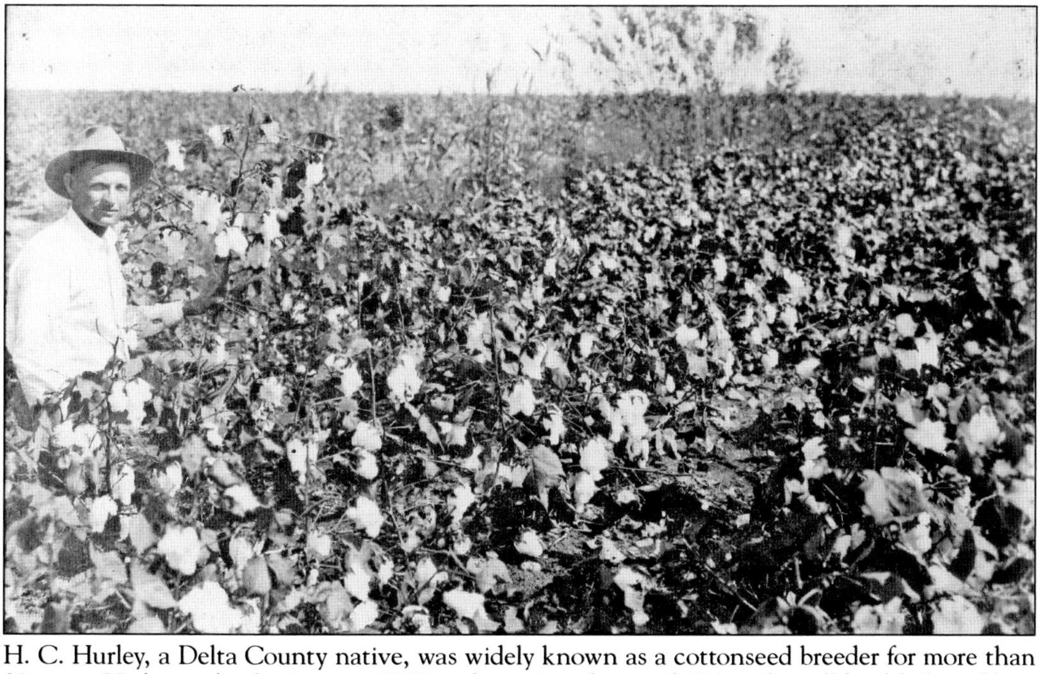

H. C. Hurley, a Delta County native, was widely known as a cottonseed breeder for more than 32 years. He began his business in 1912 and continued it until 1944, when ill health forced him to retire. He and his son, Dahl Hurley, purchased a gin, which he helped operate until his death. (Courtesy of Patterson Museum.)

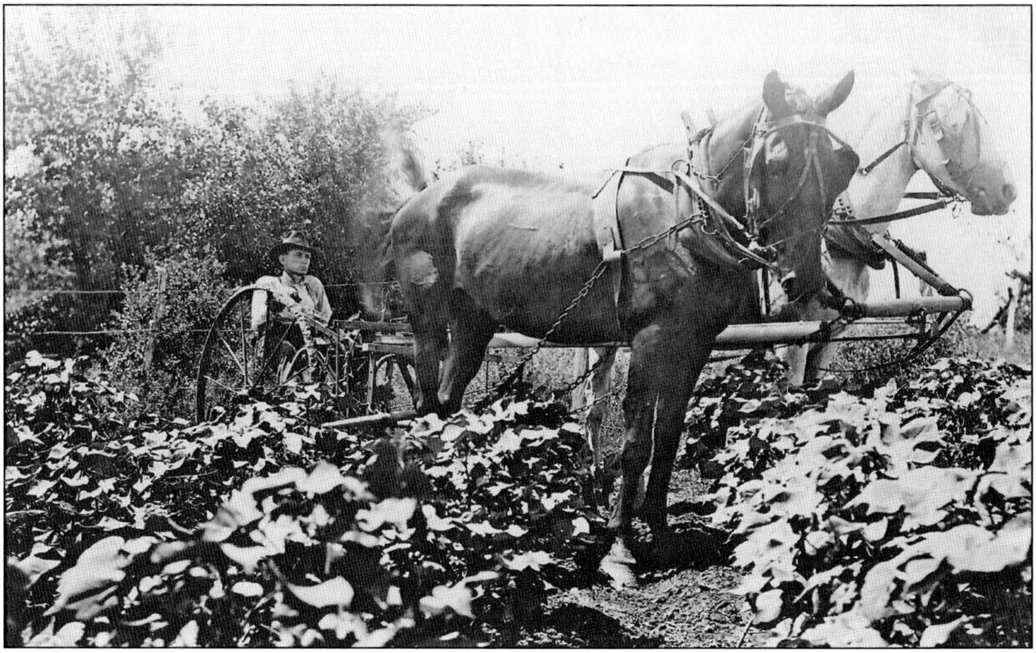

Judge John T. Taylor, elected judge of Delta County for the term of 1937 through 1940, is shown with his horse-drawn cultivator. Horses or mules drawing plows and cultivators were common in getting gardens and fields ready to plant. The picture was taken in Brushy Mound. (Courtesy of Laura Jo Taylor.)

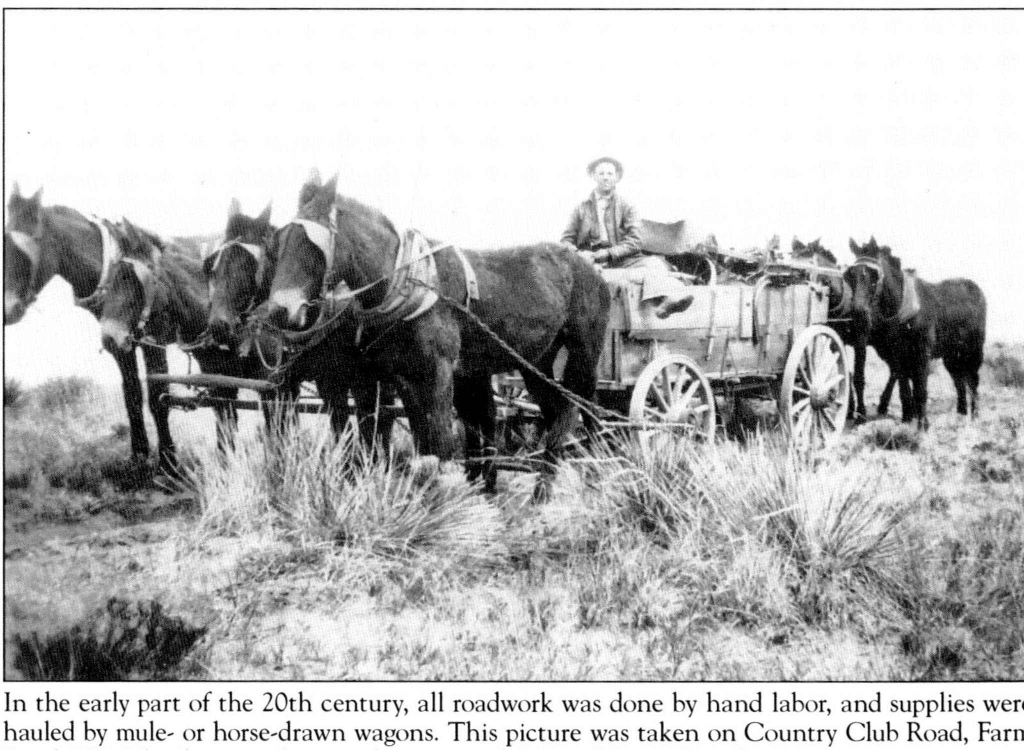

In the early part of the 20th century, all roadwork was done by hand labor, and supplies were hauled by mule- or horse-drawn wagons. This picture was taken on Country Club Road, Farm Road 1529. The date is unknown. (Courtesy of E. J. and Joyce Cates.)

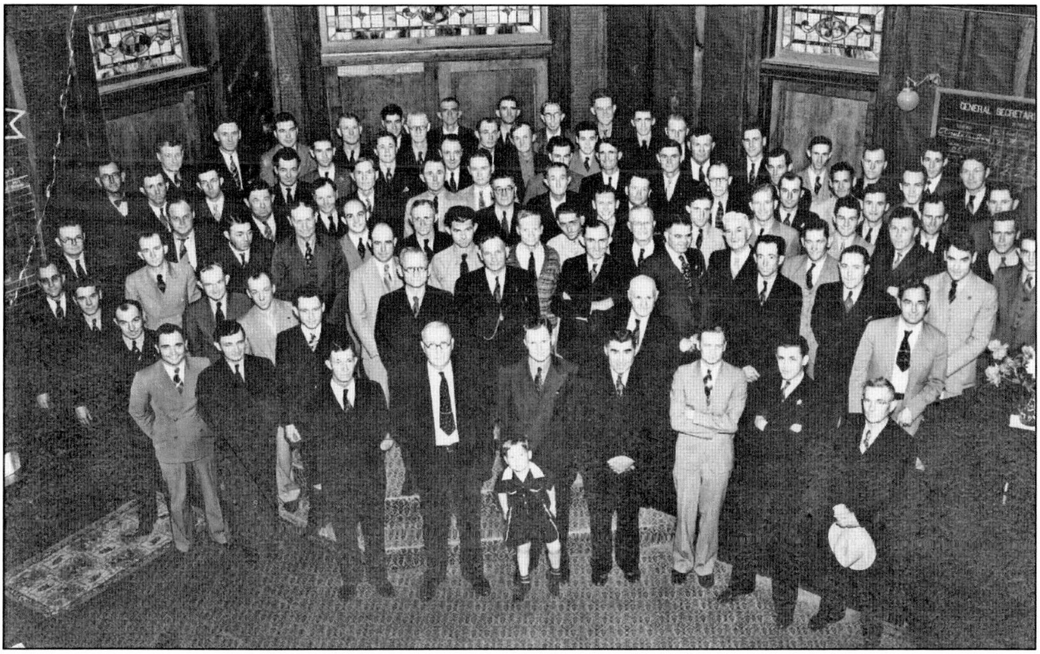

The Baraca Men's Class of the First Baptist Church in Cooper posed for this picture in June 1938. (Courtesy of E. J. and Joyce Cates.)

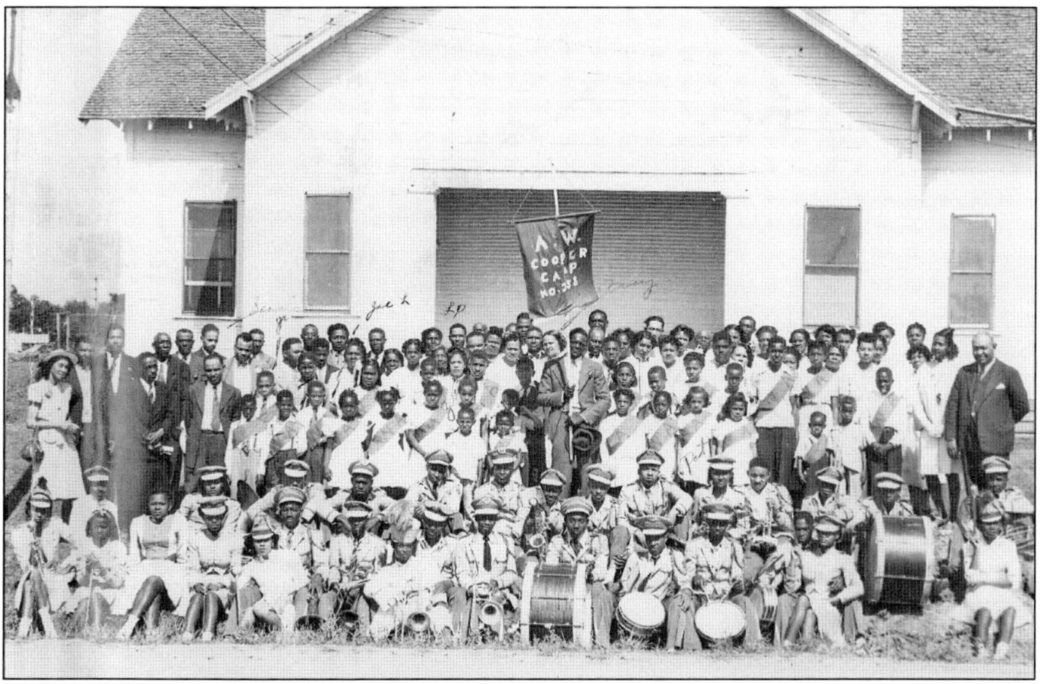

This picture was taken in front of the First Baptist Church (New Zion Baptist Church today) on Seventh Street, and the celebration event was sponsored by American Woodmen Insurance Company, Cooper Camp 258, organized by Magnolia Roseman. The band is thought to be the Gibbons High School Band of Paris, which came frequently to perform at events in Cooper. The preacher is B. T. Mitchell. (Courtesy of Carlton Thomas.)

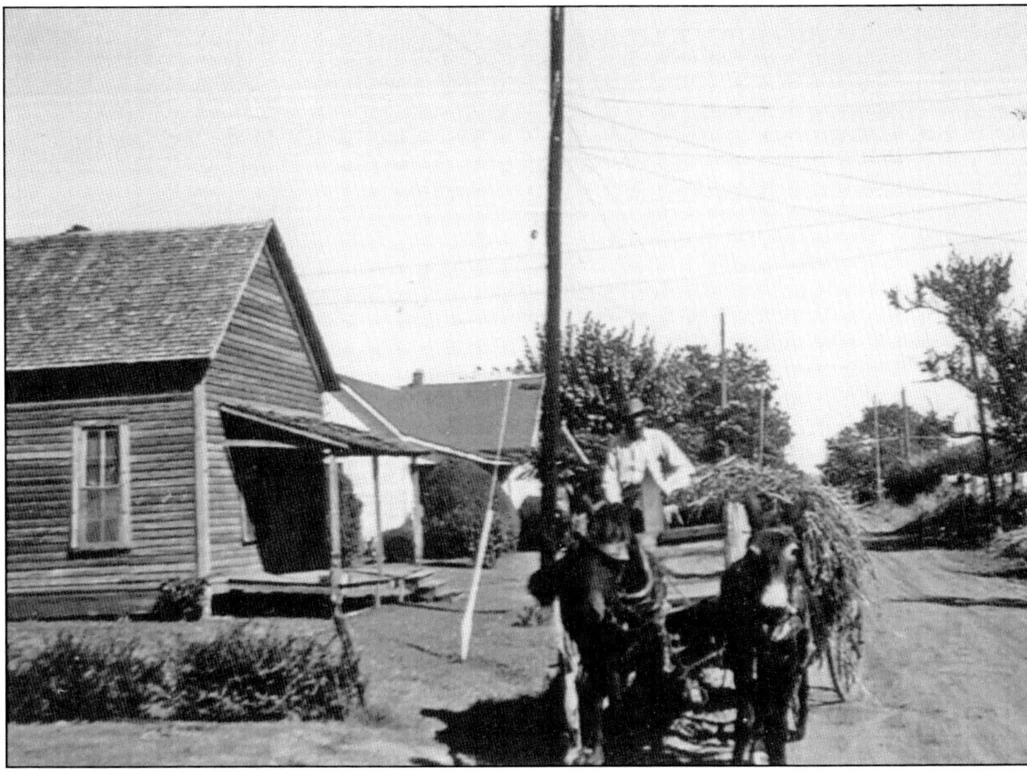

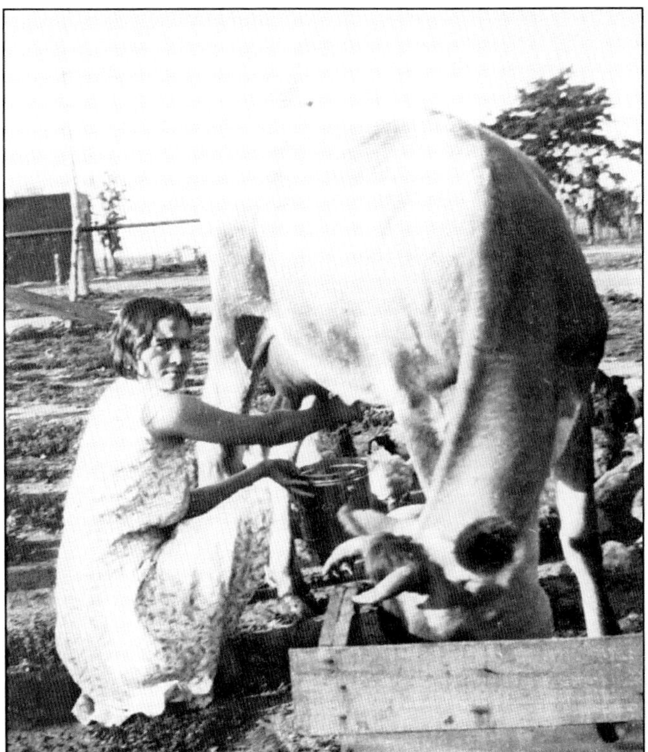

Sweet Shanklin is shown here in the 1940s on Northwest First Street with his mule-drawn wagon hauling hay for his animals. In the 1930s and 1940s, he had a business hauling debris out of the city with his mule-drawn wagon. (Courtesy of Willie Bear Wilkins.)

Opal Cates, the mother of E. J. Cates, is shown milking her jersey cow. Milking cows was necessary in rural areas and in cities until the 1950s, when electricity became widely available and people were able to purchase refrigerators and store pasteurized milk. (Courtesy of E. J. and Joyce Cates.)

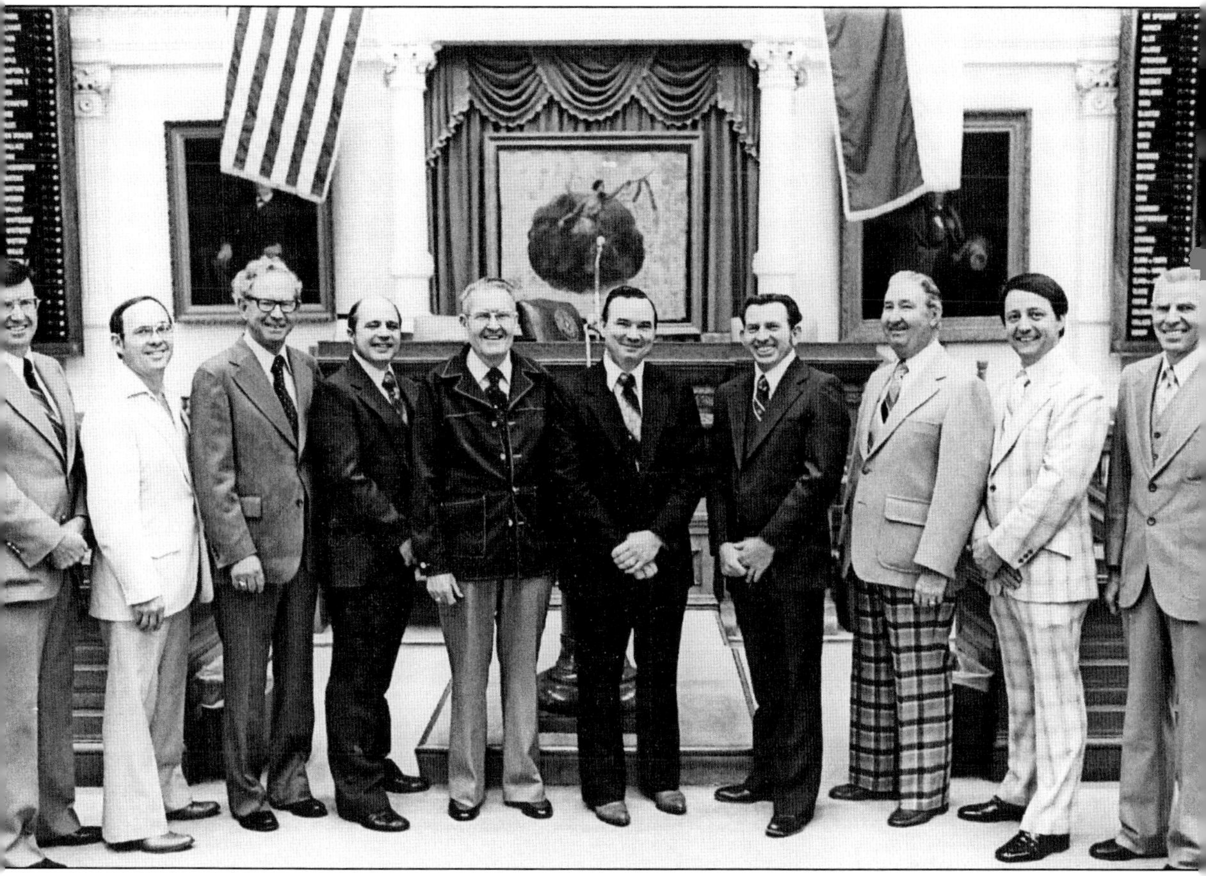

The Delta County Industrial Foundation was formed in the 1970s to encourage industry to come to Delta County. Here Morris Partain, Pike Burkhart, Troy Kern, Marion Miller, Curtis Pardue, Pete Patterson, Bobby Irvin, Curtis Hicks, Fred Wilkerson, and Thomas Allen visit with state representative Pete Patterson in the state capitol on April 25, 1979. (Courtesy of Marion Miller.)